The Art of Alfred Hitchcock

SECOND EDITION:
COMPLETELY REVISED
AND UPDATED

ANCHOR BOOKS
DOUBLEDAY
NEW YORK LONDON TORONTO SYDNEY AUCKLAND

The Art of Alfred Hitchcock

FIFTY YEARS OF HIS MOTION PICTURES

Donald Spoto

AN ANCHOR BOOK

PUBLISHED BY DOUBLEDAY
a division of Bantam Doubleday Dell Publishing Group, Inc.
666 Fifth Avenue, New York, New York 10103

ANCHOR BOOKS, DOUBLEDAY, and the portrayal of an anchor
are trademarks of Doubleday, a division of Bantam Doubleday
Dell Publishing Group, Inc.

The Art of Alfred Hitchcock was originally published in hardcover by
Hopkinson and Blake in 1976.
First published in paperback by Dolphin Books/Doubleday, a division of
Bantam Doubleday Dell Publishing Group, Inc., in 1979.
This completely revised and updated Anchor Books edition is published
by arrangement with Doubleday, a division of Bantam Doubleday
Dell Publishing Group, Inc.

DESIGNED BY ANNE LING

Library of Congress Cataloging-in-Publication Data

Spoto, Donald, 1941–
    The art of Alfred Hitchcock: fifty years of his motion pictures /
by Donald Spoto. — 2nd ed., completely rev. and updated.
        p.   cm.
    "Anchor books."
    Includes bibliographical references and index.
    1. Hitchcock, Alfred, 1899–1980.—Criticism and interpretation.
I. Title.
PN1998.3.H58S68   1992
791.43'0233'092—dc20   91-3438
                                                            CIP

ISBN 0-385-41813-2
Copyright © 1976, 1992 by Donald Spoto
All rights reserved
PRINTED IN THE UNITED STATES OF AMERICA
1   3   5   7   9   10   8   6   4   2
FIRST ANCHOR BOOKS EDITION:
JANUARY 1992

for James T. Caroscio
1946–1986

INTRODUCTION TO THE SECOND EDITION

In 1972, I was asked to contribute an essay on Alfred Hitchcock's *Vertigo* for a book about classic motion pictures. The editor was satisfied with six pages but I was not, and soon after was born the idea for *The Art of Alfred Hitchcock*—a detailed critical appreciation of his work, film by film, the first such book by an American.

My movie-watching and note-taking progressed in retrospective theaters round the world and in homes where private prints were screened for me (in those days when videotape was not the ubiquitous commodity it is today), but soon I discovered that Hitchcock's early films were not easy to see. In fact, it was necessary to spend a month at the British Film Institute, London, watching rare copies of mostly unknown pictures like *Champagne*, *The Manxman* and *The Skin Game*.

With a few notable exceptions, his first seventeen films are historical curiosities—interesting works by a gifted novice rather than cinematic masterpieces—and so in 1975 I chose to treat somewhat more briefly the works from 1925 to 1934, a decision retained in preparing this revision. Of Hitchcock's fifty-three features, there is only one I have not seen: *The Mountain Eagle,* produced in 1925 and lost soon after. Additionally, I have omitted consideration of *Bon Voyage* and *Adventure Malgache,* two short films he directed for a European acting troupe, to honor the French Resistance during World War II; I finally saw them in 1981 when I was preparing his biography, but they were never released theatrically in America and have been unavailable to the public for almost fifty years.

From 1974 to 1976, a very rich kind of material was provided by interviews with people who worked with Hitchcock. In this regard, I was fortunate to have the cooperation and encouragement of Dame Peggy Ashcroft, Ingrid Bergman, Hume Cronyn, Joan Fontaine, Princess Grace of Monaco (the former actress Grace Kelly), Tippi Hedren, Tom Helmore, Ernest Lehman, Simon Oakland, Jessica Tandy, Samuel Taylor and Teresa Wright. Princess Grace, after reading the first draft of the book, generously offered to contribute a foreword. Hers was one of several friendships—like unexpected benedictions—which came from this project.

Hundreds of hours, of course, were spent in the dark, at film archives. Invaluable assistance was provided by Patrick Sheehan at the Motion Picture Division of the Library of Congress, Washington; by Jeremy Boulton at the National Film Archives, London; and by Charles Silver at the Museum of Modern Art, New York, where Mary Corliss, surely the most knowledgeable and unfailingly gracious film stills archivist in the business, enabled me to find many rare photographs. Tippi Hedren also made available her extensive personal collection of stills from the productions of *The Birds* and *Marnie*.

As I drew near to concluding the first draft of *The Art of Alfred Hitchcock*, he and screenwriter Ernest Lehman were preparing *Family Plot*, Hitchcock's fifty-third (and, as it happened, his last) movie. For courtesy's sake, I sent a few chapters to Hitchcock, typescript pages on *Sabotage*, the second version of *The Man Who Knew Too Much* and *Frenzy*. Within days, I had a telegram at my home (then in New York), inviting me to watch him at work on *Family Plot* in Hollywood. When I arrived, he also granted me an extended interview, the first of many meetings in the last five years of his life.

The original edition of this book was published in the autumn of 1976, and I sent the first copy to Hitchcock; he responded by preparing a lengthy and very generous public endorsement—another first in a series of happy surprises that contributed to making

The Art of Alfred Hitchcock something of a standard work. Since that time, Alfred Hitchcock died (in 1980), my biography of him (*The Dark Side of Genius,* 1983) has been published in many languages, and his primacy as one of the few great artists of the cinema has been confirmed worldwide and without question.

From 1975 to 1986, I was fortunate to teach Hitchcock's films year-round, on a rotating cycle, at The New School for Social Research in New York; additionally, I was often invited to lecture on one or another film or theme in Hitchcock's work at festivals and at colleges and universities round the world, as well as at series for the American and British Film Institutes. As I continued to study this extraordinary body of work and listened to the questions and comments of audiences, it became clear that there was very much more to say. Thus I was delighted when Martha Levin at Doubleday inquired if I had some additional thoughts when a new printing was being prepared. I quickly replied that I had many such thoughts—too many for a few mere paragraph substitutions here and there, in fact—and she readily agreed to this completely revised edition.

Frequently, if not usually, critics speak and write as if their interpretations of art were the last words—as if their insights, as bridges from artist to audience, close the door to meaning, and thenceforth no dog should bark. I do not think this is the function of the interpreter. In this book I have simply tried to widen the scope of the creative, critical dialogue about one man's work—a half century of work.

Obviously, the passion a critic brings to the study of specific works of art reveals much about the critic himself. In setting forth certain themes, ideas and images in the art of Alfred Hitchcock, I think I have made it clear that they have special significance for me. The act of interpretation, after all, interprets the interpreter to himself. In any case, this writer has discovered as much about himself as about one artist's work, and that is no small dividend.

Finis coronat opus—the end crowns the work, according to a curious old adage. But in a work of criticism, the end should only bring us back to the beginning, to the works of art themselves. If the reader is impelled to see again the films of Alfred Hitchcock, I shall have considered my work successful.

. . .

Many people have deepened my appreciation of Hitchcock over the years—more than ten thousand students at The New School and perhaps as many more in audiences round the world—and to them all I am keenly indebted for their comments, suggestions, corrections and criticisms. I am also grateful to Douglas Alexander, who edited the text of this second edition and raised questions about some matters unclear and neglected. The dedication page bears the name of a gifted physician who was also an ardent moviegoer, a cherished friend who never tired of hearing me talk about Hitchcock.

D.S.
Los Angeles
February 25, 1991

A WORD ABOUT THE MACGUFFIN

From time to time over the years, Alfred Hitchcock referred to "the MacGuffin" in a story—some object which appears to be of importance to the characters but is actually of little interest to the director (and consequently, at last, to the audience). Examples abound: the secret formula in *The 39 Steps* and *Torn Curtain;* clauses of peace treaties in *The Lady Vanishes* and *Foreign Correspondent;* uranium in wine bottles in *Notorious.*

The origin of the word has been variously explained, but Hitchcock always thought it could be traced to a hoary anecdote:

Two men were traveling by train from London to Edinburgh. In the luggage rack overhead was a wrapped parcel.

"What have you there?" asked one of the men.

"Oh, that's a MacGuffin," replied the other.

"What's a MacGuffin?"

"It's a device for trapping lions in the Scottish Highlands."

"But there aren't any lions in the Scottish Highlands!"

"Well, then, that's no MacGuffin."

There's a lot to look for in Hitchcock's films, but watch out for the MacGuffin. It will lead you nowhere.

A COMMENT

BY PRINCESS GRACE OF MONACO

Very often I see no reason for a book to have a preface. An annoying few paragraphs demanding to be read when you really don't want to do anything of the sort.

But this book is about someone I love and respect, and I find irresistible the opportunity to add a few words of my own.

It was my good fortune to have worked in three of Alfred Hitchcock's films. I was able to observe and appreciate his special talents as a director of motion pictures, with the multiple skills that that job requires. I also came to know him as a warm and understanding human being.

Mr. Hitchcock often is reputed to hold actors in disdain. But he actually has a special way with them, and is able to get exactly what he wants in the way of a performance. His inimitable humor puts them at ease, while his enduring patience gives them any confidence they may need. Of course, sometimes he merely wears them down until he gets what he wants.

Working with Hitch is a fascinating experience, and reading this book will be just that for his many admirers and fans. They will discover the many aspects of his creativity in developing characters and plots, and will understand better his technical skills and use of camera to build mood and suspense.

Donald Spoto has done a remarkable job of research, and he has written a detailed and interesting account of Alfred Hitchcock's art and achievements in an extraordinary career that now spans fifty years. He is the master of suspense, and Dr. Spoto gives us an enlightening study of his work.

(From the First Edition, 1976)

CONTENTS

The Art of
Alfred Hitchcock

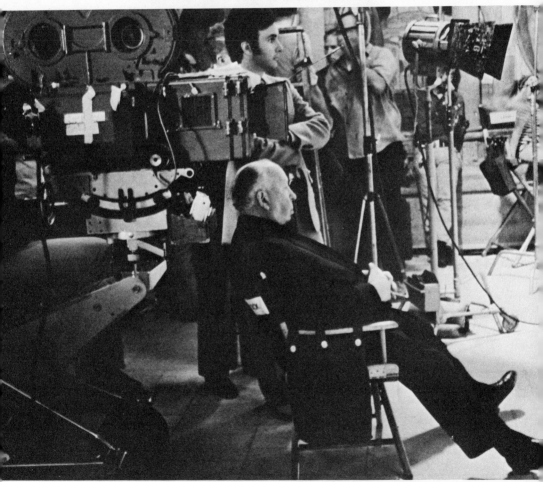

*"We try to tell a good story and develop a hefty plot.
Themes emerge as we go along."* (Hitchcock to the author.)

1

THE SILENT FILMS

(1925–1929)

So full of artless jealousy is guilt,
It spills itself in fearing to be spilt.

HAMLET

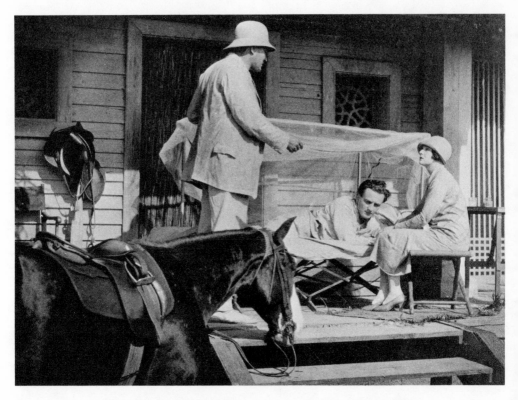

The Pleasure Garden, Hitchcock's first feature (1925).

Alfred Joseph Hitchcock was born in London on August 13, 1899, the youngest of three children of Emma and William Hitchcock, who was a moderately successful poultry dealer and grocer. Young Alfred was educated at Saint Ignatius College (a preparatory school) in his teen years, but the death of his father pitched him into the work force during World War I and he never formally attended university. His first jobs were minor technical assignments with an electric cable company, for whom he also designed advertisements.

In 1921 and 1922 he submitted to Famous Players–Lasky several portfolio of designs to accompany the intertitles of silent films: *The Call of Youth* and *The Great Day* (both directed by Hugh

Ford), *The Princess of New York* and *Tell Your Children* (directed by Donald Crisp) and George Fitzmaurice's *Three Live Ghosts*. Film crews were small and talent was quickly recognized, and soon there came a directorial assignment—*Number Thirteen* (1922) with Clare Greet and Ernest Thesiger, but the budget collapsed and the film was never completed. That same year, Hitchcock and actor Seymour Hicks edited the final version of *Always Tell Your Wife* when its director fell ill.

The parent American production company of Famous Players-Lasky abandoned its London studio in 1922, and almost immediately executive producers Michael Balcon, Victor Saville and John Freedman formed Gainsborough Pictures at the same location in Islington. From 1922 to 1925, Hitchcock was an assistant to director Graham Cutts, for whom he wrote the scenarios and designed sets for *Woman to Woman, The White Shadow, The Passionate Adventure, The Blackguard* and *The Prude's Fall*. The editor of *Woman to Woman* was a highly intelligent, vivacious young Englishwoman named Alma Reville, who in 1926 became Mrs. Alfred Hitchcock; her influence and creative collaboration on her husband's work were gradually more and more important to their success, and she often worked (sometimes credited, sometimes not) on the treatments, screenplays and continuity for Hitchcock's masterworks.

In 1925, producer Michael Balcon offered Alfred Hitchcock the opportunity to direct his first motion picture—in Munich, Germany, where facilities were far more lavish than in London and where Balcon had negotiated a coproduction deal (the better to insure European distribution of his picture). Assisting the neophyte technician were screenwriter Eliot Stannard, cinematographer Baron Ventimiglia and assistant director-editor Alma Reville.

The project was to be a potboiler based on a popular novel by Oliver Sandys called *The Pleasure Garden,* about a chorus girl named Patsy Brand (Virginia Valli) who befriends Jill Cheyne (Carmelita Geraghty) and helps her land a job as a dancer at the Pleasure Garden music hall. Soon Jill is engaged to Hugh Fielding (John Stuart), whose work takes him to the tropics. In his absence, her career and her social life flourish, and before long she is mistress to (among others, it is implied) a dashing continental playboy.

Patsy, meanwhile, marries a friend of Fielding named Levett (Miles Mander), and after their honeymoon at Lake Como he sails to the Far East on business. When Patsy learns her husband is ill, she goes out to care for him, but finds that he has taken to both drink and native girls. In alcoholic dementia, Levett drowns a hapless object of his attention, and when the poor girl's ghost comes to haunt him he turns on Patsy, threatening her with a sword until a local doctor shoots him dead. Fielding, forgotten by the madcap Jill, meets up with Patsy, and the story ends with the beginning of their life together. There's certainly little exceptional in the content, but Hitchcock invested the film with a fascinating structure: his primal concern is the two sets of lovers, for Patsy and Levett (and their various ideas about fidelity) are everywhere visually contrasted with Hugh and Jill.

The film opens with an extraordinary shot of leggy chorines hurriedly descending a spiral staircase and rushing onto the stage of the Pleasure Garden, where they dance with the wild abandon typical of the Jazz Age. The movement is so animated and the cuts so swift that this silent film suddenly becomes a kind of vivid and funny musical flip-book. The camera then cuts to a man in the theater audience, avidly watching the chorus girls' legs through binoculars. In fact these opening images announce a great deal that will be mainstream Hitchcock for the next half century: the theatrical setting where players become protagonists in bizarre real-life dramas, the camera observing an observer, the rapid cuts from the watcher to the watched, the dizzy circular staircase—and the puckish humor: "What every chorus girl knows," announces a title card, and then we're shown a woman washing her stockings in a basin.

Life within and outside this pleasure garden, from London's cramped West End to the wide open spaces of the tropics, is a perilous, fallen paradise—thus Hitchcock's insistence on the ominous snake, entwined round a tree in the title cards he himself designed (thus giving another meaning to the theater of the film's title). The chase and the nick-of-time rescue he learned from D. W. Griffith, and the camera's wonderfully realized, hallucinatory dream imagery from several of his German technicians. But every sequence shines with an astonishing originality: characters gazing directly at the camera, long takes and few intertitles, an emphasis on the tiny, revelatory gestures instead of the broad, sweeping histrionics dear to silent filmmakers. *The Pleasure Garden* was certainly an auspicious debut for a director who departed England on assignment, and when Balcon arrived to see the rough cut he was sufficiently impressed to ask Hitchcock to remain in Munich for a second picture. A major career was moving forward.

The progress, however, was not so evident from his second film. *The Mountain Eagle* (made in Munich in the autumn of 1925 and released the following year) starred Nita Naldi and Malcolm Keen and dealt with, of all things, the hillbillies of Kentucky—not a subject of great familiarity to Hitchcock, his English screenwriter Eliot Stannard or his German crew. In America it was released under the title *Fear o' God* (the name of the wacky recluse played by Keen), but very soon it vanished into oblivion, and in fact no print of *The Mountain Eagle* has existed for very many years. This was, according to Hitchcock, no tragedy; it was, he always insisted, "a very bad movie."

But like history, he holds a considerably different opinion of his next film, *The Lodger* (1926), subtitled "A Story of the London Fog," his first English movie. "It was the first time I really exercised my style," he said later. "You might say *The Lodger* was my first picture." This may be the noisiest silent picture ever made, each shot carefully planned and edited, with swift action in every crowded frame, and the intertitle cards so sparse that we don't regret the lack of spoken dialogue.

The film's opening is a superbly elliptical montage, compacting all the major motifs into six or seven minutes of screen time. First we see a close-up of a fair-haired woman, screaming in terror right toward the camera, and the image is so startling that the silent film seems almost to burst with sound. Precisely the same image recurs in later Hitchcock films—in the first shot of *To Catch a Thief,* for example (a woman screams that she's been robbed of jewelry), in *The Man Who Knew Too Much* (Doris Day's scream at the Albert Hall fills the screen) and in *Psycho* (Janet Leigh screams as she sees her attacker).

After cutting to the blinking lights of a theater marquee announcing "To-Night, Golden Curls," Hitchcock cuts back: the woman who screamed is dead, the latest victim of the madman terrorizing London by killing young blondes; his demented signature card ("The Avenger") has been left on the body. The details immediately following fascinate Hitchcock—the press reports, the busy teletype, the dispatchers in the news offices—and he chooses this swift montage for his first cameo appearance, his back to us as he telephones in a news editing room. To convey the city's terror at this latest murder, he then shows us people listening to radio reports and blond chorus girls backstage at "Golden Curls" (shades of *The Pleasure Garden*). It's interesting to see one young chorine hearing the latest news with a kind of wistful, fearful rapture as another touches her own blond hair, clearly thinking, "Am I next?" For Hitchcock, victims must be as fascinated by the horror as the victimizers (and the audience).

Now we meet the heroine, Daisy Bunting (played by the actress June Tripp, known professionally by only her first name), who seems to be a wealthy woman, glamorously outfitted—but the camera pulls back, and the reality is very different. She's a

Ivor Novello and June in *The Lodger*.

mannequin modeling high-fashions, and in the very next shot we see her modest home life with her simple Cockney parents (Marie Ault and Arthur Chesney). Her boyfriend Joe Betts (Malcolm Keen), an ambitious detective, is a frequent visitor there: "I'm keen on golden hair myself," he tells her parents, "same as the Avenger is."

With the arrival at the Bunting home of the nameless lodger (Ivor Novello, acting with dated theatrical gestures that make his performance virtually a definition of high camp), the atmosphere changes morbidly. He asks that the Victorian paintings of blondes be removed from the room he rents ("They get on my nerves"), and he manically paces his floor—so much, in fact, that his footsteps disturb the family. (The "sound" is rendered visually by Hitchcock's design of a thick plate glass ceiling on which Novello walks; we see pacing feet as the family hears him from the room below.)

Next evening, while Daisy and the lodger play chess, he remarks on her lovely hair. Later, Joe arrives and announces to Daisy's parents that he's been assigned to the Avenger case: "When I've put a rope round the Avenger's neck, I'll put a ring round Daisy's finger." He chases Daisy and playfully claps handcuffs on her, but this backfires: she's terrified, and when set free, quite annoyed. (This funny-sinister connection between marriage and bondage will be carried forward in the famous handcuff episodes of *The 39 Steps* and *Saboteur*.)

That night, Daisy's mother watches the lodger leave the house, and when another murder is discovered next morning, her suspicions are heightened. Joe's jealousy of Daisy is the source of *his* suspicions about this strange, epicene lodger, however ("Sorry I lost my temper," Joe says to Daisy, "but there's something about him I can't stand"), and at this point we have Hitchcock's pointed theme of the triangle, a geometric shape that is on the movie's opening designs and intertitle cards. (Hitchcock himself was first employed as a studio title card designer at Islington.)

Soon the lodger is Daisy's greatest admirer, attending her modeling shows, watching her walk about and buying her the expensive frocks she cannot afford. At the same time, the police close in on the Buntings' neighborhood as the locale of the Avenger's recent crimes. The next Tuesday evening—always the night when the murders of young blondes occur—Daisy and the lodger go out. They meet Joe, whom Daisy dismisses when he again acts like a jealous schoolboy. Left alone, Joe imagines that the lodger must be the Avenger, and Hitchcock shows us the detective's mental process with only the most economical visuals: connective images of the lodger pacing, of the lodger's strange black bag, of the Avenger's note, all passing over his footprint in the mud, at which Joe stares.

The close-up during the lovemaking scene between the lodger and Daisy at home (and in the film's final shot) foreshadows several similar kissing scenes in later Hitchcock films (from Ingrid Bergman and Gregory Peck in *Spellbound* to Tippi Hedren and Sean Connery in *Marnie*). The couple is then interrupted by Joe and his colleagues, who find in the Lodger's satchel a gun, a map and a collection of news stories about the Avenger's victims, one of whom, the lodger says, was his own sister. Joe orders him arrested, against Daisy's protests. The handcuffs are clapped on and the man is taken away, but when Mrs. Bunting faints at the unpleasant turn of events, the lodger escapes amid the confusion. Daisy meets up with him, and he tells her that indeed his own sister was the Avenger's first victim; he has, in effect, set out to avenge his sister.

She takes him to a pub for a restorative brandy—a drink that will make a crucial cameo appearance in every one of Hitchcock's films. But his handcuffs are spotted by someone, and soon the crowd is after him, very nearly tearing him to pieces. Just at that moment, the real Avenger is arrested, the lodger is cleared and we have a happy ending, with Daisy blissfully in the arms of the (still nameless) lodger at his own house—quite a mansion, as it turns out.

The film's series of silent shrieks recall Edvard Munch's famous painting, and the expressionist lighting, severely raked sets, disturbing mirror reflections, angular shadows and dizzying staircase shots were clearly influenced by Hitchcock's work with German movie technicians and his observation of other directors in Germany the previous year. *The Lodger* is a remarkably effective combination of style and content, and in spite of Novello's performance of the lodger as a distracted neurasthenic, there is a delicate poise between paranoia and security. The final macabre joke, of course, is that Daisy's life with the lodger is visually associated with the opening announcement of murder: again "To-Night, Golden Curls" flashes on the background marquee. Hitchcock, who wanted the lodger to be guilty, had to yield to the producer's demand for a happy ending, but convention has rarely seemed so unappealing. Nothing about this couple looks very promising.

The Lodger is in every way a remarkable achievement, and it justified Michael Balcon's continuing confidence in Alfred Hitchcock's talent. Witty, visually inventive, genuinely disturbing despite its conventions, understated and economical (especially in its use of dialogue intertitles), it withstands multiple viewings and is virtually a textbook for Hitchcock's later work. There is, most of all, his favorite theme: an innocent man wrongly accused of a crime. This plot device is brilliantly linked to a deeper moral ambiguity, for using the most fragile circumstantial evidence, the detective—jealous of his fiancée's friendship with the lodger—constructs first in his own mind and then in the suspicions of others a case for an innocent man's guilt.

This theme will recur with startling regularity in Hitchcock's work—most notably and problematically in *Suspicion.* And both films have suffered from serious subsequent misperceptions deriving from Hitchcock's own public statements. He contended that the popular images of Ivor Novello (in *The Lodger*) and of Cary Grant (in *Suspicion*) made it impossible for them to be seen as villains. He would, he claimed, have liked to have had the lodger simply disappear into the night, without ever establishing his innocence or guilt. And in the later film, he would have preferred Johnny Aysgarth (Grant) to have actually murdered his wife with poisoned milk and not (as the finished film has it) be revealed as innocent of such an intention. But in fact, these endings would have blurred the significance of everything that preceded, which makes for a much more disturbing and mature tale of psychological turmoil and manufactured guilt.

In *The Lodger,* the ambiguity of the situation derives only partly from the deplorable lengths to which the detective's jealousy leads him. The lodger is himself far from innocent, since he has in fact planned to murder the real killer all along. He arrives with a revolver and a carefully marked map of the crimes, and sets himself up as the real avenger of his own sister's death—a kind of Victorian vigilante. Intending to kill the killer (whom we never see), he is guilty of a carefully premeditated act of hatred. This is hardly innocence, and so our reaction to the supposedly happy ending is tempered. The identical theme operates, with even more relentless cynicism, in *Frenzy* (1972), in which the man innocent of the rape-murders seethes with violence and plans revenge on the real killer.

Hitchcock's fourth film, *Downhill* (1927), was based on a series of sketches about school life by Ivor Novello, whose popularity as a matinée idol had already been well exploited by Balcon in *The Lodger*. Isabel Jeans, another famous stage actress, was engaged to costar, and Hitchcock and writer Eliot Stannard set themselves the task of stitching together the sprawling and diffuse sketches. The result was a story remarkable mostly for its introduction of another mainstream Hitchcockian concern, that of guilt shared by two friends—a theme to be emphasized again and again, from *The Manxman* through *Strangers on a Train, Frenzy* and *Family Plot*. The opening title announces the tale of "two school boys who made a pact of loyalty—and one kept it at a price."

Ivor Novello in *Downhill*.

Novello was cast as Roddy Berwick, a (rather overgrown) boy who takes the blame for a schoolmate's offense, is expelled from home and school and embarks on a path "downhill" until he is finally restored to respectability. Though innocent, he learns about his own capacities for wickedness during this journey, which becomes a kind of moral education before the somewhat simplistic conclusion. Roddy is thus grandfather to all the Hitchcock heroes who learn that a recognition of their true humanity requires an excursion to the frontiers of their shadowy side.

As in *The Pleasure Garden* and *The Lodger,* Hitchcock here indulged his predilection for the swooping camera movement over staircases, the better to visualize the motif of "descent." We see, for example, a subjective (i.e., point of view) shot of Roddy descending in the London underground—"the quickest way to everything," as the intertitle card proclaims with pointed ambiguity.

The world of social and academic respectability and the canonization of class distinctions are neatly punctured in *Downhill,* too, and Hitchcock returns lovingly to the theatrical setting, "the world of make believe" (thus the titles) concretizing "the world of lost illusions" that comprises Roddy's inner journey—far more exotic and, finally, more significant, than his trips to Paris and Marseilles. Technically, the picture is superior to just about anything that was made in England that year: there are perfectly matched dissolves to relate characters and themes; a fine dream sequence; and astonishingly stable follow shots with a hand-held camera along the docks of Marseilles. The sets, to be frank, are more convincing than some of the acting.

Easy Virtue (1927), based on a controversial Noël Coward play, was Hitchcock's fourth film under contract to Michael Balcon at Gainsborough Studios. The director seems to have acquiesced dutifully rather than accepted cheerfully, and the nature of the material generally lacked interest for him: Beautiful Larita Filton (Isabel Jeans), once the defendant in an ugly divorce case, meets and marries John Whittaker (Robin Irvine), a handsome but weak young man, the son of a wealthy, class-conscious English family. Larita's new mother-in-law (Violet Farebrother) learns that Larita was (unfairly, as we know) accused of impropriety in the earlier divorce case, but the very idea of scandal is unacceptable to the family, and John is unwilling and unable to stand by his wife against his mother's moral outrage. The story ends unhappily, with Larita's marriage over and her reputation permanently destroyed.

Typically, Hitchcock took refuge in devising fresh cinematic gestures and camera techniques to avoid the proliferation of title cards. He also wisely chose to contrast the grimly severe features of the mother-in-law with the sharply handsome features of blond Isabel Jeans. *Easy Virtue* is remarkable, in this regard, for the number of close-ups in which a player gazes directly at the camera—expressions overwhelm us, and thanks to the marvelously plastic features of this talented British cast, there is subtlety in these expressions, not merely exaggerated silent screen reactions.

The opening shot is at first unclear—a white field with a carved circle—until we see that it's the top of a judge's wig. He lifts his head, gazes at us, and from his point of view we see a blurry image of a crowded courtroom. He then raises his monocle before the camera, and into clear focus, framed in the monocle, a lawyer rises to face the judge.

"I must ask you," says the attorney to Larita, "to repeat your statement with regard to this decanter"—a brandy decanter, of course. From a close shot of the decanter the camera pulls back to a matched cut in a flashback scene which gave rise to the divorce trial. But Hitchcock is as impatient as any viewer with too much courtroom talk—especially in a silent film—and so he simply dissolves wordlessly from one profile of a talking attorney to a profile of a respondent, and back and forth again. Then from a close shot of the judge swinging his monocle, the image dissolves to a swinging pendulum. The passage of time is thus neatly conveyed in a few seconds.

Hitchcock is also fascinated with the way in which publicity and the ubiquitous camera probe and pry into lives. Larita leaves the courtroom surrounded by a group of eager photographers; later, her photo in a social gazette triggers her mother-in-law's memory of the divorce scandal; later still, in the depths of her anguish, Larita gazes at a camera and angrily hurls a book at it; and the conclusion—again after a divorce trial—shows Larita the victim of unwanted publicity from British paparazzi. This motif of the morality of picture-taking is a subtle but consistent one in Hitchcock, right up to *Rear Window,* wherein Grace Kelly says to chair-bound news photographer James Stewart: "Do you think it's ethical to go around the world just taking pictures of people?"

The young director's visual ingenuity shines throughout: a good example is the comic moment he devised to show us John's proposal of marriage, Larita's hesitation, his insistence and her final acceptance—all without a single title card. First we see a switchboard operator making a connection, and then we follow her successive reactions to the dialogue she overhears (but we, of course, do not)—reactions of pleasure, then dismay, then fear, encouragement and finally triumph at the stages of the conversation. Everything is conveyed through the operator's facial expressions, and this technique—never mere gimmickry—is central to the complexity of Hitchcock's representation of what characters *feel,* as distinct from what they *say.*

The design of the Whittaker baronial dining hall is also noteworthy: it's a curious anomaly, a formal room over which loom enormous painted icons of saints and patriarchs—clearly more expressionistic than realistic, more apt for a Byzantine cathedral than an English country house.

The picture ends as it began, at a divorce trial, and with the same matched visuals, the same judge and the tear-stained face of Isabel Jeans. The final close-up is one of the most affecting in Hitchcock's films—despite her closing line, which Hitchcock claimed was the worst single moment of dialogue he ever had in a movie: "Shoot," the beaten Larita tells the waiting photographers outside the court, "there's nothing left to kill!"

Hitchcock appears strolling past a tennis court, holding a walking stick and wiping perspiration from his brow. Isabel Jeans, bemused, gazes after him. She had costarred happily in *Downhill* and would play a tiny role in *Suspicion,* but she is best known to movie audiences as Aunt Alicia in the musical film *Gigi.* One of the most admired and versatile actresses of the English stage and a woman of great elegance, she died in 1985 at the age of 94.

"There were all kinds of innovations in *The Ring,*" Hitchcock said of the first original story he developed for the screen, "and I

Lillian Hall Davis and Carl Brisson in *The Ring*.

remember that at the premiere an elaborate montage got a round of applause." The appreciation was well deserved, for this traditional story of a love triangle (two men in love with the same woman) was so freshly treated, so ripe with visual and narrative invention—not to mention cynical wit—that it seems astonishing from one so young. Neither suspense thriller nor comedy, *The Ring* is instead a kind of meditation on the vagaries of love, rather like all Hitchcock's films when you stop to think about it. (They're all variations on a love theme, all types within the romance genre.)

"One Round Jack" Saunders (Carl Brisson) can knock out all challengers in a few moments—except Bob Corby (Ian Hunter), who is his rival for the affections of his fiancée Nelly (Lillian Hall Davis). But the ring is not only a boxing arena: it's a wedding ring, it's the cyclic nature of the love triangle, it's the apparent futility of romanticized tenderness—and all these rings are reinforced by Hitchcock's accumulation of circular objects. There are, to name but a few, the close-up of a drum beating out an invitation to a fairground; a revolving carousel and a turning Ferris wheel; the bracelet in the form of a snake (recalling the title designs of

The Pleasure Garden) Bob slips on Nelly's arm. The visual design of the film, then, both establishes and reinforces its theme of the cycles of love—both endless possibility and (it is implied) ceaseless disappointment.

Hitchcock's fascination for the grotesque emerges in *The Ring*, too, in the boxers' sideshow colleagues. Siamese twins fight over a pew in church, the giant arrives at the wedding accompanying the midget, the fat lady enters the church somewhat tentatively. But the picture's psychological maturity is focused in its insistence on the shifting, fickle nature of erotic love, and characters' states of mind and feeling are everywhere italicized by Hitchcock's canny use of overlays and dissolves, montages, double exposures and blurred subjective images. Jack, for example, proposes a champagne toast to Nelly—but she is out with another man, and as he glances at the untouched glasses the wine loses its sparkle, the bubbles go flat. Such touches seem obvious many years later, but this was highly inventive moviemaking in 1927. To his credit, Hitchcock never substituted mere technique for faces: his camera catches perfectly the nervous beauty of Lillian Hall Davis and the lingering confusions on her face.

Hitchcock made quite different use of Hall Davis in his next film, however. *The Farmer's Wife* was a routine assignment during his contract years at British International Pictures, and the idea for the film was simply to capitalize on a fabulously successful rustic stage comedy, but from such exigencies came a film everywhere revealing the sure hand of a talented filmmaker.

Following his wife's death, Farmer Sweetland (Jameson Thomas) scours the countryside for a new bride. His options, however, prove to be disastrous—a tearful, wizened spinster, an equestrienne just a *little* too masculine for Sweetland's comfort, and a porcine hysteric. He seems on the verge of perpetual celibacy until he looks in his own kitchen, at the housekeeper who has for years served him and his late wife so devotedly (Lillian Hall Davis)—a fragile but strong beauty who, of course, has loved him silently all along.

From this uncompelling narrative Hitchcock fashioned a terrifically funny film that is also not afraid to be quite unexpectedly tender. Most often, we see characters from others' viewpoints—thus actors face the camera directly, react out at us—and thus we spectators are identified with the one seeing (most often Sweetland). Considering how talky the Eden Phillpotts play, it is doubly impressive that there are so few intertitles. Instead—visual storyteller that he instinctively was—Hitchcock found images to convey emotions. A ring suspended from a saddle is intercut with a man's wistful look: we read his thoughts from the juxtaposition (a happy marriage past and a yearning for one in future); the sense is reinforced by confetti and rice at his daughter's wedding table and a shot of his own empty dining room.

But above all *The Farmer's Wife* is comedy, and Hitchcock never forgot that. A formal luncheon, for example, descends into something worthy of Lewis Carroll as everything is just upset enough to make the entire world seem daffy: a weepy maid cannot prevent ice cream from melting; children wreak havoc everywhere; and a sturdy matriarch tries to negotiate her way through the chaos in an enormous wheelchair whose steering device has a mind of its own.

Jameson Thomas in *The Farmer's Wife*.

Betty Balfour in *Champagne*.

Hitchcock continued in a comic vein with *Champagne,* also made
in 1928 and developed from his own idea. It's an amusing trifle
that continues the theme of the displaced rich child subject to a
moral education (introduced in *Downhill*), but here the protagonist
is a girl (Betty Balfour, one of the most popular comediennes of
her day). She's the prototypical flapper, she fears neither man nor
beast, and she flies round the world in her own biplane, determined
to prove to her father (Gordon Harker) that her boyfriend (Jean
Bradin) is worthy of her. To teach her a lesson in responsibility,
Papa allows her to think the family fortune—derived from champagne—has been lost. Betty is then propelled from the life of a
carefree child to that of an actress, toothpaste vendor and cabaret
seller of the very champagne that once meant her security. Her
father finally takes pity on her and agrees to her heart's desire.

Malcolm Keen and Anny Ondra in *The Manxman*.

Along the way, there are some splendid moments in an otherwise unremarkable narrative. The private detective (Theo von Alten) hired to trail Betty opens and closes the film, in precisely the same action—draining a champagne glass, and we not only see him do this, we drain it with him and see the background image as if through the bottom of the glass. (As in *Easy Virtue*, the film begins with a deliberately self-referential shot—a distorted point of view through an object.) He seems at first sinister, then protective, then kindly, and finally just plain lecherous—and it's always precisely the same view of the man smiling; Hitchcock insists that a shot itself is neutral, that its meaning is provided by editing and context.

Champagne is graced with neat insertions. Father presses the call buttons on his executive desk and a flock of aides rushes in, like startled pigeons. A drunk aboard ship sways from side to side when the sea is calm but walks perfectly straight when there's a storm and everyone else is off balance. Hitchcock had just developed a taste for vintage champagne, and this picture was his little homage to the bubbly.

If we take Hitchcock's opinion as the standard, then the only interesting thing to say about *The Manxman* (1929) is that it was his last complete silent film. The picture deserves a better judgment, however; in fact it's a deeply felt story, shimmeringly photographed and affectingly rendered. Adapted from a novel by Hall Caine, it tells of the cramped, stifled life of several forlorn people on the Isle of Man. Peter Christian (Carl Brisson) asks his lifelong friend Philip Quilian (Malcolm Keen) to plead his cause with the father of his beloved, Kate (Anny Ondra). Philip does so, despite his own secret desires for her. Pete leaves for Africa, to earn enough money to win Kate's hand, and during his absence Philip and Kate have an idyllic affair—which she believes can turn to marriage when the news of Pete's death is received. But Philip is in line for an inherited judgeship on Man (a position called the deemster) and his family reminds him that Kate is really beneath him socially. Peter, as it turns out, is very much alive, and when he returns he marries Kate, who (at first unknown to him) is bearing Philip's child. She leaves home for Philip and when he rejects her she attempts suicide—a crime on the Isle of Man. She is brought before Philip, who acknowledges his guilt, and, with Kate and their child, leaves Man in disgrace. The last shot is of Pete's face, grief-stricken and doubly abandoned.

To this relentlessly unhappy melodrama Hitchcock brought a sure hand, demonstrating the variety of moods, tones and tensions he could maintain in a film narrative. Looking back to *Downhill* and forward to *Family Plot* (1976), Hitchcock and screenwriter Eliot Stannard stressed the motif of ambition versus love (located in the person of Philip), complicated by the obligations—and eventual exploitation—of friendship. The opening title card, the words of Jesus in the New Testament (and not an epigraph to Caine's 500-page novel, published in 1894), is one of Hitchcock's least subtle indicators of the controlling theme: "What shall it profit a man if he gain the whole world and suffer the loss of his soul?"

Jack Cox's cinematography ranks with anything ever achieved on black-and-white: the love scenes on the high cliffs of Man and in the meadows nearby (shot in Devon) have an almost fragrant loveliness, and there's just the right tincture of melancholy in the great watermill sequences where the rendezvous and later the marriage are set. The deepening of love, sometimes conveyed through the changing tone of Kate's diary, is expressed in few words—as usual, it's achieved mostly through the faces of the principals, with their disaffected gazes revealing that passion soon spends itself. Perhaps the single most arresting image in *The Manxman*, however, is Hitchcock's dissolve from the black waters into which Kate leaps in her abortive suicide attempt, to the inkwell dipped by Philip's pen. Seldom has a romantic melodrama been so uncompromising about the tragic effects of ill-considered passion.

2

BLACKMAIL

(PRODUCED AND RELEASED 1929)

. . . to fear the birds of prey . . .

MEASURE FOR MEASURE

John Longden and Anny Ondra in *Blackmail*.

The American film industry made a giant leap when Al Jolson sang and spoke onscreen in 1927: at once the news about *The Jazz Singer* proclaimed the end of the silent film era. Two years later, Alfred Hitchcock had finished directing (but not editing) *Blackmail*, based on a play by Charles Bennett, when executives from British International rushed in to say they had sound equipment ready. Since he had a script and a cast still available, they asked would he like to reshoot some portions of the film they could then release as England's first talkie? He agreed at once.

There was, however, a problem. In the lead role of a Cockney coquette was the Polish-Czech actress Anny Ondra—the pert blonde from *The Manxman*—and she had a pronounced accent.

And so her scenes (among others) were reshot, and just off camera stood the English player Joan Barry, speaking Ondra's lines while Ondra silently moved her lips. (They had sound, but there was not yet the capability for postsynchronization or dubbing.) Additionally, Hitchcock reshot scenes for which he "designed the sound"—effects, distortions, surprises that went far beyond mere talk or noise. *Blackmail* remains, over sixty years later, an astonishing achievement technically—and a rich, disturbing moral thriller in the bargain.

The story line is surprisingly simple. Alice White (Anny Ondra) and her beau, detective Frank Webber (John Longden) quarrel at a restaurant, and Alice departs on the arm of a handsome, well-dressed stranger (Cyril Ritchard). As it happens, he is an artist and invites her to his studio where he persuades her to model for him in a tutu. She's coy, flirtatious, modest, but curious. He then attempts to make love and in her fear she seizes a bread knife, stabs him to death and makes her way home unseen. Webber, assigned to the case, soon suspects that Alice is the murderer, but he conceals this from his superiors. Now enters the blackmailer, who had seen Alice entering the artist's flat. Webber implicates him in the murder, a chase ensues, and the blackmailer falls to his death through the dome of the British Museum, if you please. Alice, her conscience tortured now with responsibility for two deaths, tries to give herself up—but Webber prevents her. The film ends with Alice's anguish and the couple's shared, secret guilt.

That figures representing law and order are themselves eminently corruptible is a common theme in Hitchcock's films, and in this regard he shares a kind of moral cynicism common in modern literature (Joseph Conrad and Graham Greene are only two examples) and film (Fritz Lang was among the earliest, in German films like *Spione*). Judgments about what to consider infallibly right, true and good, about what forces to label "evil" and about the prestige accorded human authority are questioned throughout Hitchcock's work with as much insistence as wit. In *Blackmail* he explored more deeply than in *The Lodger* how the righteousness of law officers is often merely apparent; how those we frequently idolize play us false; how appearances must not be confused with reality. These concerns are made plain in the structure he devised

with his writers (playwrights Bennett and Benn Levy)—a structure that moves from considerations of duty, then of love and
finally to the conflict between love and duty. The film naturally
falls into three movements encapsulating this structure.

After an opening close-up shot of spinning auto wheels, we
see the police silently move in on a crook, arrest him, record his
fingerprints and toss him in a cell. (These details fascinate Hitchcock, perhaps because of his autobiographical account of being
"arrested" as a child, taught a lesson by a policeman relative who
tossed him in jail for five minutes with a stern warning to better
conduct. Variations of the first sequences of *Blackmail* occur later
in, for example, *The Paradine Case* and *The Wrong Man*.) The
arresting detective calmly washes his hands of the matter (literally)
and tells a colleague he has a date with his girl.

We then move from duty to love, as Webber and Alice meet,
then quarrel and part; the stabbing of the artist that follows—in
a context of violent lovemaking—becomes an ironic twist on the
love motif. Arriving home before dawn and stealing into bed fully
clothed, Alice is found by her mother (Sara Allgood), and for a
long period when there is no dialogue (only her troubled features
and her attempts to compose herself), Hitchcock filled the first
English soundtrack with the loud, incessant chirping of Alice's
caged bird—the first use of birds, Hitchcock's lifelong correlative
for chaos and disorder interrupting an apparently normal routine.
From *Blackmail* through his final great poetic statement (*The Birds*),
he drew continually on the British sport of bird-watching and on
birds as the traditional symbol for danger from medieval through
Victorian art.

In the family breakfast sequence which follows, the traumatized Alice attempts the banalities of the morning routine with her
parents and a gossipy neighbor who discusses the now publicized
murder. "What an awful way to kill a man," whines the visitor,
"with a *knife*! Now a good stiff whack over the 'ead with a brick
is one thing—there's something *British* about that! But a *knife*?
No, *knives* is not right! Now mind you, a *knife* is a difficult thing
to handle. Not just any *knife* will do . . . a *knife* . . . and with a
knife . . . And if you come to Chelsea, you mustn't bring a *knife*!"
As the woman rambles on in this speech, Hitchcock moves his
camera toward Alice's face—and simultaneously he brilliantly ex-

ploited the possibilities of sound by distorting the woman's voice on the soundtrack: we hear only the subjective impression of what Alice hears. The words seem to blur and run together and only the single word *knife* stabs out at Alice and at us from the track. Alice's father then asks her to cut a bit of bread; she distractedly grasps a knife identical to the one (also on a plate of bread) she used to kill the artist; but just as the neighbor says "knife" one last time it seems to leap from Alice's hands and fly to the floor. (" 'Ere, you might *cut* someone with that," scolds her father.)

The ordinary kitchen knife will, of course, be a frequent instrument of mayhem in Hitchcock's films. Annabella Smith is stabbed in the back by the spies in *The 39 Steps;* Verloc is killed by a knife held by his wife in *Sabotage;* and Marion and Arbogast are stabbed by Norman in *Psycho.* Hitchcock refuses to stylize or aestheticize the act of murder; on the contrary, stabbing, knifing and a long penetration of the blade into flesh allow the victims fully to experience their approaching death and the killers to savor their crimes. Hitchcock insists on the horrible nature of the deed, but neither does he dwell unduly on it; there is, in fact, a kind of squeamishness not found in later filmmakers.

The third movement of *Blackmail*—the elaboration of the "love versus duty" theme—begins when Frank Webber enters to say he has been assigned to the case. As soon as it is clear from the blackmailer's information that she is guilty, Frank at once decides to cover up for Alice—without any explanation from her, without asking a single question to determine the extent of her willfulness.

The blackmailer falls to his death after lowering himself on a rope past an enormous Egyptian god's head—actually a miniature, enlarged by a trick process shot. And just when Alice tries to confess to the police, Frank interrupts her and takes her home. Her silence—like the silence of Mrs. Verloc in *Sabotage,* also effected by a passionate detective who places love above duty—finally places her and the detective in a psychological climate of mutual guilt and collusion.

Blackmail is remarkable for its lively wit (Hitchcock makes his cameo appearance in an underground train, pestered by a small boy), its vibrant sense of London life, its feeling for neighborhoods, pubs, police stations, a tobacconist's shop. Everywhere he could, Hitchcock tried to do something more with sound than merely record dialogue: like the loud bird sounds and the subjective distortion of "knife," Alice's scream overlaps with that of the landlady as she discovers the dead artist (a moment repeated in *The 39 Steps,* when a woman's scream as she discovers a crime overlaps a train's whistle). But it is impossible to watch the film without sensing the director's deepest anxiety: that the custodians of order can play us false, that passions are deceptive and that (in the words of Gabriel Marcel) we live "in a world where betrayal is possible at every moment and in every form."

3

EARLY SOUND FILMS

(1930–1934)

Sweet are the uses of adversity.

AS YOU LIKE IT

Edward Chapman, Sara Allgood, Sidney Morgan
and Marie O'Neill in *Juno and the Paycock.*

Immediately after completing *Blackmail,* Hitchcock was one of
several directors assigned to supervise portions of a revue called
Elstree Calling (1930), the first British filmed musical comedy. A
mixed pudding "with sketches and other interpolated items by
Alfred Hitchcock and with some music by Ivor Novello," Hitchcock essentially directed actor Donald Calthrop (none other than
the blackmailer in the preceding film) who insists on entertaining
an audience with bits of Shakespeare even though he's invariably
interrupted or pulled offstage. When he finally has the chance for
a scene from *The Taming of the Shrew*—with Anna May Wong as
a Chinese-shouting, pie-throwing, scantily clad Katherine—Calthrop enters on a runaway motorcycle. The farce could hardly be

broader. Hitchcock, unsurprisingly, claimed to have almost forgotten the day he worked on this.

Also in 1930, Hitchcock and his wife Alma Reville were assigned to adapt, film and edit Sean O'Casey's play *Juno and the
Paycock,* about an impoverished family during the Dublin upris-
ings. This was not a work of his choice; he dispatched it per-
functorily according to his contractual obligations; and it has, as
he told François Truffaut, "nothing to do with cinema," or at
least nothing to do with *his* cinema.

More typical was his next film, *Murder!* (1930)—of which Hitchcock (according to the frequent custom of the time) simultaneously
directed a German-language version. The script (by the director
and his wife, based on a novel by Clemence Dane and Helen
Simpson) concerns Diana Baring (Norah Baring), a repertory ac-

Herbert Marshall and Esmé Percy in *Murder!*

tress accused of murdering a friend. After serving on a jury that
finds her guilty, the distinguished actor Sir John Menier (Herbert
Marshall) changes his mind and undertakes her defense. By writing
a scene for a proposed play and inviting the man he suspects to
read a part, Sir John elicits a confession: the real killer is Handel
Fane (Esmé Percy), a transvestite circus performer who killed
Diana's friend because she threatened to reveal that he was of
racially mixed blood. Fane leaves a note admitting his guilt and
clearing Diana; he then hangs himself during a trapeze performance. At the fade-out, Diana is acting onstage with Sir John in
his new play.

    Murder! is primarily important for its theatrical setting, and for
the issue toward which that setting points. From *The Pleasure
Garden* onward (cf. *The 39 Steps, Young and Innocent, Stage Fright,*
among others) Hitchcock used the theater—and often film itself—
as a fulcrum on which to balance a story whose theme is the search
for real identity and the concomitant deception of appearances.
Here, the accused is an actress, the hero a playwright-actor, the
murderer an acrobat-actor; in addition, Hitchcock gives his leading
lady a character name identical to her real name (Baring). Throughout, the script cross-relates the relationship between art and life:
"This is not a play," Sir John tells Diana. "This is life!" And to
get at "nothing but the truth" (the title of a play in the company's
repertory), the police attend a play that shows a murderer dressed
as a woman and as a policeman—two disguises the real killer used
to escape the scene of his crime. Hitchcock then cuts at once from
the stage's curtain to the rising of the panel on Diana's cell door.
And when Sir John's detective efforts are finally successful, the
killer commits suicide within a performance and Diana enters Sir
John's home elegantly dressed—but the camera pulls back to reveal
the scene is in a play the two are acting, and a falling curtain ends
the film.

    Murder! thus becomes Hitchcock's first serious, protracted at-
tempt to blur the distinction between "playing" and "really
doing," thereby forcing a reassessment not only of the truth that
is contained in what is "false" (i.e., art) but also the false nature
of what is thought to be "true" (i.e., life). That this is mainstream
Hitchcock is demonstrated by the frequency of its recurrence.

    The long and unbroken takes for which Hitchcock later became justly famous (and which he had so admired in the work of German directors like Lang, Pabst and Dieterle) were first attempted in this film (as, for example, when two women discuss the crime, walking from sitting room to kitchen and back again: there is no cut for a full three minutes). And continuing his experimentation with sound, Hitchcock cleverly got round the problem of being, in 1930, unable to post-dub an interior monologue or an accompanying musical soundtrack. While Herbert Marshall simply shaved before a mirror, Hitchcock activated off-camera a wire recorder on which Marshall had prerecorded his monologue ("Why did I send her away? Now she's come back . . .") and he arranged for a thirty-piece orchestra to play an excerpt from *Tristan und Isolde* on the set—then his camera rolled, filming Marshall's act of shaving, and the studio microphones recorded the prewired speech and the live on-set music.

The other aspect of the film Hitchcock emphasized (and which fascinated him throughout his life) was the sexual ambiguity of the villain—he's not only a performer who often relies on drag (that's quite British, after all): he's also an epicene, rather swooning and delicate homosexual, in fact too grandly exaggerated and languorous for the film to bear. Hitchcock seems more interested in the byways of this sort of behavior than in the paths of a traditional murder mystery, and in fact the byways are somewhat muddied in this case: transvestism is here an emblem of homosexuality and that in turn is somehow linked with "racial impurity." This outdated viewpoint does not help the picture overcome its technical flaws, and finally *Murder!* seems a bit quaint for later audiences.

Alas, no such inventiveness marks his next film, a routine studio assignment to bring another play to the screen—in this case a rather damp melodrama by John Galsworthy called *The Skin Game* (1931). Hitchcock rightly called this the lowest point in his career, for neither he nor the studio executives could do very much with the story of two competitive families, one traditional and the other modern, and their feuds over land rights. During the conflicts between the aristocratic landowner Mr. Hillcrest (C. V. France) and the nouveau riche Mr. Hornblower (Edmund Gwenn, in the first of four roles for Hitchcock), the younger generation (sup-

Phyllis Konstam, John Longden and Edmund Gwenn
in *The Skin Game*.

posedly the love interest) is drawn into the strife, and only an
attempted suicide in a mansion's reflecting pool livens things up
for a few moments. The script, by the Hitchcocks, remained almost slavishly faithful to the play, which was the major problem.

But he and Alma sprang back gloriously with *Rich and Strange,*
an entirely original project vaguely based on an idea suggested to
them by Dale Collins. Hitchcock himself made the uncharacteristic
admission that there are many ideas in this picture—perhaps because it is also uncharacteristically and frankly autobiographical
and he wished to deflect attention from this fact. Like a filmed
dream, *Rich and Strange* justifies its title from Shakespeare (*The
Tempest*), to which Hitchcock calls attention in an early intertitle:
". . . Doth suffer a sea-change into something rich and strange."
    Bored with their monotonous rounds of office work and home
life, Fred and Emily Hill (Henry Kendall and Joan Barry) are
rescued from ennui by a rich uncle who leaves them an inheritance
in advance of his death, so they will be able "to experience all the
life you want by traveling." The couple take a trip round the
world, during which Emily falls in love (though chastely) with
dashing Commander Gordon (Percy Marmont) and Fred becomes

infatuated with a common adventuress posing as a princess (Betty Amann). But the romantic expectations of both Fred and Emily are dashed, and with it their unrealistic dreams. Shipwrecked in the Far East, the Hills are picked up by Chinese and finally return to the drab home life, apparently unchanged. From this thin thread is spun a series of alternately comic, tender and hallucinatory episodes on the possibility of an inner change from an outward journey, a sort of rite of passage in which people experience, endure and learn.

Rich and Strange opens with a stunning long crane shot of Fred's office. Without a cut, we follow from a vast overview of workers riveted to their desks, through the five o'clock departure, down wide staircases. Critic and satirist of the bourgeois life though he was, Hitchcock was even more critical of those who invite chaos by yearning for excitement (a common motif in his films). Exotic

Henry Kendall and Joan Barry in *Rich and Strange*.

ports of call, glamorous Paris, the mysterious East and the fabric of shipboard life—none of these are lost on Fred Hill, but he is such an overgrown baby, so susceptible to the wiles of a vamping brunette (his wife, in the Hitchcock tradition, is a cool blonde) that it's hard to feel sympathy for him when his "princess" is deposed. Which is of course precisely Hitchcock's point. "Love makes everything difficult and dangerous," remarks Emily to Commander Gordon, referring to her relationship with him and to her husband.

Many viewers have trouble with the final quarter of this picture. Rescued from their sinking ship by a passing Chinese junk, the Hills witness the birth of a baby in the crudest circumstances— but the fragile life triumphs, even on the wild sea, even when there's only salt water to bathe the newborn. They also stand in horror as one of the Orientals slips on deck, his foot caught in a rope: his mates calmly watch as the man dangles slowly headfirst into the water and drowns. Could they not have moved, hurled themselves over the side to help? What might have been done to save the man?

The two episodes focus the entire point of *Rich and Strange,* which has something to do with the extremes of life and death, and the *acceptance* of life and death on their own terms. The reactions to the two events by the Chinese are entirely appropriate to an Oriental philosophy, if not to polite middle-class Britons. What Fred and Emily see is the exact opposite of their own constant *yearning,* their dissatisfaction with their lot. Moments later, while enjoying a supper their hosts have offered them, they see a cat's skin nailed to the ship's side; realizing what they've eaten, they then rush to the side to vomit it. And even this scene supports the idea and finally reveals the film's several earlier references to seasickness, nausea and vomiting. Supper was delicious. Why do the Hills think otherwise when they're told what it was? *Rich and Strange* remains just that years later: a film ripe with an almost spiritual sensitivity, yet wonderfully odd in execution.

With his next two contract films, Hitchcock and his public could never have known that much greater renown and artistic success was but a little more than two years away. Before that, however,

John Stuart and Anne Grey in *Number Seventeen*.

he managed to dispatch two pictures that can only be called as boring as the home life of Fred and Emily Hill.

First, Hitchcock greatly altered Jefferson Farjeon's novel and play *Number Seventeen* for BIP's 1932 film of it. The narrative line—something about a safe house, thieves, a dead body that seems never explained—is hopeless, and Hitchcock seemed to settle for atmosphere as he accumulated Gothic elements: cobwebs, shadows on doorknobs, strange noises, vanishing corpses. A young detective and a girl (John Stuart and Anne Grey) are handcuffed to a railing which collapses, leaving them suspended in midair, an image which seems to have neither context nor clarity here—but which will be greatly exploited in *Young and Innocent* and *North by Northwest*. From there, the only thing worth mentioning about *Number Seventeen* is the final chase involving a train and a runaway bus and the great crash aboard a cross-channel ferry, realized well enough so that you forget it was all done with miniatures and studio tricks.

Waltzes from Vienna (1933), however, is just plain dull. Based on a popular West End musical about Johann Strauss the elder and younger, it was pure kitsch, presented with a minimum of music and a maximum of sight gags. Fay Compton and Edmund Gwenn,

both giving vivid, even sometimes subtle performances, cannot
redeem the film from a fatal lethargy, and Hitchcock—doubtless
aware that he was outside his métier, simply kept his camera
moving. He always called the making of this picture the point at
which he had almost completely lost confidence, and it is easy to
see why. The musical was certainly not his genre—so much he
knew in 1933. But which way to turn?

He refound his path—and progressed considerably on it—with
The Man Who Knew Too Much (1934), the first of two versions of
a story about a couple on vacation whose child is kidnapped to
prevent them from divulging what little they accidentally learned
about a plot to assassinate a foreign statesman in London. This
earlier version was a huge critical and popular success and remains
so sixty years later. There is, in fact, a kind of snobbishness about
it: precisely because this film was crudely and quickly made in
grainy black-and-white, with holes in the plot large enough to
accommodate a Sherman tank, it is (so the outré opinion has it)
vastly superior to the 1955 Hollywood remake, which was in

Edmund Gwenn and Esmond Knight in *Waltzes from Vienna*.

Technicolor and VistaVision, with lavish sets and songs and all the resources of later filmmaking (elements which somehow, for some critics and viewers, automatically stigmatize a picture). This is utter nonsense, for reasons which at once become clear when the remake is assessed.

On its own terms, however, this first version is entertaining enough, and with this remarkably piquant seriocomic thriller Hitchcock began a quintet of brilliantly conceived British films, each of them noteworthy for tight construction, a quirky blend of suspense and humor and an emotional impact that gradually deepens in all of his greatest works to come. Supervising a genial team of writers who gave him acute dialogue, he broke cliché after cliché, turning an espionage melodrama into a suspenseful account of a family threatened with dissolution.

The first and last images of the film are neat reversals and clues to Hitchcock's carefully planned, interlocking structure: the opening on the bright ski slopes of St. Moritz begins a tale that ends

Nova Pilbeam, Leslie Banks and Edna Best
in *The Man Who Knew Too Much* (1934 version).

on a dark, sloping rooftop in London. Within this framework is a story designed entirely in terms of related contrasts: the glamorous Alpine resort is contrasted with the grimy alleys and sooty slums back home; an elegant Swiss hotel and its glittering public spaces are reversed by dingy, narrow staircases and eerie shadows in which the later action occurs. *The Man Who Knew Too Much* in fact creates and sustains tension by becoming ever more claustrophobic; lighting and set design do not merely locate the story, therefore, but also create mood. Hitchcock had learned well from his apprenticeship as set designer and assistant director of silent films.

The structure is sharply realized in terms of narrative as well as visual design. In St. Moritz, it's clearly established that Jill Lawrence (Edna Best) is an expert at skeet shooting, and an oily, well-dressed gentleman challenges her to a contest. She loses the match when she's distracted by an innocent interruption from her young daughter Betty (Nova Pilbeam). "Let that be a lesson to you," she tells her opponent. "Never have any children." She then says to her husband (Leslie Banks): "You take this brat," adding a curiously crude but lightly spoken regret: "You *would* have this child!" And with that Jill departs with a family friend, the handsome Frenchman Louis Bernard (Pierre Fresnay). Nearby are a moon-faced stranger named Abbott (Peter Lorre) and his strange woman companion, identified only as his "nurse"—is this a cover for their real relationship, or is he ill? This Hitchcock never clarifies.

After losing the match, Jill promises to beat the challenger at some future contest, and he gallantly replies, "I live for that moment." This is, of course, precisely how the film will conclude. The challenger turns out to be an assassin involved in the politically motivated kidnapping, and Jill wins the final "match" and saves the daughter she casually dismissed by shooting him from a London rooftop.

The evening after the opening match, the Lawrences dine in the hotel ballroom and Jill dances with Louis Bernard. A shot is fired, and the Frenchman dies in Jill's arms—but not before uttering an odd request: "In my room—a brush—tell Bob to take it to the British consul—and don't breathe a word to anyone!" Moments later, Betty is kidnapped, taken hostage so that the Lawrences will reveal nothing told to Jill by the dying Louis Bernard, who, we learn, was killed because he knew of a plot to assassinate a foreign statesman.

Only after we've seen the whole picture can we appreciate that Hitchcock continues his carefully planned circular structure in this taut ballroom sequence: dance music accompanying the scene points forward to the organ music played at the Tabernacle of the Sun, to drown out the noise of Bob's fight with the kidnappers, and even more clearly to the concert at the Albert Hall.

Typically, Hitchcock situates all the chaos in places that seem distant from evil and safe from danger—locations that are glamorous (a ski resort) or respectable (a concert hall). In his later films, similar terror will erupt in equally unexpected venues—at Radio City Music Hall and the Statue of Liberty, for example (*Saboteur*); at a venerable California mission church (*Vertigo*); at the United Nations and at Mount Rushmore (*North by Northwest*); in a peaceful, sleepy northern California village (*The Birds*).

The Man Who Knew Too Much is peppered with sharp motifs, apparently throwaway items that become the carriers of important ideas. Bob's inability to communicate in German to the Swiss police—all he can manage to stammer is *"Der britische Konsul"*—casually alludes to the ominous political situation then brewing in Hitler's Germany, which was a major concern for England in 1934. Lorre (who had played a child molester in Fritz Lang's 1931 German film *M*) is a kidnapper with a disturbing streak of sophistication—he loves classical music and a good wine—and even of exaggerated politeness. He and his lady friend-nurse are killed in the final shootout (note Lorre's grief when she dies in his arms) and moments later the child is "reborn" to her family, saved by her mother's sharpshooting.

In all Hitchcock's apparently political spy-chase thrillers, the international issue is merely his pretext for examining quite personal and emotional issues—thus his refusal to specify a "cause" or to identify the nation involved. This plot pretext is what he famously referred to as the "MacGuffin"—what the spies are after, what gets the action going but fades into insignificance for the characters and the audience. We're never told, after all, just what country is represented by the man targeted for assassination, nor whence the kidnappers and assassins hail. Topical stories are dated once the issues no longer prevail, but Hitchcock knows that tales focusing on recognizable human feelings are perennials. His concern, therefore, is for the beleaguered family: witness, for example, the hitherto unexpressed tenderness, the increasing closeness that prevails between husband and wife when they're united in anxiety about their daughter.

Hitchcock called this first version of *The Man Who Knew Too Much* the work of a talented amateur, the remake that of an accomplished professional. He was quite right. For 1934, this must have been a welcome and exciting film, and it certainly advanced Hitchcock's cachet. But his next picture, *The 39 Steps,* was vastly superior, and with it may be marked a major turning point in the art of Alfred Hitchcock.

4

THE 39 STEPS

(PRODUCED AND RELEASED 1935)

Talk to him of Jacob's ladder,
and he would ask the number of the steps.

DOUGLAS JERROLD,

A MATTER-OF-FACT MAN

Madeleine Carroll and Robert Donat.

"What is drama," Alfred Hitchcock once asked, "but life with the dull bits cut out?" For Richard Hannay, the unwitting hero of *The 39 Steps,* all life's dull bits are suddenly and completely excised, and the ensuing drama leaves him and the audience breathless, intrigued, sometimes amused and titillated. The event that sets off this spy-chase thriller is (as often in Hitchcock's tales) an accident, a trick of happenstance that could befall anyone at any time.

Some critics have dismissed the film as little more than a pleasant diversion (which it certainly is), but a merely pleasant diversion does not continually generate fresh interest and disclose new richness after multiple viewings and the passage of decades. *The 39 Steps,* on the other hand, stands alone in the genre as a survivor of time and fashion precisely because—casually, humorously—it is concerned with issues of very great earnestness; indeed, it improves with age and familiarity. *The 39 Steps* may be Alfred Hitchcock's first indisputable masterpiece, and it marks a major shift in his career. In his previous seventeen films, he had been seeking a style and a vision that were uniquely his own; with this film he established the terms of the style and the beginning of a consistent vision.

Based on an interesting but distressingly complicated novel by John Buchan, the scenario by Charles Bennett and Hitchcock simplifies everything in the novel and addresses the human stakes of the espionage game, a concern already introduced in *The Man Who Knew Too Much* the previous year. Here, a Canadian on holiday in London named Richard Hannay (Robert Donat) has to establish his innocence of a crime—the knife murder of a mysterious brunette spy (Lucie Mannheim)—and simultaneously prevent a national secret from passing out of the country to "the enemy," whoever that may be. To do this, Hannay must discover and bring

Lucie Mannheim and Robert Donat.

to justice a ring of spies known as "the thirty-nine steps," and in his efforts he is at first hindered and finally helped by a beautiful blonde named Pamela (Madeleine Carroll), the counterpart of the attractive brunette spy. The secret (the so-called "MacGuffin" that gets the story going but quickly dwindles into insignificance) concerns a line of fighter planes, but this we are told only in the last moments of the film, and Hitchcock has even less interest in it than we do.

Hitchcock's comic thrillers from this point on most often present an innocent man, wrongly accused of a crime and sought by the police, who's forced to embark on a madcap journey and to trust a new relationship with a dubious blonde. This is precisely the format of *Young and Innocent, Saboteur* and *North by Northwest.* In the case of *The 39 Steps,* the cyclic journey takes the hero from London to the Scottish Highlands and back again, in an odyssey of self-discovery and fresh perceptions. For this, the single unifying motif is the assumption of roles and the setting of the theater, where the film begins as Hannay buys a ticket and the camera follows so that *we* move down the aisle with him to a seat. Ninety minutes later, the story ends at another theater, and between these two moments we have a series of assumed names and disguises as each character prevaricates or plays a role. Spies masquerade as police. Professor Jordan (Godfrey Tearle) isn't a professor at all, but the dangerous anti-British spy with part of his small finger missing, against whom the dying brunette had warned Hannay. "What would people think," he asks Hannay, "if it were known that I am not—how shall I put it?—what I *seem*?" Minor characters prevaricate, too: the crofter, for one example, is ostensibly religious but is really a venal brute. "All the world's a stage," indeed. But the main "actor," of course, is Hannay himself, and he assumes at least four disguises and identities to elude the police: that of a milkman, an auto mechanic, a politician, and a newlywed.

For Hitchcock, all these shifting identities are emblematic of the disparity between appearance and reality, of the unpredictable bases of relationships and the precarious necessity of trust—a complex of ideas made clear in each sequence of the picture. Trust and betrayal are the central concerns of a remarkable number of Hitchcock films (*Shadow of a Doubt, The Paradine Case, Strangers on a Train, Vertigo, North by Northwest, Frenzy* and *Family Plot*), and

Robert Donat, John Laurie and Peggy Ashcroft.

in each this motif is either a new addition to the literary material
on which the script was based or receives an emphasis the original
material did not offer.

In the beginning of *The 39 Steps,* for example, the beautiful,
mysterious spy coyly calls herself "Smith." Her aim is to prevent
a secret from being discovered—"not because I love England but
because it will pay me better that way." She trusts Hannay to hide
her from the pursuing enemy agents. Once he's on the run to
escape unjust accusation for her death that night, Hannay trusts
(foolishly, at first) Annabella's opposite, the blond Pamela (Madeleine Carroll). And Richard and Pamela are balanced by two other
couples whose relationship is marked by trust and the lack of trust,
and these couples complete a kind of quadrille—four sets of people
who illuminate the theme. This is clearly appropriate to a spy
story, since spies by their very nature and work are characterized
by the lack of trust they must induce in others.

The first couple is the suspicious, foul-minded Scottish crofter and his young wife (John Laurie and Peggy Ashcroft). A religious fanatic, he sees wickedness everywhere and beats his wife after she helps the innocent Hannay to escape. Her sad, longing gaze when Hannay departs is one of the subtlest and loveliest touches in Hitchcock's films: she seems to see any possibility for freedom disappear into the night with this handsome stranger.

Opposed to them and further highlighting the motif of bonded couples is a second pair, the innkeeper and his wife; like the crofter's wife, she's especially helpful, tolerant, gentle and encouraging. These are two of the most engagingly drawn women characters in Hitchcock's films, and their scenes advance a delicately balanced structure. Hannay, who had prepared a fish supper for "Annabella Smith," is later offered a fish supper by the crofter's wife and a supper of sandwiches by the innkeeper's wife; his initial act of kindness, in other words, is reciprocated twice at crucial moments in his journey.

It is possible, in fact, to see all the characters of *The 39 Steps* in terms of the degree of trust that maintains between couples. The forced closeness (by handcuffs) between Hannay and Pamela eventually leads to real romance, and the final shot shows them reaching out toward one another; and the forced and loveless relationship between the crofter and his wife is contrasted with the unpretentious gentleness of the innkeeper and his wife. The structural linchpin for the film is the wondrous Mr. Memory (Wylie Watson), based on a vaudeville performer Hitchcock saw as a youngster. An innocent performer at the beginning, he's the innocent victim at the end: fidelity to his talent, as Hitchcock pointed out, demands that he utter the secret, and this causes his death.

It's astonishing that this romantic thriller has such deft comedy, too: the vaguely kinky lingerie salesman on the train to Scotland who loves to talk about corsets and brassieres when he isn't telling obscene limericks; the political double-talk concocted by Hannay as he masquerades as a candidate for God knows what; Hannay taken away from the conference hall in handcuffs to the cheers of his new "constituency" after he promises them nothing, but does so with such charm that they find him irresistible. *The 39 Steps* is remarkable for its unforced wit—and for the fact that this, too, does not grow stale with time.

. . .

When *The 39 Steps* was released, Hitchcock urged audiences to
see it and all his films "at least three times, in order to pick out
all the details and the intention behind them, and in order to get
deeper into things." This movie is so much fun that it would be
easy to dismiss it as "mere" entertainment and not get deeper into
things. But no doubt the Greeks, sitting on the hillside, thought
Aristophanes' *The Birds* was just great fun, and the folks attending
the Globe Theater were just hugely entertained by Shakespeare's
Twelfth Night and *A Midsummer Night's Dream*. *The 39 Steps* is that
sort of comedy—inevitable and fresh, funny and tender, but with
a concomitant gravity. Like all great comedy, it wondrously survives the particularities of its own era.

5

SECRET AGENT

(PRODUCED 1935, RELEASED 1936)

I shall endeavour to enliven morality with wit,
and to temper wit with morality.

JOSEPH ADDISON IN

THE SPECTATOR, 1711

Madeleine Carroll, Peter Lorre and John Gielgud.

One of Alfred Hitchcock's rarely seen and least-appreciated works, *Secret Agent* was based on stories by Somerset Maugham. Working again with the great scenarist Charles Bennett, the director fashioned a work that continues his cycle of films on the decadence and perversity of the spy's world. Here, he explores what might be called the evolution of moralities—shifting attitudes toward a task undertaken in the name of patriotism that is really nothing but political expediency ending in murder. The movie is one in an unbroken series of masterworks from *The 39 Steps* through *The Lady Vanishes,* five altogether superior achievements in less than three years.

The story is set during World War I and moves from London

to Switzerland, and thence on a climactic train journey through middle Europe. After the opening credits the camera pulls back from a covered coffin to show visitors at a wake. Like everyone and everything in the story to follow, however, this is a sham: the casket is empty. The mourned man, novelist Edgar Brodie (John Gielgud), soon confronts head agent "R" (Charles Carson) and demands an explanation of the news of his own death. He's told that the war in the Middle East is at a critical stage and that Brodie—renamed as spy Richard Ashenden—is to be sent to Switzerland to locate and "eliminate" a German agent.

Brodie/Ashenden arrives in Switzerland with his accomplice, called the General (Peter Lorre), an Eastern European who says he is a noble Mexican. There they meet their cohort assigned to act as Mrs. Ashenden, the blond Elsa Carrington (Madeleine Carroll), and Robert Marvin (Robert Young), an apparently innocent American infatuated with Elsa. When Ashenden and the General think they have found the German spy they've been sent

The director and cast after the chocolate factory sequence.

to kill—a harmless soul named Mr. Caypor (Percy Marmont)—
Ashenden reluctantly participates in the deed, although from a
distance. But then they learn they have eliminated the wrong man:
it is actually Marvin they seek, and en route to enemy territory
the train carrying them all is wrecked. Marvin shoots the blood-
thirsty General before expiring of his own injuries; survivors Elsa
and Ashenden/Brodie resign their jobs and marry. The concluding
frames announce General Allenby's victory in the Middle East, a
crucial victory of World War I.

There are two narrative movements in *Secret Agent*—not *The
Secret Agent,* as filmographies so often misstate; the correct title is
important, for there are several secret agents in the story, which
explores the very nature of what it means to be a secret agent. At
first, Elsa sees the business of spying as "something worth-
while"—even the prospect of committing murder in the line of
duty is "a thrill, excitement, a big risk, danger!" She's delighted
at the thought of mayhem and disappointed when she can't assist
at the killing of Caypor. But at this point Ashenden is still a

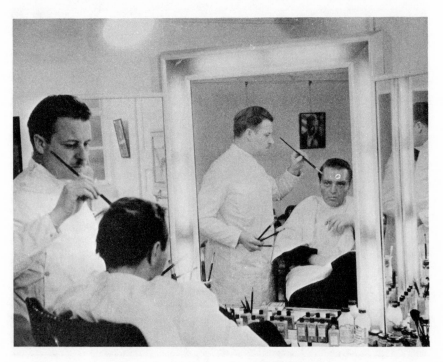

Peter Lorre becoming the General.

reluctant spy and he corrects her: "It's murder," he insists, "and you call it fun."

But Elsa repents of her attitude and is shocked into a recognition of the horror of it all when they learn that the wrong man lies dead. Now the second narrative movement begins, for when Ashenden learns that the real enemy is Marvin, he moves in for the kill and it is Elsa who objects: "It's murder! I'd sooner see you dead than see you do this. What do I care about them or him? It's us! I'm not going to have this on our consciences!" Passionate and active, Elsa does more than hesitate as Ashenden did: she backs her assertions with threats, holding Ashenden and the General at gunpoint until the train crashes moments later under an air attack. The moral positions, in other words, have completely reversed.

Subtly but deliberately, the film links the political expediency of murder with an abuse of language. Instead of enabling people to communicate, speech and language in *Secret Agent* are always confusing for the characters, always deceptive, never clear—precisely because as spies they distort, encode, and manipulate language for their own amoral purposes. Ashenden must painstakingly decode messages. The Swiss coachman can't understand simple English. The guard at the railway station doesn't comprehend the General's instructions. Elsa is forced to stay at the hotel and learn German (the enemy language) from the Englishman's German wife as Hitchcock cuts to the murderous mountain-climbing expedition with the General, who repeatedly misstates simple English proverbs as he's about to kill the wrong man. Even Elsa and Ashenden have their problems: "Speak English!" she urges when he uses fancy words like "uxorious" and "connubial"—words relating to marriage, words of which she is aptly unaware. Thus human language is reduced to a confusion of sounds and syllables; it's something to be decoded or interpreted, a hidden message from home that contains deadly orders.

This leads by the film's structural logic to another important motif, the increasingly chaotic, deafening noises that interrupt communication and are signs of a world in moral disarray. The bombs and sirens in London, the insistent ringing of the Langenthal church bell, the single keyboard note depressed by the dead organist, the dog whining when his master dies, the monotonous dirge wailed by the peasant singers, the whirring belts at the choc-

olate factory and the long, loud fire alarm there—all these cacoph-
onous sounds move toward the final train wreck. The world of
spies is increasingly disordered, broken by disarticulate speech and
shattered by noise. "The funeral will be quiet and private, in the
country," lies the guard at the fake funeral. But when we move
to the countryside, it's in Switzerland, where nothing is quiet and
private: everything becomes progressively louder until at last the
opening false funeral has turned into a series of real, multiple deaths
and a single, final crash.

As in *The 39 Steps* but with more ominous significance, everything
is deceptive: the reluctant spy Ashenden is really the novelist Brodie; Elsa is "issued" as a false wife; Marvin appears charming but
is really the villain; the bearded Swiss grandfather buying chocolate
is involved in espionage, and his candy contains a secret message;
a picturesque country church is the scene of a brutal murder; the
German-speaking Englishman with his German wife are not
enemy spies but innocents; the "hairless Mexican General" is not
a general at all, nor Mexican nor hairless. The world of appearance,
casually and lightly introduced as a Hitchcockian motif in *The 39
Steps,* is here developed with obvious insistent gravity.

It is in fact this General who is the story's most immoral character, he who insists on committing a murder after he's been paid
to do it, for it's a matter of his "honor." Exploitation virtually
defines spies, and Hitchcock concretizes exploitation by locating
it within the General's viciously manipulative seductiveness. His
first appearance establishes him, in Brodie's words, as "a lady-
killer"—the phrase is wittily, ominously ambiguous as we see him
chasing a servant girl; later he pursues hotel maids and, most
nastily, Elsa. The same is true of Marvin, whose essential perversity is finally revealed, for after pursuing Elsa romantically, he
admits, "You know I don't love you. I never did"—and then he
kisses her, wildly, brutishly. It's a brilliant touch, and sometimes
audiences laugh ruefully at this moment, perhaps because we see
how empty is the gesture of passion, how inappropriate to his
words.

The moral tone of *Secret Agent* provides its bite and its complexity, and we are left with no doubt about the whole wretched
business of killing under the pretext of national purpose or inter-

Madeleine Carroll, Peter Lorre, Alfred Hitchcock
and Robert Young.

national security. Behind and beneath the exigencies of a wartime
tale, Hitchcock clarifies his observations on the basic depravity of
espionage. Everything is tainted in this kind of world, and sexual
exploitation disguised as romance is the worst fraud of all.

6

SABOTAGE

(PRODUCED AND RELEASED 1936)

Some of our most exquisite murders have been domestic, performed with tenderness in simple, homey places like the kitchen table.

HITCHCOCK, TO THE FILM SOCIETY
OF LINCOLN CENTER, 1974

Sylvia Sidney and Oscar Homolka.

This may be Hitchcock's greatest (if not his most popular) British film; it's certainly a taut, densely structured moral thriller with all the concerns of the first-rate Joseph Conrad novel on which it's based (*The Secret Agent*), but updated to London 1936 and made specifically Hitchcock's own. As in *The Man Who Knew Too Much* and *The 39 Steps,* he has no interest at all in why the spies are doing what they're doing, what international situation prevails, or who's working for whom. His concern is rather with the dark underside of human nature, the pervasive nature of iniquity and the suffering of innocents that inevitably attends acts of political terrorism. Bombings in Piccadilly Circus might have seemed fantastic to Londoners sixty years ago; today, *Sabotage* has the alarming look of a documentary film.

The story concerns Detective Sergeant Ted Spenser (John Loder), pretending to be a greengrocer to uncover the details of a terrorist plot to destroy London: he sets up shop adjacent to the Bijou Cinema, managed by Karl Verloc (Oscar Homolka) who uses the place as a front for spies. Verloc's nameless young American wife (Sylvia Sidney) and her brother Stevie (Desmond Tester) are ignorant of the man's activities, and one day Verloc asks the boy to deliver a package of films which secretly contains a time bomb set to go off on deposit and destroy portions of central London. But Stevie is delayed on his errand, and he and a busload of people are killed. When Mrs. Verloc learns the truth about her husband, she longs for vengeance, and in fact her husband dies— but ambiguously, as he seems to walk into a knife she holds at the dinner table. She is full of remorse and guilt and desires to talk to the police, but Spenser—who has fallen in love with her— will not allow her to divulge her conscience and takes her away (in a final scene lifted directly from *Blackmail*). Underneath this

Sylvia Sidney.

Sylvia Sidney, Desmond Tester and Oscar Homolka.

tale Hitchcock offers a dual analysis: of the audience watching the film, and of the chaos at the fringe of ordinary experience.

Hitchcock and screenwriter Charles Bennett made significant changes from the Conrad novel, the most crucial being that Verloc's tobacconist shop has become a movie theater. This enabled the director to reflect on the nature of film-watching itself, since most of the story's action occurs in a cinema. The Verlocs live *behind* the movie screen; it's hard not to think of Hitchcock's injunction to "get behind the movie" to consider its serious themes and ideas.

The film's structure is carefully built, and the action occurs over four tense days. On Wednesday, we first see an audience sent away from the Verloc movie theater when electricity fails, thanks to Verloc's sabotage of London's main power plant. But the effect of the electrical failure on the public is disappointing to the saboteurs: hearty Londoners are unfazed, there are headlines about "laughter in the dark" and a general spirit of patient bravado prevails. All this annoys the coven of spies, who have paid Verloc to pull off something designed for more dramatic effect.

In the Verloc private quarters behind the theater, Stevie is then introduced comically, but he's also associated with accident and destruction in a way that prefigures his ultimate death: as he tries to help prepare the family supper, we first see his head wrapped in a shroudlike towel; he accidentally tears an apron; he smashes a plate; he pops a boiling potato in his mouth and tries not to wince when he's caught.

At once, the detective-grocer enters, and Hitchcock establishes the self-referential nature of *Sabotage*. "I thought someone was committing murder!" he says when a window creaks open and the sound resembles a woman's scream. "Someone probably is," replies Verloc with a smile, "up on the screen there!" Verloc points to the opposite wall of the family quarters, adjacent to the movie theater, but his remark points to the film we're watching—where someone is indeed committing murder, right up on the screen there. The murderous nature of what's happening on the screen— and the movie audience "laughing in the dark"—will be located with a vengeance in the brilliant sequence of the Disney cartoon later, when *Who Killed Cock Robin?* portrays a stylized murder that evokes children's laughter.

The character of Mrs. Verloc is now clarified at the family dinner, in the first of three meal sequences in the film, each more ominously marked by the potentially dangerous gestures accompanying the carving of meat—a ritual which finally becomes deadly. Here we see her as a good-natured, energetic, innocent and attentive wife, grateful for her husband's generosity to her young brother.

On the second day, Hitchcock makes explicit the nature of "watching destruction" and insists (as he had in *Secret Agent,* through Ashenden's watching the murder of Caypor through a long-range telescope) that gazing at evil without consideration of its nature is not morally neutral. Verloc meets his superior at the London Aquarium, where he's told to plant a bomb in Piccadilly Circus on Saturday, the Lord Mayor's Show Day. Left alone to contemplate the deadly effect of his task, Verloc gazes at a rectangular fish tank, and from his point of view we see the swimming fish. The image at once dissolves to Verloc's imagination—a scene of Piccadilly Circus, still within the tank's rectangle, and then with him we see the collapse of all the buildings in a massive explosion. Finally, the image redissolves back to the peacefully swimming fish. Water, archetypally, is the source of life and also of primal chaos.

Only when Verloc leaves the aquarium and is—for our amusement—caught in the revolving door, can we see Hitchcock's final purpose for the sequence: "laughter in the dark" again, this time associated immediately with the character of Verloc. We laugh at Verloc: London life is becoming a sort of black comedy, as the opening news headlines proclaimed. In this regard, we now understand why all the films being shown at Verloc's cinema are violent movies, and why the movie audience there *laughs* at them. (And laugh, of course, is precisely what *we* do at this and every Hitchcock thriller.)

Also on this second day (Thursday), Hitchcock introduces his bird imagery, his ultimate marker of chaos not only in this picture but in very many of his films right up to *Psycho* and *The Birds*. Taking his cue from art history and literature, Hitchcock employs birds as destruction caused by human frailty—and sometimes of monstrous evil unleashed by situations often thought to be petty and inconsequential. Stevie, soon to be the innocent casualty of Verloc's sabotage, is shown in Trafalgar Square surrounded by birds, he feeds the birds, tries to befriend them—and presently he becomes the recipient of a gift of birds from Verloc. The boy is, then, constantly associated with "the birds that will sing on Saturday," which phrase is the spies' code for the bombing of Piccadilly Circus. Innocence is swallowed up in a caldron of unthinking evil.

Stevie is subsequently told by Verloc to "kill two birds with one stone" by delivering film tins which (he is unaware) contain explosives—bombs Verloc has collected from an accomplice who, we might have guessed, tends a bird shop. Hitchcock has reached his stride at this point, for now we have a complete fusion of the *film* imagery with the *bird* imagery; he has not only linked the Verloc movie cinema with death and destruction, he has also pointed brilliantly to the ultimate significance of the murderous bird cartoon later. In this regard, it's no accident that after Stevie's death Verloc kneels before his wife in contrition, but when she rises abruptly to leave him, the camera pulls back and we see Verloc kneeling before the caged birds, those metaphoric carriers of the destruction he uncaged.

On Friday, the role of the grocer-detective is clarified as we see his moral dilemma, for he's clearly smitten with Mrs. Verloc. Perhaps no two Hitchcock antagonists are more disturbing than these two men. Spenser is no virtuous guardian of justice, for he will quite readily place love above duty and use his official capacity to press his romantic intentions—shades of Frank Webber, the detective in *Blackmail*—and in fact Spenser himself becomes the saboteur of law and order. Equally disturbing, equally upsetting of our easy judgments is the residual humanity of Verloc, who is reluctant to obey orders if innocent lives are endangered. Weakness propels him, however.

The fourth and final day—Lord Mayor's Show Day—synthesizes every accumulating image and every ethic of this extraordinary film. The birds, as threatened, sing indeed at 1:45, as the bomb explodes, killing Stevie and other passengers in a bus. Boldly, Hitchcock cuts from this dreadful image to Spenser and the Verlocs *laughing* (at what we don't know). All that remains is the third and final dinner, in which Verloc and we see what is going on in the mind of his wife as she carves the meal: the knife seems to leap from her hands, her thoughts turn to avenging Stevie's death as she gazes from the knife to her husband. Then, in a brilliant cinematic rendering of dual intentions, Verloc seems to walk into the knife, to kill himself—and she seems both to will and not to will killing him.

This is precisely why Mrs. Verloc must then stumble into the cinema—dazed, almost catatonic—and take her place with the children laughing gleefully at the Disney cartoon *Who Killed Cock Robin?* She and we watch the screen; it's the only movie-within-the-movie we can really identify and understand in *Sabotage* (although the other fragments also show dreadful events oddly accompanied by the audience's inappropriate laughter). We watch as a murderous bird shoots a deadly arrow into another bird, a rival for the attention of a seductress-bird (obviously modeled by Disney on the great comic seductress of the 1930s, Mae West). This cartoon excerpt is in fact the entire narrative of *Sabotage* in miniature, encapsulated in a few seconds of Disney cartoon.

And so we see and hear the film's conclusive laughter in the dark, prepared from the opening scene, and now we can move with Hitchcock to his final, inexorable moral logic. Just as at the finale of *Blackmail,* Detective Spenser, pleading his love for Mrs. Verloc, prevents her from unburdening her conscience to the police, prevents her from telling what happened between her and her husband. Whereas *Sabotage* began with people sent away from a theater because lights went out, they are now sent away because lights go on, as police search the place for terrorists. Conveniently, the cinema is then blown up (by the bird shop proprietor's bomb), leaving no trace of the circumstances of Verloc's death. And because the detective will not allow Verloc's wife to unburden herself of the ambiguous circumstances of that death—not, as everyone thinks, because of the bomb but because of her knife—she and Spenser will be forever locked in moral collusion, frozen together in a silent guilt.

The last words of the film are a subtle but pointed exposition of a film watcher's discontinuous memory: "That's strange," says the chief of detectives, "she said he was dead *before* the explosion— or *was* it after? I can't remember." The birds singing at 1:45 have thus become a terrible omen, a warning that looks forward to a man's hobby of stuffing birds and to the death of a Crane from Phoenix (in *Psycho*); and to an invasion by forces of alienation and division unleashed by human weakness (in the ultimate avian movie, *The Birds*).

Sabotage is a film of such resonant moral complexity that it is astonishing to realize it has been accomplished in only a few minutes longer than an hour. The economy is everywhere admirably exquisite, and seldom had a Hitchcock film so ominous a fade-out. In it, Hitchcock examines the thin veneer of security that overlays the destructive elements of life; he also probes the disturbing mixtures of innocence and guilt in all the major characters, thus making an easy judgment difficult. We have been led, then, from the darkness of a movie theater to a deeper darkness within, to an exploration of the potential to sabotage our own lives and the lives of those near us. Politics is not the issue, nor even the state of the nation. Rather it is the buying and selling of one's own soul, using the front of a cinema or the role of a grocer— using anything as "cover" to manipulate others. And the role of the audience in *Sabotage*—like our role as we watch it—is part impartial observer (which is itself an indictment) and part accomplice, for our loyalties never lie very strongly with the forces of justice in this story. Every expectation is overturned, so that even the comfort of armchair philosophy is denied us. Hitchcock has performed the ultimate act of sabotage.

7

YOUNG AND INNOCENT

(PRODUCED 1937, RELEASED 1938)

The ceremony of innocence is drowned.
YEATS, ''THE SECOND COMING''

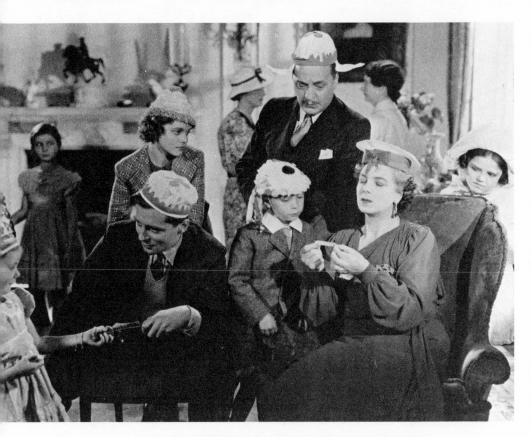

Derrick de Marney, Nova Pilbeam, Basil Radford
and Mary Clare are the adults.

After the dark, grave halftones of both *Secret Agent* and *Sabotage,*
Hitchcock wisely (and perhaps necessarily) chose to alter the mood
in his next film. Until the 1970s, *Young and Innocent* was not
generally known in America and had been not much esteemed
even in Britain. Now widely available, it is surely the most openly
affectionate of Hitchcock's English films—and the most emotionally whole. Moreover, its comedy is never merely a relief from
suspense but is rather the carrier of precisely the gentleness and
truthfulness that the film postulates as constituting genuine maturity. It has none of the severe undertaste of *Secret Agent,* nor the
serious moralism of *Sabotage.* But its lightness and warmth—and
the charm of both the characters and the actors portraying them—

do not make for either a saccharine or shallow movie. Even at his most benevolent and pacific, Hitchcock is ever the ultimate moral cynic. For all its casual humor and its easy, uncomplicated flow, the material of *Young and Innocent* is no less rich than its predecessors.

After the success of *The 39 Steps,* Hitchcock knew that the innocent man on the run was a compelling protagonist for audiences. In this case, the hapless hero Robert Tisdall (Derrick de Marney) again depends on a blonde, but Erica Burgoyne (Nova Pilbeam)—unlike Pamela in *The 39 Steps*—willingly goes along for the ride. To make matters more complex and to give the film a richer emotional texture, she's the daughter of the chief constable (Percy Marmont), and like the leading man, she's both young and innocent. She's also Hitchcock's most fully realized woman so far (but not much more than a girl, in fact: Nova Pilbeam—the kidnapped Betty Lawrence of *The Man Who Knew Too Much*—was eighteen when this film was made).

The picture's first shot is a tight close-up of a dark-haired woman, who at once cries, "Don't shout—don't shout, I tell you!" and without a cut she walks back and away from us as a nervous man, smoking furiously, steps in front of the camera. At once we notice that he has a severe nervous tic which makes his eyes twitch. They argue violently as he accuses her of cavorting with "boys," and the entire unpleasant exchange is filmed without a cut, the camera holding close on the couple, barely allowing them room to move. Only after she slaps him hard and he goes to a door is there a cut onto a terrace overlooking the sea. Fade-out. Next morning her body is discovered washed up onshore, and we certainly do not think that the killer was Robert, a screenwriter down on his luck who knew the murdered woman and who just happens to be strolling by; he discovers the corpse.

The apparently casual, stormless, lightweight, and benign tale that follows—of innocence vindicated—is actually a network of significant motifs. The murdered woman is a film star, the man accused of her death was her screenwriter, the murderer is a musician (with a nervous tic) who wears blackface in a jazz band, a tramp is disguised as a dandy, and Hitchcock makes his cameo appearance holding a tiny camera, trying to photograph the swirling activity outside the local constabulary. Everyone, in other words (as in *The 39 Steps*), externalizes in some way the clash between the world of appearances and real life; everyone deals in illusion.

If youth and innocence (Robert and Erica) are more to be admired and trusted than jealousy and rancor (the murderer and his victim), it's only because their sight is clearer, their perceptions uncluttered—thus Hitchcock's insistence on the innocent man's sharp vision and the guilty man's nervous, twitching eyes. To focus this (as it were), Hitchcock introduces in *Young and Innocent* the motif of vision, which he will systematically deepen over the next several decades.

This motif of vision is the single most important clue to the director's ethic here. A murderer has troubled eyes; an indifferent and suspicious lawyer (assigned to defend the innocent man) can't see a thing without his thick spectacles; the heroine's young brother warns that a man wanted by police will die of starvation "with rooks pecking at his eyes"; and at the structural midpoint of the film—in a scene Hitchcock called "a deliberate symbol"—is the children's birthday party where, significantly, the game of blind-man's bluff finds only an adult wearing a blindfold, while the children see clearly. Everyone in the adult world of *Young and Innocent* is fumbling in the dark, all the grownups are role-playing, and the police are (as usual in Hitchcock) slightly daffy or at least not inclined to see things clearly (as, for example, when Robert is questioned on the beach and at the constabulary).

The emphasis on eyes, blindfolding and eyeglasses has, then, a real purpose. They will also be important in *Suspicion,* wherein the neurotically suspicious and imaginative young wife (Joan Fontaine) constantly puts on and removes her glasses. The eyeglasses of Constance Petersen (Ingrid Bergman) in *Spellbound* are also shown in close-up as she holds them and watches her patient sleep; she will be transformed from clinical observer to fellow sufferer. The strangling of Miriam Haines in *Strangers on a Train* is seen reflected through her glasses, which fall to the ground. Midge (Barbara Bel Geddes) in *Vertigo* needs eyeglasses, an apt symbol for her well-meaning but bungling attempt at emotional fulfillment with Scottie Ferguson (James Stewart). And there is a brilliant and telling close-up in the attack on schoolchildren by *The*

Birds: as a child falls, eyeglasses are shattered, the image filling the screen. In each case, eyeglasses are Hitchcock's variant on the Venetian mask—they enable one to see but they disguise, and they are a marker of frailty, of a flaw in vision.

Contrariwise (as did Stevie in *Sabotage*), it's the young people in *Young and Innocent* who carry the story's benevolence and evoke our positive response. Young Erica is a mother surrogate to her four young brothers; we presume their own mother (the chief constable's wife) has died, and Erica's meals with the boys in fact clearly convey deeply affectionate attachment. Consider, in this regard, the ingenuous smiles by one, the tentative reaching out of a concerned hand by another. Seldom has family feeling been so acutely rendered in a Hitchcock film.

The motif of vision is synthesized in *Young and Innocent* by use of the camera eye itself and *what the camera is doing*—constantly a point of self-reference (Hitchcock makes his cameo as a cameraman, after all). The crucial sequence for this is set in the ballroom of the Grand Hotel, a scene requiring considerable rehearsal for the stunning double crane shots. From a vast overview of dancing couples, the camera glides down almost two hundred feet, moving swiftly and fluidly over the heads of the dancers and up toward the musicians until it comes to rest on a tight close-up of the twitching eyes of the murderer. Moments later, the shot is reversed. (Similar camera technique will be employed in *Notorious* and the remake of *The Man Who Knew Too Much*—in the former, the long shot to the close-up of the key in Ingrid Bergman's hand; in the latter, the single long shot of the opening credits, from a view of an entire orchestra to a tight shot of a cymbalist.)

Also remarkable and equally significant is the collapse of the underground mineshaft, as Robert rescues Erica from a falling car and certain death. (Here, as for the ballroom sequence, the vast resources of the largest stage at Pinewood Studios were required.) The situation of a clinging couple directly prefigures—almost shot for shot—the penultimate sequence of *North by Northwest,* in which Cary Grant strains to reach the dangling Eva Marie Saint. In neither film is the sequence mere cinematic wizardry, as if a director, his production designer and his cinematographer simply show (or show off) a tense, suspenseful shot. Rather, the content *determines*

The famous crane shot: from a high-angle overview of the ballroom to a drummer's eyes, without a cut. The crane in reverse moments later (below) required an entirely new set-up.

the technique: the sequences are powerful not because they simply manipulate suspense, but because they relate us to the characters about whom we care.

The film's final image exactly reverses its first. The sharp-featured, angry, shouting brunette of the opening is now replaced by the smiling, silent blonde. The freewheeling wife confronting her snarling mate at the opening is now replaced by the innocent girl safely stationed between the father who has been the central man in her life up to now and the young man who will be henceforth. The opening violent argument has become a gentle reconciliation, and the caring Erica, who at the outset revived the fainting Robert with brandy, now saves him by reviving the murderer with brandy and eliciting the confession that exculpates Robert.

"Father, don't you think we ought to invite Mr. Tisdall to dinner?" Erica's last words bring to a final focus the crude supper Erica brought to Robert in the barn, the victory dinner he later promised her and the several interrupted dinners at the Burgoyne dining table. This is the warmest, most confident of films, without cloying artifice or dewy romance, full of seasoned sentiment. It offers in every sequence a celebration of innocence vindicated and youth triumphantly anticipating maturity.

THE LADY VANISHES

(PRODUCED 1937, RELEASED 1938)

The MacGuffin should turn out to be as trivial and absurd as the little tune of The Lady Vanishes.

FRANÇOIS TRUFFAUT TO ALFRED HITCHCOCK

Dame May Whitty as Miss Froy.

This peerless comic thriller with its script by Sidney Gilliat and Frank Launder (based on a novel by Ethel Lina White) is certainly one of Alfred Hitchcock's two or three best known and most popular movies. It's also the film whose international success clinched Hitchcock's attraction for the American producer David O. Selznick, who was negotiating to bring him to America the following year. How magnificently ironic, therefore, that *The Lady Vanishes* is one of the very few projects Hitchcock undertook rather late in preproduction—after the script was virtually completed, the cast set and almost everything in place for another director. But he added grace notes and one major motif to the story.

The Lady Vanishes tells of Iris Henderson (Margaret Lockwood), on holiday at a Tyrolean inn, who meets charming old Miss Froy (Dame May Whitty), a governess and music teacher. They depart aboard the same train for London, but soon Miss Froy seems to have vanished; in her place is a stony-faced woman who hardly resembles her at all. Iris turns for help to Gilbert (Michael Redgrave), a young musicologist she had met (and disliked) at the hotel, and to a motley crew of fellow travelers. But everyone denies having seen Miss Froy, and Iris is neither helped nor believed—especially when Dr. Hartz (Paul Lukas) explains that Miss Froy was merely a figment of Iris's imagination, the result of a disorienting blow on the head at the railway station. Suspicions are aroused, however, over a nun curiously outfitted with high heels, and a bandaged patient who, when unwound, turns out to be none other than Miss Froy. It's then revealed that she is a counterespionage agent trying to smuggle an important secret back to London—a secret coded in a popular folk tune. Several other passengers turn out to be part of an enemy spy ring led by Hartz, whose purpose is finally foiled as Miss Froy eludes her pursuers. She is reunited back in London with Iris and Gilbert, who also make a nick-of-time escape. The title then discloses its neat double edge. Just like Miss Froy, Iris Henderson is a vanishing lady, too: in the final moments of the film she escapes the searching gaze of her fiancé and leaps into a waiting taxi with Gilbert.

As in *The Man Who Knew Too Much* and *The 39 Steps,* the politics are again vague, but here the reason was as much the restrictions of British censorship as much as the writers' deliberate ambiguity: in 1937 and 1938, English films had to maintain a steadfast neutrality about events in Germany and about German expansion throughout Europe. But this requirement paradoxically freed *The Lady Vanishes.* Instead of serving a specific politic, the film became a tightly woven tale in which all appearances are deceiving and characters are sprung free for new relationships.

The film marked the first appearances of the prototypical British gentlemen abroad—Charters (Basil Radford) and Caldicott (Naunton Wayne), who would appear in several later films. Here, they seem like ungrownup schoolboys, more interested in cricket results than in spies and a smoldering world crisis. Todhunter (Cecil Parker), a barrister with an eye on a judgeship, has been on holiday with his mistress (Linden Travers) and avoids any involvement with Iris and her troubles, lest his name turn up in news accounts. A magician, his wife and son turn out to be part of the plot against Miss Froy, too—and his act includes a "vanishing lady" trick. A sinister baroness (Mary Clare) is also involved, and a Cockney lady (Catherine Lacey) is disguised as a nun. None of these characterizations is gratuitous, since each carries forward the theme of appearance versus reality, a sort of "Now you see him/her, now you don't." And all of them point to the great conundrum in the plot, the charmingly malevolent Dr. Hartz, who operates on heads.

Again, as in *The 39 Steps* (and, later, as in *Shadow of a Doubt*) a tune becomes the carrier of significance—here, it's a folk melody that contains the MacGuffin, "the secret clause of a peace treaty between two countries," as tweedy Miss Froy reveals in a triumph of unrevealing obfuscation.

Linking every sequence and all relationships are two motifs, sleep and music. At the inn in Brandrika, Iris cannot sleep because of Gilbert's music and the peasants' dancing. On the train, her troubles begin (and Miss Froy is abducted) when Iris goes to sleep. Later, she and Gilbert feign sleep to escape a worse fate (poisoning) at the hands of Dr. Hartz. This motif is not the bearer of a *theme*—*The Lady Vanishes* doesn't go quite that deeply with its own devices—but it is a linking technique in the various parts of the whole.

The motif of music is fuller, however. It's entirely appropriate, first of all, that a peace clause be conveyed in music, which always represents harmony and the opposite of chaos. The spy, Miss Froy, is a music teacher who plays the piano. Gilbert is also a musician, studying complex tunes indigenous to middle Europe; it's a neat twist, at the end, that he forgets the crucial melody Miss Froy asked him to remember, and can only hum the Wedding March.

Appearances in the world of espionage are deceptive, of course. The frumpy British nanny is a fearless spy, dashing across the European countryside on behalf of—something. The elegant Dr. Hartz is really the enemy, a deadly brain surgeon instead of a compassionate healer. A nursing nun is no nun at all, but an accomplice of Dr. Hartz; she defects to "our side," however, when she learns what Hartz plans to do with nice old Miss Froy, and

Naunton Wayne, Dame May Whitty, Cecil Parker,
Linden Travers, Basil Radford, Margaret Lockwood,
Catherine Lacey, Michael Redgrave.

she gets to make up for her past by bravery in action (getting shot but not killed).

The secret is finally meaningless, and we care only about the safety and romantic future of Iris and Gilbert, two handsome, plucky people whose frankness, courage and charm will reverse the pathetic situation of Todhunter.

Although *The Lady Vanishes* hasn't any of the rigor or gravity of mainstream Hitchcock, audiences love its grainy appeal, and several images stick in the mind's eye: Miss Froy's handwriting on the train window, which disappears just when Iris needs to prove the old lady's presence; the eerie appearance of a bandaged patient; Gilbert spotting a telltale tea label on the window; and the now almost legendary shot of a nun in full medieval habit and fashionable high heels. With Hitchcock up front stoking the cinematic engines, this charmer continues to chug merrily along its irresistible route.

9

JAMAICA INN

(PRODUCED 1938, RELEASED 1939)

I must down to the seas again,
to the vagrant gypsy life.

JOHN MASEFIELD,

''SEA FEVER''

Leslie Banks and Charles Laughton.

"*Jamaica Inn* was an absurd thing to undertake," Alfred Hitchcock said of his last assignment before leaving England for an American contract; as usual, he was right. The period photoplay based on Daphne du Maurier's novel was not congenial for Hitchcock's contemporary sensibilities, and it leaves the impression of a bored director marking time. With *Waltzes from Vienna* and later *Under Capricorn*, *Jamaica Inn* forms a trio of costume dramas, a genre Hitchcock never otherwise undertook. The feeling and tone of this genre always eluded him, and a fatal lethargy usually crept over everything. Despite screenwriting contributions from Sidney Gilliat, from Hitchcock's assistant Joan Harrison, from Alma Reville Hitchcock and from playwright J. B. Priestley, *Jamaica Inn* is a picture in search of a predominant mood and tone. Perhaps because of that lacuna, it offers some robust pleasures.

The story is set in 1819 on the Cornwall coast, before the British Coast Guard was in service. After the death of her mother in Ireland, Mary Yellen (Maureen O'Hara) comes to Jamaica Inn to stay with her Aunt Patience (Marie Ney) and her Uncle Joss Merlyn (Leslie Banks). The place is a den of thieves and wreckers who, under Merlyn's direction, lure ships off course, kill the crews and plunder the cargo. One of the gang has been hoarding booty and Jem Traherne (Robert Newton), newest to join them, is suspected. Mary saves him from being lynched by his mates, and together they seek out the local justice of the peace, the loony Squire Pengallan (Charles Laughton). Traherne then reveals he's a Royal Navy lieutenant traveling incognito to uncover the mastermind behind the pirates' gang. Pengallan agrees to help, but soon it becomes clear that *he* is the villain behind Merlyn's activities. He turns Traherne over to the pirates and kidnaps Mary. About to leave the country, the squire is caught and throws himself down to the deck from the masthead of a ship.

Frankly disaffected by all this Regency hoopla, Hitchcock was interested only by the possibilities of various contrasts—mostly between the Squire's opulent home and the rude inn. The introduction to the former, a mansion, is accomplished deftly, by a series of gradual, ever closer cuts until we settle in a candlelit dining room where the Squire dines sumptuously, surrounded by a horde of vulgar sycophants overeating and drinking. When Pengallan calls for his favorite horse, the animal is calmly led into the room, and there is given at once the impression of the squire's deranged mind. At once Mary arrives, on her way to Jamaica Inn amid a fierce storm, and the squire inspects her much as he did the horse.

From the brightly lit interior of this little castle the narrative moves to the dingy crudeness of the inn, and the ironies accumulate. (Almost the entire first half of the film is weirdly claustrophobic by being shot within the confines of these two houses.) Just as Pengallan presided over a gathering of nobodies, Merlyn directs a band of scheming cutthroats—and introduces a prize horse to search for his niece when she escapes. Both men leer nastily at poor Mary, as willowy a gothic heroine as ever graced the pages of a dime novel. Jamaica Inn and the squire's mansion, it is implied, are simply two aspects of the same spiritual estate. Appearances, as always, belie reality.

The design of Jamaica Inn is remarkably inventive, drawing on all the resources of contemporary stagecraft: there are trapdoors, winding staircases, oddly beamed rooms and low, swooping ceilings contrasting with the studied elegance, shining marble and wide foyers of Pengallan's house—but both are locales of moral decay, and the production consistently links them.

Most interesting, however, is what might be called "Mary's moral dilemma"—the fact that her aunt is the wife of the chief pirate. Will Mary aid Traherne, bring the wreckers to justice and thus risk Auntie's life? Additionally, will nice old Auntie stand by her husband and be party to another imminent shipwreck and the deaths of innocent men? "People can't help what they are—you don't understand," Aunt Patience tells Mary when the girl begs her to quit Jamaica Inn. The remark will be presently relevant to Pengallan's dementia. But Auntie's problem is neatly resolved in traditional romantic-melodramatic fashion: Joss is shot by one of his own men, Aunt Patience by Pengallan. The only Hitchcockian wit introduced into all this is the dullness of Traherne, guardian of the law. He has to be told the truth about Pengallan *by* Pengallan, whose perfidy he hasn't the alacrity to guess.

The squire is, of course, the film's most interesting character— either despite or because of Laughton's mincing, huffing, selfindulgent performance. Madly obsessed with booty and beauty, this bloated dandy believes that "What's beautiful is worth men's lives"—his justification for killing sailors for exotic silks. Pengallan identifies himself with the end of the Age of Elegance, and at the finale, when he kills himself in a mock-heroic gesture, he climbs to the topmast and calls to the crowd below: "What are you waiting for? A spectacle? You shall have it! Tell everyone how the Great Age ended!" In hurling himself to his death, he recapitulates the film's opening image, in which shipwrecked men threw themselves into swirling, dangerous waters only to be killed by Pengallan's thugs.

If Pengallan is the film's colorful character, he points to the only intriguing theme—the possibility of being saved. The film opens with an old Cornish prayer for poor seafarers, and one of the pirates—named Salvation, played by Wylie Watson, who was Mr. Memory in *The 39 Steps*—wonders aloud about what they're all doing. Interestingly, the only active repentance is offered by Joss, who dies in his wife's arms and offers regrets for having caused so much pain for so long. This theme is clearly focused in the Mary/Traherne relationship: "You saved my life, you're responsible for me," he tells her. (In *Vertigo,* Scottie tells Madeleine/Judy, "You know, the Chinese say that when you save a person's life you're responsible for it—so that makes me responsible for you.") For Hitchcock, redemption is very much of the present, a matter of being saved for meaning in human relationships.

There is, in this regard, one glowing moment of real pathos amid all this crude melodrama. In the gang is an adolescent lad relegated to servant status among them, and when the group is arrested, the handcuffs slip from his slender wrists and he must be bound with rope. But he objects: "I don't want to be tied with a rope! Why can't I be handcuffed like the rest—I'm going to be *hanged* like the rest!" He then realizes what he's said and his voice breaks: "I'm going to die! I don't want to die, I'm only seventeen!" His tears well up, he begins to weep and the camera moves slowly along the row of his embarrassed companions, genuinely touched by the single note of emotion that has broken out among them and, it is implied, feeling guilty for the death of innocence. In this one scene, the characters and story are—for just a moment—raised to something like the truth.

10

REBECCA

(PRODUCED 1939, RELEASED 1940)

I am aware of the damp souls of housemaids
Sprouting despondently at area gates.

T. S. ELIOT,

''MORNING AT THE WINDOW''

Laurence Olivier, Joan Fontaine and Florence Bates.

Hitchcock's first American film won David O. Selznick the Oscar as producer of the best film of 1940. In fact, it's more a Selznick film than it is Hitchcock. Depending on your mood, it's either impossibly dated, woefully prolix as well as comically overstated every step of its long way—or it's deliciously entertaining, the kind of gothic romantic hokum they don't make anymore. Or both.

The scenario follows Daphne du Maurier's best-selling novel closely, and the story is told entirely in flashback with a voice-over reflection at the opening. An unnamed American girl (Joan Fontaine) is in Monte Carlo as companion to Mrs. Van Hopper, a pompous, rich American matron (Florence Bates). One day she meets the rich widower Maxim de Winter (Laurence Olivier), and although he treats her with brusque condescension, he soon proposes marriage and the girl accepts. The couple return to his ancestral home, the gloomy estate Manderley, in Cornwall; there they are greeted by an enormous staff supervised by the intimidating Mrs. Danvers (Judith Anderson). The new Mrs. de Winter quickly learns that the memory of her predecessor fills the house and that she is most unwelcome: even her husband will not speak to her of Rebecca. After a complex investigation, it turns out that the beautiful mistress of Manderley was really an immoral tramp and, aware of her approaching death from cancer, actually committed suicide in such a way as to imply that her husband had killed her. Because she cannot live with the revelation of this truth about her beloved Rebecca, Mrs. Danvers burns herself and Manderley in a great fire, freeing the couple from the tyranny of the past.

It's hard to reflect on *Rebecca* as if it were a Hitchcock film. The production values were entirely Selznick's, the crew was Selznick's, the casting was entirely overseen by Selznick. But there are remarkable visual touches which (because we see them in other films by the director, pre- and post-*Rebecca*) enable us to locate some of his particular contributions.

The opening long shot accompanying the heroine's voice-over introduction—directing our gaze from the exterior gates of Manderley right up to the burnt structure half-glimpsed in shadow and moonlight—was accomplished in a single, fluid, meticulously rehearsed take. (What we see is not, of course, a roadway and a mansion, but a studio miniature.)

With precision and economy, Hitchcock then depended not on dialogue but on strictly visual means to inform us at the outset of the flashback that a woman has come upon a man about to throw himself over a precipice to a watery death. A man looks down, he looks back; he looks after the interrupting girl, looks down again. Basic moviemaking technique, but through Hitchcock's "cutting in the camera"—his lean, minimal shooting—he made sure the editor (and the eternally interfering Selznick) would be left only with what he wanted for this sequence.

In a way, the entire first portion of the story, set in Monte Carlo, is its most entertaining—not merely because of its robust

Laurence Olivier, Florence Bates, Joan Fontaine.

humor and swift pacing (both of which almost vanish once we get back to Cornwall and the ridiculously mammoth Manderley) but also because of its brightly lit interiors and the delicious performance by Florence Bates as Mrs. Van Hopper. She had been a latecomer to professional acting, and Selznick and Hitchcock had seen her onstage at the Pasadena Playhouse. Casting her was much easier than filling the role of the second Mrs. de Winter: at first Selznick wanted an elaborate search, much as he had done for Scarlett O'Hara in *Gone With the Wind* the previous season. Many tested for this role, but Hitchcock's choice of Joan Fontaine wisely prevailed. It may be the best performance of her career; certainly it was the one which established her as a credibly shy English rose.

The repartee of these early sequences is deft and bright. But there are splendid visuals, too. With Selznick's encouragement, Hitchcock and his writers drew a marvelously effective portrait of Mrs. Van Hopper and stressed her control over Fontaine by placing the girl (in the first hotel lobby sequence) constantly on the extreme right of the frame, almost pushed off view by the busty Bates and the overwhelming glamour of Olivier.

Rebecca may be the most straightforward film in the Hitchcock canon, a fact due entirely to Selznick's insistence on strict adherence to the novel. It's also a dangerously literal kind of filmmaking to which Hitchcock would rarely return, although there's no doubt he took full advantage of the superb American technical possibilities: the pinpoint spotlights on Fontaine (in the home-movie sequence at Manderley, and again at the end, as Mrs. Danvers prepares to set the house afire), for example, and the sudden evaporation of Gladys Cooper from the image as Fontaine turns in profile, shocked when Cooper says about Mrs. Danvers, "Why, she simply *adored* Rebecca!"

Apart from these cinematic grace notes, there's not much room left in the script for Hitchcock's touch. Selznick, for example, kept italicizing every important moment in the script by ordering up an exaggerated score from the great Franz Waxman. When Fontaine asks Olivier (on the terrace in Monte Carlo) if he's ever afraid of drowning, there's a burst of violins in scary glissando, telling us—even as we see Olivier turn away from the camera—that this

Hitchcock on the set with Gladys Cooper,
Nigel Bruce and Joan Fontaine.

is a topic that oughtn't to be mentioned to the poor man. This kind of offscreen interference was an early lesson to Hitchcock in America, and it's interesting to observe how sparingly and wisely he allowed music when he was his own producer.

Once we're in Manderley, it's also interesting to see how Hitchcock's camera associates Mrs. Danvers with Mrs. Van Hopper. The latter made her exit from the Monte Carlo hotel room by opening a door and surveying the young girl contemptuously from head to toe—a long shot repeated exactly moments later, with the same action and glance offered to the girl by Judith Anderson in the first bedroom sequence at Manderley.

These touches sharpen and enliven an essentially talky and (in the latter third) dreadfully complex story, and somehow the film seems to end three or four times. But *Rebecca* enables us to understand the meaning of gothic romance, and for this fidelity to a vanishing genre we have to thank the classy Selznick management as much as Hitchcock's intuitive understanding that there's real horror in thinking that someone dead may be watching and inviting your doom. To this premise Hitchcock, of course, returned with a vengeance in both *Vertigo* and *Psycho*.

11

FOREIGN CORRESPONDENT

(PRODUCED AND RELEASED 1940)

You may dive into many waters,
but there is only one social Dead Sea.

ARTHUR WING PINERO,

THE SECOND MRS. TANQUERAY

Robert Benchley and Joel McCrea.

Just prior to America's entry into World War II in 1941, the Hollywood anti-Nazi film took on an added dimension. "War propaganda," the exhortation to the American public to support actively those countries falling under the scourge of Hitler, was the honest professional effort of several producers and directors. In 1940, four films foresaw the nation's growing involvement, and each supported it with varying artistic success. Mervyn LeRoy's *Escape* and Archie Mayo's *Four Sons* are little discussed today. Frank Borzage's film of Phyllis Bottome's novel *The Mortal Storm* is archly sentimental but is saved by the fervent and appealing acting of the principals (Margaret Sullavan, James Stewart, Frank Morgan, Irene Rich) and by the exquisitely moving, tragic finale.

But Hitchcock's *Foreign Correspondent* has best withstood the years, and even after just one viewing, the picture clearly reveals concerns beyond its concluding propaganda statement (tacked on by producer Walter Wanger). Charles Bennett's and Joan Harrison's screenplay is adventurous and entertaining, and the brilliant production design by William Cameron Menzies made for a film of astonishing visual complexity. In its meticulous structure, its disarming humor and its multileveled humanity, *Foreign Correspondent* remains without doubt a Hitchcock masterwork.

The story concerns Johnny Jones (Joel McCrea), a dull-witted

Eduardo Ciannelli and Albert Basserman.

reporter who is sent to Europe in 1939 to replace Stebbins (Robert Benchley), an alcoholic malingerer. In London, Jones—rechristened Huntley Haverstock to give him cachet (" 'Jones' will handicap you—no one will believe it")—contacts Professor Van Meer (Albert Basserman), a Dutch diplomat privy to the secret clause of a peace treaty, and when Van Meer proceeds to Amsterdam, Jones/Haverstock follows. Thenceforth Jones is accompanied by Carol Fisher (Laraine Day), whose British father Stephen Fisher (Herbert Marshall) does not in fact head a peace organization (as he pretends) but rather works for the enemy. After numerous complications, the action returns to London, where the hero, averting death at the hands of Fisher's hit man Rowley (Edmund Gwenn), boards a plane bound for America. But the plane is shot down by the enemy, and the film ends at a London radio studio, as the foreign correspondent, having survived, delivers a ringing message home ("Keep your lights burning, America!").

Much in this narrative has the familiar traits of, for example, *The 39 Steps* and *Secret Agent*—the journey, the forced change of name and identity, the need to trust, the perfidy of spies and espionage, and so forth. *Foreign Correspondent* begins very much as *The Lady Vanishes* and *Rebecca* had: in a single shot, from the far to the near perspective—in this case, from the spinning globe atop a New York skyscraper, the camera glides swiftly down to a bank of windows, then seems to sweep inside to a newspaper office (the globe and building are modeled on the *New York Times*).

The structure of the picture recalls *The 39 Steps* and anticipates both *Saboteur* and *North by Northwest*—a picaresque, elliptical journey in which a man unwittingly becomes a hero (although in this case without being falsely accused of a crime). It's important, in this regard, that the journey of the attractive but slightly dim Johnny Jones not only evokes his courage at the finale, it also forces the American audience to confront what's happening in war-torn Europe during the summer of 1939—while America was still pursuing an isolationist policy.

At first shot, Jones is a lazy fellow cutting out paper designs at work, blithely oblivious to world affairs:

Mr. Powers (newspaper publisher, played by Harry Davenport): What do you think of the current world crisis?

Jones: What crisis?

Joel McCrea and Edmund Gwenn.

Powers smiles, since, as he says a moment later, he wants to send over to Europe "a fresh unused mind" to work as foreign correspondent.

Ostensibly, Jones's mission is to get information from Van Meer, "the keynote in the European situation today . . . If he stays at the helm of his country's affairs, it may mean peace in Europe . . . He's Holland's strong man, one of the two signers of the Dutch treaty with the Belgians. I want you to talk with him, find out what's in that treaty and what he thinks is going to happen."

There's our MacGuffin. Now the story can get on with the business of educating Jones, sending him from New York to London to Amsterdam, then out to the Dutch countryside for the astonishing windmill sequence that is the structural midpoint of the film. Thenceforward, the journey is exactly retraced—back to Amsterdam, then to London, and finally (by telephone and radio broadcast) to New York, although our hero returns to London.

Foreign Correspondent is certainly one of the most visually inventive, brilliantly designed of Hitchcock's masterworks, with perhaps more elaborate set pieces than any other: the Amsterdam town hall meeting in the rain, with the murderer escaping through a sea of bobbing umbrellas; the intricate, interlocking cogs of the giant windmill, with a crane-mounted camera sweeping up, in and around the mill's levels; and the final crash into the sea. It's also one of the funniest scripts Hitchcock directed, one in which the villain has never before been so ambiguously portrayed as a smooth, attractive, devoted father.

The design of the film, by the great William Cameron Menzies, conveys a sense of cramped enclosures, from the New York newspaper office to the London and Amsterdam hotels to the menacing windmill interior to the terrifying airplane crash in the sea, viewed from the claustrophobic cockpit. This accumulation of small spaces is ironically reversed when the band of survivors clings desperately to a piece of fuselage, with the wild, infinite sea stretching round them.

The recently transplanted Englishman Hitchcock employed a prototypical prop in *Foreign Correspondent*—a detail that points beyond itself to become a kind of punctuation mark. Johnny Jones proudly sports a new bowler hat as he departs New York: he's adopting a British gentleman's respectability, after all, and has just been dubbed Huntley Haverstock by his boss. But his young niece and nephew filch the hat and he departs without it. In London he replaces the bowler but then absentmindedly leaves it in a taxi during his first meeting with Van Meer. This, too, is replaced— only to be lost a third time when a breeze snatches it away at the windmill. Only when we hear the repeated dialogue about "talking through your hat" and about "using English clearly" does this significance of the bowler hat become clear: a facile sense of respectability and merely polite diction are no defense, no "cover" in wartime. Connected to this is the running commentary in the film about good manners and polite conversation, all of them

futile—right up to the woman in the airplane whose adherence to
etiquette results in her death. (And note Hitch's cameo: walking
past McCrea, reading an American newspaper and wearing an
American fedora, not an English bowler.)

The hero of this unerringly entertaining film is a man of sin-
gular simplicity, the quintessential American nice guy in a situation
beyond his mental abilities but admirable precisely for his pluck,
his decency and his innate courage. He can't see that the chap
assigned to him as bodyguard is actually trying, rather obviously,
to murder him, and he's slow to see the truth about Carol Fisher's
father and the complexity of their relationship. For all this, he's a
man who wins by displaying honor and fortitude in specific situations—in the car chase after the murder of Van Meer's double;
at the windmill; escaping from the Amsterdam hotel room at night;
and then taking charge during the crash into the sea.

That final crash remains one of the most remarkable and effective sequences in the cinema, even considering advances in moviemaking technique fifty years later. First, Hitchcock had a short
piece of film made with the camera approaching a body of water.
This was rear-projected onto a paper-thin screen, and behind this
was an enormous tank of water. On the set he positioned his
actors—the pilot and crew—in the studio cockpit, with this second
piece of film rolling. Then, just as the plane is seen "approaching
the water" from their viewpoint, a release button was pressed and
the huge tank of water poured through the screen, engulfing actors
and set and giving the impression of a crash into the sea. The
ensuing action, moments later, when the plane breaks up in the
ocean, was filmed in a huge studio tank on the Goldwyn lot—
with rotary blades churning up waves and giant wind machines
off-camera—and with portions of the plane's fuselage tied to rails
beneath the water. With designers and technicians such as producer
Walter Wanger's budget could provide, Hitchcock's ingenuity
flourished.

Hitchcock's first American film, *Rebecca,* was made in California
but certainly looked like Monte Carlo and Cornwall, and the
whole picture was so faithful to du Maurier that it could have
been made at Islington or Shepherd's Bush. Any attendant doubt
as to Hitchcock's ability to handle something distinctively Amer-

ican was dispelled by *Foreign Correspondent*. In spite of its mostly European setting, the leading man is American and the whole tone and texture of the picture celebrates American simplicity, American savvy, and American courage. That's what the producer and the studio wanted, and that's what Hitchcock delivered with a benign vengeance. *Foreign Correspondent* has about as much to do with the details of the start of World War II as *Tosca* has to do with Napoleon's Italian campaign, which is probably why, half a century later, it's such ripping good fun.

Hitchcock's favorite player in this cast was the legendary German actor Albert Basserman, then a refugee. He knew not a word of English and memorized all his lines phonetically and quickly, without knowing much about what they meant. Hitchcock gave him swift summaries of what was transpiring in each scene just before he went on camera, and this is worth mentioning since the performance is remarkably acute. Hitchcock also enjoyed working with Robert Benchley, who poked fun at his own boozy persona in the role of the tippling Stebbins. Benchley wrote his own dialogue, to Hitchcock's great delight.

12

MR. AND MRS. SMITH

(PRODUCED 1940, RELEASED 1941)

Marriage is like life in this—
it is a field of battle, not a bed of roses.
ROBERT LOUIS STEVENSON,
''VIRGINIBUS PUERISQUE''

Gene Raymond, Robert Montgomery and Carole Lombard.

Even more than *The Lady Vanishes, Mr. and Mrs. Smith* was directed from a script with which Hitchcock had little to do. As a favor to Carole Lombard (whose home he was renting since her marriage to Clark Gable in 1939), Hitchcock agreed to direct her in a comedy. A script by Norman Krasna was ready, and RKO sprang for the deal.

The premise is simple. Wealthy Manhattan lawyer David Smith (Robert Montgomery) regularly engages in very sophisticated and prolonged marital battles with his wife Ann (Carole Lombard)—sophisticated because they have agreed to lock themselves up together until the arguments are settled, and prolonged because they can lead to a week's incarceration. After one such

conflict, he admits to Ann that no, if he had it to do over again
he wouldn't marry her—love her though he does. That same day,
a man comes to David's office with the propitious news: David
had married Ann in a town whose legal status was incorrectly
assigned to one state rather than another, and on a technicality,
"We just found out that anybody who got married between 1936
and now with an Idaho license in Nevada—well, you're not legally
married." It's easy to see where this kind of thing will go. Not
very far. Thank heavens we have Robert Montgomery and Carole
Lombard to look at; otherwise terminal boredom may have dispatched us.

Carole Lombard on the set.

It would also be easy to affect a kind of gold-digging attitude about *Mr. and Mrs. Smith,* panning through the slightest nuggets for Hitchcockian markers and signs of something deeper; such an enterprise would also be funnier than the film, which warrants only minimal discussion. Neither wild enough to be called screwball comedy nor inventive enough to engage even Hitchcock's interest, he simply photographed a finished script, adding a few touches wherever he could.

The first shaving scene after the three-day marital row and reconciliation—as Lombard wields a razor against Montgomery's face and throat—may make us feel a trifle uneasy (like the dentist sequence in the first version of *The Man Who Knew Too Much*), but it's outdone by the final shaving sequence, when the fiery Lombard has reason to be even madder at her smug husband. Just the slightest pressure on that razor, and voilà—Sweeney Todd.

People complain very loudly indeed about *Mr. and Mrs. Smith* being an inferior Hitchcock picture, a disappointment after *Foreign Correspondent,* a failed attempt at popular comedy, a poor excuse to avoid more serious subject matter. These objections are foolish. Had anyone else directed the picture, it would have been more like corduroy than the seamless velvet, low-keyed trifle it is. There were no pretensions about this movie, and the director's admirers and his critics oughtn't to have any. Taken on its own modest terms, it's engaging enough, and enables us to see that Hitchcock thought no movie genre was beneath him. He was willing to stretch his talents in America on virtually any kind of story.

13

SUSPICION

(PRODUCED AND RELEASED 1941)

"What is *he? He's a horror!"*

"A horror?"

"He's—God help me if I know what *he is!"*

HENRY JAMES,

THE TURN OF THE SCREW

Cedric Hardwicke, Joan Fontaine and Dame May Whitty.

Few Hitchcock films have aroused such argument and discussion as *Suspicion,* based on the novel *Before the Fact* by Francis Iles (pseudonym of Anthony Berkeley) and written for the screen by Samson Raphaelson, Hitchcock's assistant Joan Harrison and his wife Alma Reville. The story concerns Lina McLaidlaw (Joan Fontaine), the shy, somewhat dowdy daughter of rigidly proper, wealthy parents (Sir Cedric Hardwicke and Dame May Whitty). Against her parents' wishes, she yields to the romantic pursuit of the reckless roué Johnny Aysgarth (Cary Grant), an irresponsible but dashing spendthrift, and not long after their marriage, she suspects that he is trying to murder her. But she is proven wrong, and the film ends with the possibility that Johnny will finally act

SUSPICION   101

responsibly and will help to rebuild a relationship perilously close
to destruction.

Hitchcock always claimed that he wanted to end *Suspicion* quite
differently, with Johnny indeed killing his wife; before she willingly drinks the poisoned milk he offers—rather than face life
without her beloved—she writes a letter implicating him in the
crime, then asks him to post it. But this ending was foiled, Hitchcock maintained, when RKO refused to cast Cary Grant as a killer.
(The situation recalls the director's defense of his original intentions for *The Lodger* in 1926.)

But Hitchcock is the master of red herrings as well as of suspense, and careful research has shown that the truth of the matter
is otherwise. *Suspicion* is just what he constructed, and the ingenious disclaimer was put forth only after the picture failed to please
critics and audiences and its status among his early American films
diminished in time. Had he presented us with a woman who *rightly*
suspects her husband is her would-be killer, we'd be left with a
story of her rather demented passion unto death—not very convincing psychologically (without much possibility of audience
identification), and with no twist at the end, no payoff. In fact,
the entire Hitchcock canon is a series of films that are variations
on romances—on the vagaries of love and passion, need and obsession. *Suspicion* is no different, and the ending as we have it is
mainstream Hitchcock: in light of the final moments, everything
preceding requires revaluation.

The film opens with dialogue over a black screen. We hear a
man's voice and the sound of a train's whistle (or is it a woman's
faint moan?) before we see anything, and you don't have to have
a prurient mind to pick up the typically Hitchcockian *double entendre* (especially without the visual): "Oh, I beg your pardon, was
that your leg? I had no idea we were going into a tunnel. I thought
the compartment was empty. So sorry, I hope I didn't hurt you."
In less than a half minute and with the most economical visual
means, Hitchcock then introduces a playboy with a hangover and
a prim, tight-lipped, bespectacled spinster reading *Child Psychology*. We learn that he's irresponsible—he's riding in first class
without the proper ticket—and an opportunist, for he blithely
asks her for money to pay his fare.

This first view of a pinched, plain young lady is dramatically

The first scene sketches the entire character.

altered by the following sequence, when we see her astride her
feisty horse: she's courageous, glamorous and totally in control
of the animal. More nuanced still is the next scene, as Hitchcock
continues to use his camera to delineate character within an en-
vironment. First shot: a long and wide view of Lina, a tiny figure
before a window in the grandly formal reception room of her
family's mansion (inference: rarefied, privileged life in which she
has scarcely any identity). Hitchcock then cuts to the second shot:
a medium close-up of Lina turning the pages of a magazine (inference: boredom, loneliness). Cut to the third shot: close-up, and
now—quite apart from her setting—we see that even in simple
dress she's a woman of delicate beauty, but she seems without
purpose, romance or excitement in her life (inference: there's more
than meets the eye).

Her friends then arrive, and when Lina sees Johnny among
them she quickly removes her eyeglasses, which she thinks are
unflattering. Similar moments in Hitchcock are always important:

removing eyeglasses not only reveals characters as dramatically other than what they appear, but also makes them vulnerable—the first appearance of Madeleine Carroll in *The 39 Steps,* for example, and Ingrid Bergman in *Spellbound,* among others. Hitchcock makes of eyeglasses a modern version of the Venetian mask: they're a kind of prop or makeup, and sometimes they're a masquerading convenience.

The first hilltop sequence in *Suspicion* then occurs, as Johnny spirits Lina away from her companions en route to church. In extreme long shot, we see the hillside and its bare-branched trees, and there Johnny and Lina are apparently in combat. Cut to a medium shot, and it certainly seems as if he's attacking her—he has her by the wrists, and she's in a panic. "Nothing less than murder could justify such violent self-defense!" he tells her with a smile. But he says he was only trying to fix her hair. This could be regarded as a deliberate red herring unworthy of Hitchcock—until we see that the scene is exactly reduplicated at the film's finale—and the false emotionalism of the scene might also be easily dismissed because of the exaggerated musical accompaniment (in

Cary Grant.

the fashion of the early 1940s). But once again, a Hitchcock film is more sophisticated than the sophisticates. The hysterical score is apt as an expression of the mind of this woman—and the film is, after all, presented entirely from her highly neurotic viewpoint, that of a woman who extrapolates (from her husband's childish irresponsibility) to the wrongheaded conviction that he's a killer.

When Johnny asks Lina what she thinks of him in contrast to her fine horse, she replies with an answer straight from a college introduction to Freud: "I think if I got the bit between your teeth I wouldn't have any trouble handling you at all." This is a woman with a subtle but very definite need to control men as well as herself and her horse (as we saw in the film's first two sequences). To clinch the association of the idea of sexual control, Johnny leans over to kiss her, she glances down, and Hitchcock fills the screen with a huge close-up: Lina firmly snaps shut her handbag. The image (from Freudian dream theory again) is one of obvious sexual inaccessibility. (The first shot of *Marnie* is of a huge, tightly clutched purse; the last word heard in *Marnie* is the word "purse"; in between these two moments is a story of pathological frigidity.)

But in the next sequence, when Johnny escorts Lina home, we learn just how disturbed and exploitive *she* is. Overhearing her parents discuss their "old maid" daughter, who's "not the marrying kind," she turns round and kisses Johnny aggressively and hard, right on the mouth before rushing into the house. He will be her escape, her proof that she isn't destined for spinsterhood.

There is in fact a kind of dual exploration in *Suspicion*. Although each is genuinely attracted to the other, Lina is willing to exploit Johnny's charm for her own purposes even as he is willing to exploit her wealth for his: he's an ideal passport to freedom from her family's unworthy image of her. In this regard—by a curious inversion of expectations—Johnny's telephone call to her moments later (that he cannot meet her again that afternoon, as planned) is accompanied by her attitude of utter defiance as she returns to the luncheon table and to her parents. Lest we miss the point that this defiance also comes from her vulnerability to her own fantasies, the following shot shows her point of view: she's leafing through a magazine again (this woman is a fair target for Publishers Clearing House) and comes on a photo of Johnny. We see her remove her glasses and place them down over the picture: feelings now triumph over fear.

In a model of screenplay construction, Hitchcock offers the sparest means for describing Lina's romantic isolation without Johnny: a quick shot of her return to the hilltop where their ambivalent tryst began, then the invitation to the Hunt Ball which she declines ("Mother, I'm not going to the ball," says this despairing latter-day Cinderella) until his telegram announcing that he will be there—whereupon she leaps into a spasm of romantic elation that continues through the Hunt Ball in her auto ride with him. Kissed for the first time, she swoons with delight in a haze of romantic fixation before inviting him back to her house for a drink. She's a willing victim, yielding to a myth of her own invention.

This self-donation to fantasy and romantic obsession is, of course, a typically Hitchcockian theme, and it describes with appropriate variations the women of *Shadow of a Doubt, Vertigo, The Birds* and *Marnie*. The cinematic marker of this is Hitchcock's 180-degree tracking shot, in a semicircle round a couple as they kiss (here, Lina and Johnny, at Lina's home) and the shot draws the viewer right into their romance, in *Spellbound, The Paradine Case, Under Capricorn, I Confess, Vertigo* and *Torn Curtain.*

In the same scene, Johnny states his surprise that Lina is not nervous when *he* is clearly so. "I'm rather surprised myself," she replies, "but perhaps it's because for the first time in my life I know what I want." Her determination could be no plainer.

The future of the union is indicated plainly, for they elope to a grimy little registrar's office in a torrential downpour (shades of Joan Fontaine's arrival at Manderley in *Rebecca*). Immediately after their honeymoon she learns he has neither a shilling nor a job, and in fact he borrowed money for the wedding trip—just as he soon steals to pay horse-racing gambling debts (continuing the association of ideas established by her equestrian expertise in the film). "Johnny, I'm just beginning to understand you—you're a child," says this amateur psychologist. (The comic scene in which the chairs are delivered from General McLaidlaw highlights the fact that Johnny is a benevolent, shiftless fellow, but nothing like the murderous manipulator his wife soon suspects.)

Beaky Thwaite (Nigel Bruce) is then introduced, announcing his amusement at Johnny's irresponsibility—"That Johnny'll be the death of me," he laughs, and that's a neat plant in her mind, for presently she will most fervently imagine first that Johnny has pushed Beaky over a cliff and then that Johnny has challenged him to a brandy-drinking bout to poison him. ("I've seen this happen before," Johnny says, when Beaky collapses in a near-fit of toxic reaction after just one sip of brandy. "It'll either kill him or it'll go away by itself . . . One of these days it *will* kill him.") Lina adds two and two—and counts five.

The next round of suspicion is triggered when Johnny lies about the loss of his job. His subsequent idea to develop land for a seaside resort further arouses Lina's neurotic suspicion: her husband must be planning to kill Beaky for his partnership money! The extent of this woman's perverse psychology is then italicized by Hitchcock: she admits to Johnny next morning—her suspicions to the contrary notwithstanding—that she couldn't sleep all night because "I was afraid you'd stopped loving me." Her pathology is located in the fact that her love for him deepens in direct proportion to her conviction that he's a deranged killer. (In *Marnie,* as Hitchcock himself said, "A man wants to go to bed with a woman precisely because she's a thief.")

That very evening, as Johnny, Lina, and Beaky play a game of anagrams, Hitchcock conveys brilliantly the state of this woman's mind and her susceptibility to her own suggestions. The word DOUBT becomes DOUBTFUL, then MUD becomes MUDDER (a horse that runs well on a muddy track) which becomes MURDER and then MURDERER. Then Lina glances at Johnny and we read her shocked expression: "Of course, he's a murderer!" And in a cinematographic overshot we see her fantasy as Johnny kills Beaky. Later, her fantasy will be imposed on reality despite all evidence to the contrary. Moments later, as she reenters the house from her journey to the seaside, a dark shadow of a cloud covers the house—as later, the web-patterned windows cast an eerie shadow on her, suggesting that she's both victim and spinner of a deadly game of suspicion.

Lina is mistaken—time after time—yet she never seems to absorb the lesson of her own continually erroneous perceptions. Once Johnny begins reading a neighbor's detective thrillers, Lina

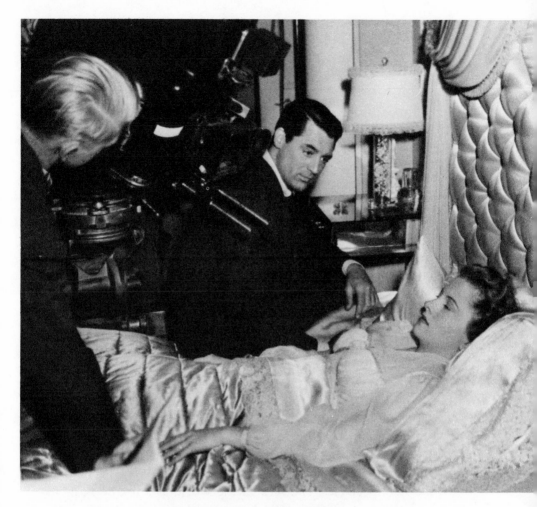

Closing in for a tight shot.

is again suspicious—especially about his curiosity for an untrace-
able poison. Now she imagines *she's* to be the murder victim, a
conviction sealed when she learns that he's been trying to borrow
against her life insurance policy, which can only pay in the event
of her death.

The final argument, as she leaps from the car as they drive
along the cliff, brings us back to the first hilltop sequence—it's
an exact duplicate of the earlier scene, with the same bare trees,
the same windy hillside, the same grappling between them, the
same attack imagined by her. And the final revelation—far from
being an inappropriate ending to which Hitchcock merely acquiesced—is in fact entirely consistent with everything that has
preceded. For over ninety minutes, we've seen a series of events

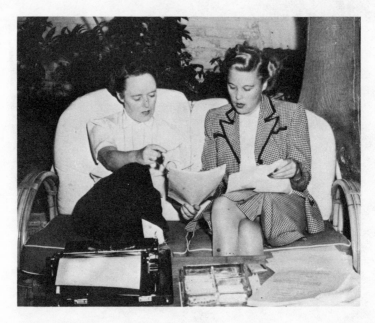

Alma Reville and Joan Harrison working on the script.

in which a woman's fervent imagination and melodramatic fantasy life have constantly misled her to rash judgments and erroneous perceptions. Lina turns venial sins into mortal, she leaps from an observation of a man's childish irresponsibility to a conviction of graver crimes. First shown to us reading *Child Psychology* from behind her spectacles, she sees all the world as a textbook in abnormal child psychology (Beaky, too, she calls a "baby" who should grow up). Now, at the end, she is forced to admit: "This has all been as much my fault as yours." And we've just seen, in this disturbing film, an examination of the dangerous potential of unbridled suspicion.

14

SABOTEUR

(PRODUCED AND RELEASED 1942)

Journeys end in lovers meeting,
Every wise man's son doth know.

TWELFTH NIGHT

Robert Cummings and Norman Lloyd.

By autumn 1941, Alfred Hitchcock had been in America over two years, and only *Mr. and Mrs. Smith* had featured an entirely American cast. For his fifth film and fourth loan-out under the terms of his Selznick contract, he offered independent producer Frank Lloyd at Universal the script of *Saboteur,* virtually an American version of *The 39 Steps.* In addition to the English-born Joan Harrison (his collaborator since 1935) and the Austrian Peter Viertel (son of the director Berthold Viertel and his wife, screenwriter Salka Viertel), the American humorist Dorothy Parker worked on the dialogue to provide a naturalism and to inject necessary humor.

Like *The 39 Steps* before it, and *North by Northwest* after, *Saboteur* is a remarkably relaxed comic thriller in the picaresque tradition: there is at the center an amiably roguish hero whose journey round the country satirizes mores and illuminates the life of the common folk. To be sure, the folk in Hitchcock's films are not exceedingly common, but the hallowed structure of a satiric journey is clearly represented. In *Saboteur* (which Hitchcock rightly said was "cluttered"), there are almost as many ideas as miles covered, and the most interesting are typical of the director—the flight of an innocent man to establish his identity, the significance of a linear journey ending in a vertical fall, the necessity of trust, the forced relationship ending in elected affinity, the disparity between appearance and reality.

The story required numerous script revisions, and the film as we have it concerns aircraft factory worker Barry Kane. The police are on his trail as the perpetrator of a factory fire that resulted in the death of his best friend, and he embarks on a long trek across the country—from Los Angeles to New York—in the course of which he must trust a blonde (Priscilla Lane) who is at first unhelpful. Handcuffed to her (as Robert Donat was to Madeleine Carroll in *The 39 Steps*), Barry meets a variety of eccentric local characters, and you can't get a more outlandish crew than *Saboteur*'s circus sideshow performers. But they're protective and compassionate toward the fleeing couple—a more fully realized microcosm of humanity than the elegant and wealthy Manhattanites we're soon to meet, who are really Nazis in mufti. Finally, Kane tracks the fifth columnists to a swanky New York mansion, and the real saboteur—named Fry (Norman Lloyd)—falls to his death from Miss Liberty's torch after blowing up a Yankee ship destined for wartime service.

It's hard not to deny that there's a certain flatness to this film; there are moments when it looks so cheap you may think it was stitched together by an admirer of Hitchcock. This is at least partly explained by film budget restrictions in early 1942, and also by the fact that the producer had spent so much money on screenplay revisions (and Hitchcock had insisted on so many expensive camera setups and a few lavish sets) that economy was invoked by a number of cheap background shots, painted backdrops, miniatures and rear projections. Hitchcock wanted Gary Cooper and Barbara Stanwyck for the leads (or at least Henry Fonda and Gene Tierney); he had to settle for Cummings and Lane, less expensive players who are not entirely believable and who lack a certain polish and forcefulness.

Although it has a somewhat casual atmosphere, *Saboteur* was not at all casually constructed; in fact, it carefully exploits the single motif first shown in the opening moments of the film. In a stunning long shot noteworthy for high contrast black-and-white photography, enormous sliding doors roll back and aircraft workers pour out for lunch at the factory cafeteria. They are deliberately seen as dark, undefined little figures, so that we clearly see dozens of them striking matches to light cigarettes. At once the motif of fire is established, and from that moment forward, fire will be the film's linking device:

The saboteur—aptly named Fry—causes havoc by putting gasoline in the fire extinguishers, thus effecting the destruction of American fighter planes and an innocent man's death.

A wise and sympathetic blind man (a character embarrassingly overwritten and overplayed) gives the hero refuge from a rainstorm and invites him to warm himself by the fire.

The saboteurs plan to blow up a dam providing electrical power to all of California, and then to explode an important American ship destined for wartime use.

To escape the nest of spies in the New York mansion, Cummings raises a match to a sprinkler system, thus setting off an alarm.

The torch of Miss Liberty herself becomes the place of final confrontation.

This deliberate use of *fire* to focus the saboteurs' nefarious acts is contrasted at each point with *water*. Much is made of the pool and poolside conversation at the Deep Springs Ranch, western headquarters of the spies; the great waters of the dam are counterpoised against the fiery explosion planned for them; a newly launched battleship, blown up, sprays water over the harbor. And for causing death by fire, the saboteur named *Fry* falls from Miss Liberty's *torch:* as a betrayer of the meaning of that torch, he need not look to it for protection and is doused in the waters of New York harbor below.

As in every Hitchcock thriller, safe places like Liberty Island become dangerous venues, and here he borrowed from *Sabotage* one of his own best "safe places," the movie theater. Here, Radio

Alma Kruger and Otto Kruger.

City Music Hall (already the premiere site of many Hitchcock films up to that time), is the place for one of his most inventive set pieces as Fry, fleeing police, runs onto the great stage. On-screen, the Music Hall's thriller movie seems to be about a couple fighting (as in *Sabotage,* the audience in the theater laughs hysterically at the unfunny movie business) and then in the projected film a woman's jealous husband enters and repeatedly shoots a man (as the Radio City audience roars even more hysterically). As this movie is screened, the saboteur makes his way across the great stage in front of the film—illusion becoming reality right before our eyes—and then leaps down *into the audience,* runs right up to the camera and stares out at us as members of the on-screen audience at last become aware that there's mayhem in the theater. Hitchcock thus presents a stunning image of the unreality of sabotage becoming deadly reality in familiar locales—even as he disturbs our neat separation of what is unreal as film from what is real in its presentation.

Saboteur gives us a wonderfully offbeat guided tour of America, and its odd touches of patriotic speeches were inserted not only as a statement of faith in the country as it entered the war (the

Patricia Hitchcock and her father, about the time of *Saboteur*.

film was shot in January and February 1942) but also Hitchcock's support of the average citizen. Here we have cowboys and helpful truck drivers, wise old blind men living in the mountains and pokey next-door neighbors who mean well but bungle their sympathy. As always, the sophisticated and respectable folks—here, Charles Tobin (Otto Kruger) and Mrs. Sutton (Alma Kruger, who was no relation) and their crowd—are, like Professor Jordan in *The 39 Steps* and many others, the real villains.

The finale—with the thin, weasel-eyed Fry falling from the torch—was brilliantly designed by Hitchcock. The actor sat on a revolving, tottering chair, and the camera was pulled up and away from him in a swift reverse crane shot. A film of this was then joined—in what is called a traveling matte—with the background, and the result is a splendidly disorienting view of a man falling away through space. (The same device was used for memorable shots in *Rear Window, Vertigo* and *North by Northwest*.) After this technical tour de force, all Hitchcock can do is restore his hero to the waiting arms of his lady before the final fade-out.

15

SHADOW OF A DOUBT

(PRODUCED 1942, RELEASED 1943)

I have a little shadow that goes in and out with me,
And what can be the use of him is more than I can see.

ROBERT LOUIS STEVENSON,

A CHILD'S GARDEN OF VERSES

Joseph Cotten and Teresa Wright.

No doubt about it, this is Hitchcock's first great American masterwork, one of his timeless, endlessly rich moral thrillers. He always spoke of *Shadow of a Doubt* with particular fondness, primarily because his association with writer Thornton Wilder had been so pleasant and because his relationship with his gifted actors—one of the greatest ensembles he ever gathered—was extraordinarily genial and professionally rewarding. His personal considerations aside, however, *Shadow of a Doubt* is a model of the kind of moviemaking that is gripping, first-rate entertainment and much more: it is also a network of important themes and ideas. If to be called "great" a work must have great concerns, then by any standard this film qualifies.

Based on an idea by Gordon McDonell, Wilder's screenplay (rewritten by Hitchcock and his wife after Wilder went off to war service, with children's dialogue added by Sally Benson), *Shadow of a Doubt* concerns a widow murderer, Charles Spencer Oakley (Joseph Cotten) who, attempting to elude the police in Philadelphia, visits his sister and her family in Santa Rosa, California. There Uncle Charlie is warmly received, especially by his young niece Charlotte (Teresa Wright)—always called "Charlie" and

Charlie Bates, Henry Travers, Edna May Wonacott, Teresa Wright and Joseph Cotten.

named for him. Gradually she suspects the truth about her uncle, and this puts her in danger, for he would willingly do away with young Charlie to save himself. Uncle Charlie is finally killed during his attempt to throw his niece from a moving train: he is himself thrown off balance by her and falls onto the path of an oncoming locomotive. The film concludes with young Charlie and her detective friend (MacDonald Carey) reflecting on the uncle's dark view of a "pigsty" world, while inside the local church Uncle Charlie is eulogized as a great man, "truly one of us."

The opening moments of the picture put us on notice as to Hitchcock's method and intent. From a vast overview of a grim section of a city (the slums of Philadelphia, 1942) the scene dissolves to a grimy street, then to a single house (aptly, number 13), then up to a window of the house. We enter as the camera moves into the smoky, dimly lit bedroom, where the nattily attired Uncle Charlie lies on his bed (on-screen left, facing right); he's staring up into space, thinking. After a moment there's a knock at the door, and a woman with eyeglasses enters, talking of men who are looking for him and of money. Moments later, he leaves the house and makes a telephone call, sending a telegram to his family in California about his imminent arrival.

The scene changes. We see a vast overview of a pleasant-looking town (Santa Rosa), and then the scene dissolves to a pretty street in it, then to a single house on the street, then up to a window of the house. We enter as the camera moves slowly into the clean, brightly lit bedroom, where the neatly dressed young Charlie Newton (she seems eighteen or nineteen) lies on her bed (on-screen left, facing right); she's staring up into space, thinking. A moment later, she's interrupted by a ringing telephone that is answered by her younger sister, who wears eyeglasses. Her father (Henry Travers) comes to the girl's bedroom door, and there's talk of visitors and of money. "I'm going downtown to send a telegram," she tells her mother (Patricia Collinge). "I know a wonderful person who'll come and shake us all up. All the time there's been one right person to save us." In the next shot, Uncle Charlie is brought to Santa Rosa by a train that belches so much black, demonic smoke that it covers the sun, envelopes the entire area and sends an arc of impending doom over the town whose charm he has come to exploit.

With this stunning double sequence and its ironic discourse, Alfred Hitchcock announces not only the structure of the entire film, but also its ethic, for *Shadow of a Doubt* explores the moral links between a psychopathic killer and the innocent niece who is named for him. More important, by extension he offers what amounts to a tract on the very nature of moral ambiguity. Uncle Charlie will indeed "come to save them." He will "shake them all up" by indicating precisely the nature of a part of life that has been ignored: the impulses to decadence that lurk within even the prettiest lives.

Like many great storytellers, Hitchcock is intrigued by the association (not the identification) between wickedness and goodness. The two Charlies inhabit the same world, and the extremes they represent coexist to a greater or lesser extent within every human being. *Shadow of a Doubt,* like twentieth-century literary works such as Joseph Conrad's *The Secret Sharer* and Graham Greene's *Brighton Rock,* offers us two apparently opposite but actually complementary, not mutually exclusive personalities. One (represented here by young Charlie) exemplifies the positive part of human nature, inclined to optimism, goodness and generosity, trust and love; the other (represented by Uncle Charlie) what is negative, decadent and yields to murderous impulses. The complementarity—the fact that these two worlds intersect—is ruthlessly established by Hitchcock's camera. By presenting these two apparently opposite dimensions *in the same cinematic format,* Hitchcock links them by association. The method is not simply perverse (much less is it an endorsement of a negative vision of human character); rather it's the means through which an ethical view is expressed. The lunatic murderer Uncle Charlie—capable, as we see, of great charm, of generosity to his family, of warmth toward his sister—shares the same blood with his sweetly virginal niece Charlie. She is capable, as we learn, of murdering her uncle.

Shadow of a Doubt is a perfectly realized film because its method and its matter coincide precisely. The idea that we are all to some extent combinations of angelic and demonic impulses, that we have dual forces at war within us, is as old as the Greeks and the

Judaeo-Christian tradition; even the Oriental yin/yang shares the concept. To convey this idea, Hitchcock accumulates an astonishing number of *pairs* and *doubles* which link by association Uncle Charlie and niece Charlie, the two characters who are emblems of this division.

The long series of doubles in *Shadow of a Doubt* includes (but is not limited to): two pursuing detectives in Philadelphia and two in Santa Rosa; two criminals sought (Uncle Charlie, and another who is captured and killed); two occasions on which Uncle Charlie is amusingly but ironically called "the spoiled one"; two women with eyeglasses (the landlady in Philadelphia; young Charlie's friend Catherine—and two Santa Rosa girls with eyeglasses, Catherine and little Ann); two dinner sequences at the Newton home; two celebratory toasts (one at dinner, one after Uncle Charlie's speech); two amateur sleuths have two conversations (one on the back porch at night, one at the dinner table), about methods of committing murder.

Also: two occasions when Herb (Hume Cronyn) interrupts family activities at the Newton home; two young Newton children (Roger [Charles Bates] and Ann [Edna May Wonacott]); two school friends meet when uncle and niece go out at night; two grown children of the Oakley family (Uncle Charlie and his sister Emma Newton [Patricia Collinge]); two railway sequences (the arrival and departure of Uncle Charlie); two women (Mrs. Green and Mrs. Potter) who come into the bank where Joe Newton works; two doctors (one on the train bringing Uncle Charlie, one at the house party after Uncle Charlie's speech); two visits by the police to the Newton house; two sequences outside a church; two scenes in the garage (one a love scene, one an attempt at murder); two scenes with Uncle Charlie drinking brandy (in Philadelphia, in Santa Rosa at the bar); two double brandies ordered by Uncle Charlie at the "Till Two" bar, where he's served by a waitress who says she has worked there for two weeks; two attempts to kill young Charlie (on the outside staircase and in the garage) before the final harrowing murder attempt on the train; two converging sets of train rails seen from young Charlie's point of view. This extraordinary—almost obsessive—accumulation of doublings will recur, and for the same reason, in *Strangers on a Train*.

Additionally, both dialogue and camera movement continually associate the two Charlies. A tune, for example, "leaps from head to head," as young Charlie says of the telltale "Merry Widow Waltz"—a clear reference to Uncle Charlie's widow victims. Again: "If I fold it carefully, he won't notice," young Charlie says as she tries to put her father's evening paper back together—and the camera shows us, *as she speaks,* Uncle Charlie, folding the torn excerpt carefully and pocketing it, so that she won't notice.

So that we are very clear on the association of the two Charlies, on the disturbing idea that they share a common humanity, Hitchcock gives us a "wedding" scene that firmly establishes the spiritual link between them. Shortly after his arrival, Uncle Charlie presents gifts to the entire Newton family. Moments later, alone with his niece, he offers her an emerald ring he slips on her finger in a kind of perverse parody of a wedding scene; the accompanying dialogue stresses the union between them:

> SHE: I'm glad that Mother named me after you and that she thinks we're both alike. I think we are, too. I know it . . . We're not just an uncle and a niece. It's something else. I know you. I know that you don't tell people a lot of things. I don't, either. I have a feeling that inside you there's something nobody knows about . . . something secret and wonderful. I'll find it out.
>
> HE: It's not good to find out too much, Charlie.
>
> SHE: But we're sort of like twins, don't you see? We *have* to know!
>
> HE: Give me your hand, Charlie.

He slips a ring on her finger.

> SHE: Thank you.
>
> HE: You didn't even look at it.
>
> SHE: I don't have to look at it.

And later, she tells the young detective Jack Graham (MacDonald Carey), "It's funny, but when I try to think of how I feel, I always come back to Uncle Charlie . . . Are you trying to tell me I

Wallace Ford, Teresa Wright, MacDonald Carey
and Patricia Collinge.

shouldn't think he's so wonderful?" With those words she clasps
her wrist in remembrance of the previous evening, when her uncle
grasped her wrists so tightly in anger that the bruise still smarts.

Uncle Charlie's major monologue at the second dinner table
sequence, when he speaks of his contempt for rich old widows,
indicates that he (the prototypical serial killer) sees his mission to
kill them as almost a divine mandate: "Silly wives . . . and what
do these women do? You see them in the best hotels. Eating the
money. Drinking the money. Losing at bridge. Smelling of
money. Proud of it but of nothing else. Fat, wheezing animals.
And what do we do to such animals when they get too lazy and
too fat?" His speech is at once followed by the arrival of the
family's neighbor, Herbie Hawkins, who chats with his buddy
Joe Newton (Henry Travers) about ways of committing murder
without being detected. They are the amateur sleuths who miss
the murderer under their noses.

But it is at the smoke-filled bar moments after this that the
structural midpoint of the film occurs, the sequence wherein the

lunacy of Uncle Charlie is clearly identified with his contempt for the world and his distrust of everyone in it. Herein, for Hitchcock, lies madness and death.

> UNCLE CHARLIE: "Oh Charlie, something's come between us. I don't want that to happen. Why, we're old friends—more than that. We're like twins, you said so yourself."
> He reaches out to touch her hands, but she pulls back.
> NIECE CHARLIE: "Don't touch me, Uncle Charlie."

She returns the emerald ring. His speech—one of the longest any character has in the Hitchcock filmography—locates the source of his madness as his contempt of humanity.

> HE: "You think you know something, don't you? You think you're the clever little girl who knows something. There's so much you don't know, so much. What do you know, really? You're just an ordinary little girl living in an ordinary little town. You wake up every morning of your life and you know perfectly well that there's nothing in the world to trouble you. You go through your ordinary little day and at night you sleep your untroubled ordinary little sleep filled with peaceful stupid dreams. And I brought you nightmares. You live in a dream. You're a sleepwalker, blind. How do you know what the world is like? Do you know that the world is a foul sty? Do you know if you rip the fronts off houses you'd find swine [which recalls his earlier description of rich widows as fat, wheezing animals]? The world's a hell! What does it matter what happens in it?"

Later, after Charlie learns that her uncle is trying to kill her, he says he intends to continue hiding out in Santa Rosa. The scene is brilliantly designed. Uncle and niece stand on the upper porch at night, both of them in profile, facing each other. But they are lit from behind and with a high key light source; thus they are deeply in darkness, their features indistinct to us. We see only shapes and shadows as he says he intends to stay with the family. And then we see the extent to which young Charlie has been demoralized by the knowledge and presence of her malignant relative: "I don't want you here. I don't want you to touch my mother. Go away, I'm warning you. Go away, or I'll kill you myself. See? That's the way I feel about you!"

So that we are entirely clear on the signs and symptoms of Uncle Charlie's pathology, Hitchcock concludes the film with young Charlie's remarks to the detective, Jack Graham: "He thought the world was a horrible place. He couldn't have been very happy, ever. He didn't trust people. Seemed to hate them. He hated the whole world. You know, he said people like us had no idea what the world was really like."

"It's not quite as bad as that," replies Jack. "Sometimes it needs a lot of watching. It seems to go crazy every now and then—like your Uncle Charlie."

While World War II raged and an allied victory was far from certain, Hitchcock and his writers constructed one of the cinema's indisputable masterworks on the nature of evil. Rather than locating it within an anonymous enemy—"them, over there"— *Shadow of a Doubt* took a position far more risky. In our hometown, he postulates, in our securest settings, right in our own dining room, wickedness can sprout like malignant weeds. The tendency toward that is in our blood, just as strong as the tendency toward goodness, light and trust—thus Hitchcock's insistence on the relation between uncle and niece, the blood connection, the telepathic intimacy that links them and makes them "more than twins." Of all Hitchcock's heroines, it is young Charlie Newton whose moral education is the severest.

It's easy to forget—because it all seems so natural—that *Shadow of a Doubt* contains some of the best acting we're likely to see in film. When we recall that films are shot out of sequence—with all scenes in one locale photographed, then all in another, that perhaps the first week's shooting is of scenes toward the end of the picture, the next week's of early scenes, with no necessary connection from one day's work to the next—it is nothing less than astonishing to see the portrait of the heroine created by Teresa Wright.

Then twenty-four, and with a background of successful stage appearances, she was recommended to Hitchcock by Thornton Wilder, in whose great play *Our Town* she had appeared. This was her fourth film (she had been Oscar-nominated for every perfor-

"Peaceful, quiet Santa Rosa . . ."

mance and won for *Mrs. Miniver*), and she demonstrates in every scene a natural suppleness of understanding, so that the character's ordeal seems both shocking and inevitable. Her appeal and her sweetness are never cloying, her charm never manufactured. In her scenes with veteran performers Henry Travers and Patricia Collinge, she is such an acute listener to their dialogue that you listen with her, and your identification with her character deepens. Opposite the handsome, pliant charm of Joseph Cotten—with whom another ingenue might have seemed diminished because his role is so strong and idiosyncratic—Teresa Wright allows the maturing of a young woman to emerge without force. She offers virtually a handbook on nuanced, exquisitely rendered characterization. Present in almost every sequence, she gives this masterwork very much of its coherence, force and complexity.

Paradoxically, then, Uncle Charlie's darkness reveals the shadows in young Charlie's apparently unalloyed purity, and at the center of the film is her moral education. In this regard, any appreciation of *Shadow of a Doubt* benefits from comparisons with Joseph Conrad's novella *The Secret Sharer* and Graham Greene's novel *Brighton Rock*. In each case there is a killer who feels guiltless about others' deaths; in each case their "double" meets them in curious accidents; the villains are charming and polite, indistinguishable from respectable citizenry; the secrets are shared under cover of darkness or at night; and an unsolved killing and a fugitive provide the framework for the moral education of the "untried" individual forced to confront a "double." The narrator in *The Secret Sharer,* Rose in *Brighton Rock* and young Charlie in *Shadow of a Doubt* must explore the dark undersides of their own personalities; they must realize that their capacities for goodness and idealism stand alongside capacities for degeneracy. Their initiation into maturity involves both a knowledge and a testing, and in all these works the characters who are apparently innocent must temporarily identify themselves with destructive, primitive characters. In their unconscious minds there lie infinite capacities for criminal reversion, and their survival and maturity depend on a frank recognition of those capacities. Thus the pure adventure story, in the hands of Conrad, Greene and Hitchcock, becomes a vehicle for the exploration of self. Each villain forces his double to embark on a journey through a hitherto unacknowledged self, the "shadow" that must be seen and acknowledged for the moral problem it is.

The whole person is thus challenged, for no one can become conscious of the shadow without considerable moral effort demanding the recognition of dark aspects of the personality. Progress is made only by an exploratory descent into the primitive sources of being, and this journey exacts a price in danger and demands. Young Charlie risks her own life and at the end is disillusioned, less idealistic than before. Rose (in *Brighton Rock*), by confronting her lover and moral counterpart Pinky, loses her security and must feel "the greatest horror of all" when she learns of his hatred for her on a recording. And Conrad's captain of the *Sephora* will have to work out his new knowledge and justify his dangerous approach to the reefed shore when he finally returns from the sea, the archetypal image of the unconscious. Thus the shadow—one of what Jung called the "archetypes of the collective unconscious"—represents first and foremost the personal unconscious with its unrealized world, "as though I had been faced by my own reflection in the depths of a somber and immense mirror," as the captain says in *The Secret Sharer*.

The complex theme of initiation and a moral education about the shades of moral grayness that infest the world links these works. "Good and evil lived in the same country," wrote Greene, "came together like friends, feeling the same completion." Like Conrad and Greene, Hitchcock struggled with a Gnostic-Puritan ethic on one hand and a Judaeo-Christian ethic on the other. If goodness is really beyond nature, and if evil sprouts all around like weeds (thus Gnostic Puritanism), they still suspect that humanity is capable of transcending itself in love, and that relationships—which so often play us false—can still potentially provide a link and a hint towards divine love. These views are at constant odds in these and other works, which describe and illuminate the darkness for a world which believes it possesses the light. In this regard, *Shadow of a Doubt* could indeed be called a film about what theologians call original sin—a condition of selfishness, a conviction about a basically imperfect world, country, family, individual—radically incomplete, virtually defined by its need of transformation, of redemption.

There is a direct, relentless moral honesty about this film, which stands as one of Alfred Hitchcock's clearest statements about the ambiguity of the human condition. Produced during the war, when Hollywood films generally celebrated a naive sentimentality about the American way of life, it is remarkable in its dispassionate, cool assessments. The two Charlies are linked by more than blood relationship: they are linked by a common humanity, and it is this point that places Hitchcock among the great creative moral cynics of our age. For if young Charlie aspires to a happy life, she realizes at the end that it can only be striven for in this tangled, fallen garden that is no longer a paradise. She will have to live and die with her "shadow of a doubt" about what has gone into her blood, what makes her what she is. She has to realize that "things go crazy" in what e. e. cummings has termed "this so-called world of ours."

16

LIFEBOAT

(PRODUCED 1943, RELEASED 1944)

We said there warn't no home like a raft, after all.
You feel mighty free and easy and comfortable on a raft.

MARK TWAIN,

THE ADVENTURES OF HUCKLEBERRY FINN

Under the credits and in huge close-up, a ship's smokestack whines and slowly descends into the sea; when it's completely submerged, we see the detritus of its former life: a deck of cards floats by, then a liquor bottle, a copy of *The New Yorker* and finally a dead man, still wearing his ineffectual life preserver. The setting for the remainder of this motion picture is its title. In *Lifeboat*, Hitchcock restricted his camera and action to what may be the narrowest acting space ever filmed, thereby setting himself the challenge of something technically demanding and innovative— as, in other ways, he did with *Blackmail, Foreign Correspondent, Rope, Under Capricorn* and *Rear Window*. He also seems to have wanted to do a film without the vast sets and expansive vistas of

Foreign Correspondent and *Saboteur*. Three writers—John Steinbeck (who wrote the original story), MacKinlay Kantor and Jo Swerling—worked at various times with the problems of the scenario.

When a freighter is torpedoed by a German submarine during World War II, the survivors make their way to a lifeboat. On board are journalist Connie Porter (Tallulah Bankhead); left-wing crew member John Kovac (John Hodiak); Gus Smith (William Bendix), a seaman with a serious leg injury; the ship's radio operator, Stanley Garrett (Hume Cronyn); the ship's steward, Joe Spencer (Canada Lee); nurse Alice MacKenzie (Mary Anderson); millionaire businessman Charles Rittenhouse (Henry Hull); and Mrs. Higgins (Heather Angel), an Englishwoman carrying her dead child. They are soon joined by Willi (Walter Slezak), the sole survivor of the enemy U-boat, which has also sunk. The group decides to let him remain aboard, for he is an expert naval officer.

Days pass, food and water diminish and the fierce heat and alternately chilling cold take a toll on the survivors. Willi, as it happens, is deliberately turning the boat from its homeward course toward the position of an enemy supply ship. He is also a surgeon, and he saves Gus's life by amputating his gangrenous leg under these primitive conditions. But then it is Gus who discovers that the Nazi has both a compass and extra drinking water, and Willi pushes Gus overboard while the rest sleep, telling them later that the poor man committed suicide. They then discover the extra water he has been hoarding for himself and learning the truth about him, they beat him to death and toss his body overboard. As they come dangerously close to the German supply ship, it is sunk by an allied vessel, which hastens to their rescue.

In *Lifeboat*, Hitchcock seems to have disobeyed his own primary rule of filmmaking—never to depend merely on "pictures of people talking." No matter how witty or adult or thought-provoking the talk may sometimes be, it's simply uncharacteristic of this most pictorial storyteller to rely on so much discourse. There's not a wide field for visual storytelling here, and so the film offers annoyingly constant conversation, some of it repetitive. No doubt for its wartime setting, however, *Lifeboat* earned Hitchcock an-

John Hodiak, Walter Slezak, Tallulah Bankhead, Hume Cronyn,
Henry Hull, Heather Angel and Mary Anderson.

other Academy Award nomination as best director of the year.
(He was also nominated for *Rebecca, Foreign Correspondent, Rear
Window* and *Psycho.*)

Two points deserve emphasis. The principal character is certainly Constance "Connie" Porter, a reporter covering the war,
outfitted with camera and typewriter she's managed somehow to
salvage. Played with touching vulnerability and feisty self-assur-
ance by the redoubtable Tallulah Bankhead, Connie appears as a
shadowy figure, emerging out of the smoky air, perfectly coiffed,
wearing a large diamond bracelet; she's cool and smart, she smokes
a cigarette and looks monumentally bored, concerned most of all
about a run in her nylon stocking. Connie is roused to action only
by the prospect of shooting film of the other survivors as they
join her in the lifeboat. (Connie is nothing so much as Bankhead
herself, and she addresses every other character by her own char-
acteristic real-life appellation—"dahling"—her own addition to
the script, of which even Hitchcock could not disabuse her. Nevertheless, for her performance she was properly cited by the New
York Film Critics as best movie actress of the year.) The character

is Hitchcock's exponent for a concern first evident in *Easy Virtue* (and even more explicit in *Rear Window*)—the ethics of picture-taking:

Bankhead: I got some priceless pictures—some wonderful shots on deck of a lot of people on one of the lifeboats. They looked slow and heavy and fat with their lifebelts on—so lonesome. Then a shell hit the lifeboat. They all jumped overboard. I got a beautiful shot of the gun crew firing at the submarine . . . [Her voice rises higher and higher with enthusiasm.] I got the freighter going down, one of the lifeboats caught in the suction and pulled under! I got some of the U-boat crew jumping overboard! And I also got—[she sees a baby bottle floating in the water]—look! That's a perfect touch!

Kovac dunks the baby bottle to prevent her filming it.

Connie: What did you do that for?

Kovac: Why don't you wait for the baby to float by and photograph that?

A moment later, he jumps up and accidentally knocks the camera from her hands into the sea—the first of many items she loses. Later, her fur coat is lost when the young bereaved mother (to whom she had loaned it for warmth) goes overboard. Then she loses her typewriter when the foremast strikes it from the lifeboat. "Little by little," she reflects, "I'm being stripped of all my earthly possessions!" And last, her diamond bracelet—the single most prized item, a treasured belonging that marks her rise from Chicago poverty: it becomes fish bait. But Connie is not, of course, the only person to endure loss: a young mother loses her baby, a sailor loses his leg, the entire crew loses direction and, most poignant and necessary of all, they lose a sense of supremacy once they commit a murder.

Connie's moral education—and that's not too strong a term when we hear how much wiser she becomes, how much stronger a modulating influence on the others as the story progresses—is suggested by Kovac: "You've been all over the world and you've met all kinds of people. But you never write about them, you only write about yourself. You think this whole war's a show put on for you to cover like a Broadway play!"

. . .

The moral education includes everyone. There's a running argument aboard this lifeboat about the functions people play in times of crisis, about how individuals on both "sides" are treated during a war and especially how the predicament of these survivors relates to a larger world situation:

Rittenhouse: The more we quarrel and criticize and misunderstand each other, the bigger the ocean gets and the smaller the boat.

Kovac: The boat's too small right now for me and this German!

Rittenhouse: If we harm this man, we're guilty of the same tactics that you hate him for. On the other hand, if we treat him with kindness and consideration, we might be able to convert him to our way of thinking. That's the—uh—Christian way.

With considerable boldness and moral complexity, the script then goes on to examine the unpleasant truth that the Christian way does not always effect the desired results; pragmatism, after all, is not the rationale for the gospel. Not merely an academic, philosophical discussion, the issue of how to treat a Nazi face-to-face becomes a great, unanswerable inquiry by the final moments of the film, when we meet the second Nazi sailor, an apparently innocent young man they haul into their lifeboat. But he pulls a gun. They wrest it from him and for a moment consider killing him. "They [all the Germans] ought to be exterminated!" shouts Rittenhouse.

His companions rightly reject that outburst, but they have, after all, murdered Willi, in whose killing only the devout black man (the steward Joe) refused to participate—and only he tries (in vain) to prevent another from doing so. *Lifeboat* does not answer the questions of moral responsibility, since the film does not conclude, it just suddenly stops. But we're left with an uneasy sense of ethical drifting and uncertainty. And we hardly applaud the lynch-mob murder of Willi, no matter how foul his deeds.

The ultimate terror generated by *Lifeboat* derives from its setting rather than from any specific action within it. With no music (except under the opening and closing titles) and with no sound but wind and waves, thunder and storm, the film conveys a hor-

rific sense of endless floating, with no sure port. There's no background but the infinite water, no escape from the sea that beckons
to death and invites annihilation as the ultimate liberation. *Lifeboat*
has, finally, a hallucinatory quality, a nightmare sensation with
an overwhelming sense of imminent doom. Even the protracted
talk cannot diminish the film's overarching atmosphere of dread.

"I don't understand any of it," says Nurse MacKenzie plain-
tively. "I don't understand people hurting each other and killing
each other. I just don't understand it." What, then, asks Kovac,
is she doing in a uniform? "I'm doing the only thing I can—trying
to put [the wounded] together again if they get hurt." Such human
moments grace a very chilly film.

17

SPELLBOUND

(PRODUCED 1944, RELEASED 1945)

Fortunately, analysis is not the only way to resolve inner conflicts. Life itself still remains a very effective therapist.

KAREN HORNEY, *OUR INNER CONFLICTS*

Ingrid Bergman and Gregory Peck.

I n 1944, the idea of a romantic thriller set against a background
of Freudian dream theory intrigued producer David O. Selznick,
to whom Hitchcock was still contracted and who was himself
undergoing psychoanalysis. Based very loosely on a novel by Francis Beeding called *The House of Dr. Edwardes,* the script by Ben
Hecht concerns Dr. Murchison (Leo G. Carroll), the director of
the mental asylum Green Manors, who is about to retire. He awaits
the arrival of his successor Dr. Edwardes (Gregory Peck), who
soon falls in love with colleague Dr. Constance Petersen (Ingrid
Bergman). But Edwardes behaves strangely: emotional outbursts
are curiously triggered whenever he sees parallel lines on a white
surface. Constance discovers that he is in fact no psychoanalyst at

all but an amnesiac doctor who believes he has killed the man whose name and identity he has assumed. Unwilling to accept this or to turn him over to the police for the murder of the real Edwardes, she takes him to the home of her former mentor Dr. Brulov (Michael Chekhov), and there both of them attempt to analyze their patient's strange dreams and apparently unreasonable guilt. It turns out that the young man has always felt responsible for the accidental death of his brother when they were children, and it was not he but Dr. Murchison who murdered the real Dr. Edwardes to save his own position. At the conclusion, Murchison kills himself, and Constance and her patient—by now revealed as Dr. John Ballantine—leave for marriage and a new life together.

The basic idea—love-smitten lady analyst plays detective to prove the innocence of haunted patient accused of a crime—was only partly Hitchcock's cup of English Breakfast tea, but with the brilliant and prolific Ben Hecht as his screenwriter and with two of Selznick's most attractive contract players, *Spellbound* overcame

Michael Chekhov, Ingrid Bergman and Gregory Peck.

its own limitations to become a crowd pleaser in 1945. So it remains almost fifty years later, although we may have trouble with the idea of an analyst treating her lover.

The movie is rather a straightforward narrative with not much subtlety, and both the dream sequences and the complexities of the manhunt story required virtually constant spoken elaboration—especially for a 1945 audience unfamiliar with psychological theory and jargon. But it's fascinating to see how every sequence contributes to the overarching concern of the film, which is a love story: typically, Hitchcock made his thriller a romance, and his interest here is squarely on the couple as a new variety in the panoply of male-female relationships.

We're first introduced to psychiatric patient Mary Carmichael (Rhonda Fleming), who speaks seductively to an orderly and then cruelly digs her nails into the back of his hand, forming the parallel lines that will presently be the major motif of the picture. The exposition in the following dialogue between Mary and Dr. Petersen is structured to reveal that residents of Green Manors are basically haunted by delusions of neurotic guilt caused by past traumas—precisely the sort of thing soon to be revealed as the hero's dilemma. But this opening dialogue also sets forth the cool, slightly shocked reaction of Constance to Mary's statement, "I hate men!" The doctor herself has ignored or at least suppressed her womanly feelings, subordinating them to her work and career; this is pointedly emphasized in the ensuing comic dialogue with Constance and Dr. Fleurot (John Emery).

In a quite concrete manner, then, *Spellbound* becomes the story of a twofold transformation. First, it's the rather simplistic (and unlikely) treatment and eventual cure of John Ballantine by the generous, loving help of Constance as analyst. But it's also the story of the freeing of Constance: the very act of treating him releases her to explore and enliven her own womanly feelings. Hitherto, the deepest relationship in her life has been nonromantic, as she admits—with her mentor, the fatherly Dr. Alex Brulov.

The first mention of Dr. Murchison (Leo G. Carroll, who had been in *Rebecca* and *Suspicion,* and who would turn up again in *The Paradine Case, Strangers on a Train* and *North by Northwest*) is a direct clue: "Murchison," says Dr. Fleurot, "must be out of his

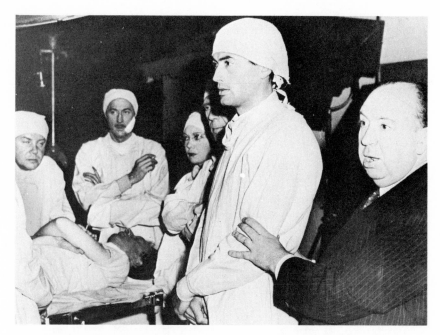
Hitchcock rehearses Peck for the operating room sequence.

mind to assign Carmichael to you." So Murchison is, and so we will discover.

As with Mary Carmichael, we learn from the scene with Garmes (Norman Lloyd) that the problem of neurotic guilt leads to the potential for all kinds of exploitation later in life. This man's delusion will lead directly to the problem of John Ballantine: Garmes thinks he killed his father (Oedipus, phone home) as Ballantine, having buried the memory of *accidentally* killing his brother, will be fair prey to Dr. Murchison, who uses him for a tool in the murder of Dr. Edwardes. (The idea of exploiting another man's psychological weakness to cover for a murder is of course central to the great *Vertigo*.)

In fact the entire key to the solution of the mystery is suggested early on, just after the arrival of the false Dr. Edwardes, when Constance tells Garmes: "People often feel guilty for something they never did, and it usually goes back to something in their childhood. A child often wishes something terrible would happen to someone—and if something does happen to that person, the child believes he has caused it, and he grows up with a guilt complex over a sin that was only a child's bad dream."

· · ·

The emotional appeal of *Spellbound* never derives from its byzantine plot. Neither is the popularity due to the overstated and exaggeratedly romantic *look* of the film—and the *sound* of the film, with its ever intrusive musical score by Miklos Rozsa, which won an Oscar and established the theremin as Hollywood's official musical instrument to suggest psychosis. The appeal of the picture has very much to do, on the other hand, with the entirely natural and understated performances by Ingrid Bergman and Gregory Peck, both of whom portray with a kind of ingenuous astonishment their discovery of previously unrecognized and unrealized feelings. Each of them embarks on a frightening journey of self-realization—and that this dual journey is so unlikely is just the point.

Hitchcock created the proper atmosphere in which these performances could emerge, and it is with films like *Spellbound* that we see how very much an *actor's director* he was in spite of the legend he fostered that actors should be treated like cattle: a reiterated remark like this was simply part of his puckish and perverse humor. (What he *really* resented was the inflated salaries paid to many unworthy practitioners of the craft.) In the naturalness and fragility of Bergman's portrait of Constance, in the way she turns her head, folds her hands, stifles an inchoate sob, there are all the qualities of finely modulated screen acting. Consider especially her scenes with Michael Chekhov: these are much more complex than they seem at first sight, for she is playing a colleague, a woman in love, and a devoted ex-student.

In the dark, angular appeal of the young Gregory Peck there's just as much to admire—the wide streak of vulnerability that is not weakness and the romantic fear linked to both warm humor and a willingness to transcend himself. Peck has always been expert at this sort of thing; he has an amalgam of qualities that made him more than merely a sex symbol and less than intimidating. His character here is willing to take responsibility for himself, but he clearly conveys the awesome nature of that responsibility. Hitchcock's arrangement of the actors within the frame, his altering the size of the image to suit the emotional need of the shot, his unerringly right placement of them against backgrounds, his work with cinematographer George Barnes on lighting and shadow, his respect for Ben Hecht's script—the director's method discloses how much he had his actors in mind. Those who would credit only Selznick with these contributions to *Spellbound* cannot have seen very many Hitchcock films; precisely the same virtues are everywhere evident in, for example, *Shadow of a Doubt*.

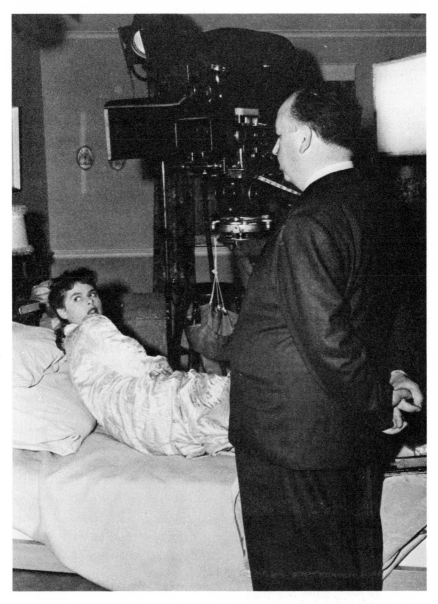

Miss Bergman prepares for a close-up.

Emotional complexities are evoked from Hitchcock's actors—not mere technique in the service of a raw emotion. And he always provided them with the breadth and space for their talents to emerge, never overdirecting them, never intruding on their own understanding of a moment. A good example of this is the evening scene in which Bergman comes to Peck's room with a copy of his book. He's seated in a chair, having fallen asleep. She then admits that she's not come to his room to discuss his book.

The ensuing scene—with the kiss, the embrace and the montage of a series of opening doors to suggest the release of long repressed love—should not be considered amusingly dated because it is so highly stylized; in fact, despite the silly doors, this may be a more realistic scene between adults precisely because it *isn't* more explicit at this point in their relationship. The credible acting makes this scene believable, in addition to the manner in which Hitchcock moves his camera around this couple with their restrained passion and their charged feelings of hesitation. As so often in such moments, he positions his couple by making us viewers identify with both characters: Bergman and Peck face the camera directly, he moves toward the camera, and each of them faces us until they kiss. This subjective-objective transference throughout the scene (used identically in *Rebecca, Shadow of a Doubt, Vertigo, The Birds* and *Marnie*) is essential when Hitchcock wants us to *feel* the dual reactions of both characters.

The psychological apparatus by which the mystery is solved in *Spellbound,* in other words, is itself in fact the MacGuffin, as the film presents a romantic situation with dreadful obstacles which we believe will be overcome. In *Shadow of a Doubt,* young Charlie had to learn that the idolization of her uncle was misplaced; in her moral education, she was freed to transfer her inchoate romantic feelings to another man (the detective). In *Spellbound,* both Constance and John have to be freed of former blockages in order to establish a valuable relationship. The psychoanalytic apparatus is simply a device for them to get over, and so should we.

The visuals are, of course, endlessly fascinating. Hitchcock wanted something other than the usual blurry images for the dream sequences, so he and Selznick brought in Salvador Dalí, who gave Hitchcock the De Chirico-like effects he wanted. But however beautiful and hauntingly provocative these images remain, they are but a few of what the artist provided Selznick and Hitchcock for the film. For years, Hitchcock mentioned only that there was also a statue that was to "crack like a shell falling apart, with ants crawling all over it, and underneath, there would be Ingrid Bergman. It just wasn't possible!"

But the actress's recollection was more detailed, as she told the author of this book: "It was a wonderful, twenty-minute sequence that really belongs in a museum. The idea for a major part of it was that I would become, in Gregory Peck's mind, a statue. To do this, we shot the film in the reverse way in which it would appear on the screen. They put a straw in my mouth so I could breathe, and then a statue was actually made around me. I was dressed in a draped, Grecian gown, with a crown on my head and an arrow positioned so it seemed to be through my neck. Then the cameras rolled. I was in this statue, I broke out and the action continued. We ran it backward, so it would appear as if I became a statue. It was marvelous, but someone went to Selznick and said, 'What is all this drivel?' and so they cut it. It was such a pity."

What fell to the cutting-room floor was more than gimmickry, for the piercing of Constance's neck with an arrow suggests just how far, in his own mind, Ballantine's anger and guilt may go: there is a clear connection between his belief in his capacity for murder and his ambivalent feelings about Constance as healer and lover. And the statue conveys his sense of her as a mother-goddess figure (thus the Venus/Cybele costume), with the arrows reminiscent of the spiked fence that caused the death of Ballantine's brother. Constance-as-statue also suggests that he sees her as classically cold, artificial, remote, untouchable. The unedited original might have conveyed even more surreally the tragically compatible emotions of love and hate, desire for help and mistrust of helpers, and the fear of discovery.

Other inventive moments managed to survive the finished film, however. The scene in which Peck drains the glass of drugged milk is wonderfully realized: a giant pail was held in front of the camera which photographed Dr. Brulov in the background as the milk was poured into a trough. And the penultimate shot (of Dr. Murchison's suicide) was possible by constructing a huge wooden hand holding a gun. This was mounted under the camera and

The stars of *Spellbound* chat with the director during
a break in shooting the asylum sequences.

turned round just toward it, so that Bergman could be kept in
clear focus beyond; the red explosion was hand-tinted onto the
black-and-white image. These touches are dandy, but Bergman
and Peck gave *Spellbound* its humanity.

18

NOTORIOUS

(PRODUCED 1945–46, RELEASED 1946)

No, no, go not to Lethe, neither twist
Wolf's bane, tight-rooted, for its poisonous wine.

KEATS, ''ODE ON MELANCHOLY''

Leopoldine Konstantin, Ingrid Bergman and Claude Rains.

To put the matter plainly, *Notorious* is Alfred Hitchcock's most complex and compelling romance up to his great masterpiece *Vertigo*. Right after watching it, you may tend to forget its plot about Nazis working with uranium ore in Brazil, in a race to develop the bomb at the end of World War II. What sticks in the memory is rather the tale of a couple—a needy woman and a frightened man—and of another man betrayed by both his own devotion and by the political expediency of the couple. *Notorious* is as fine an exploration of adult confusions as one could ask for. It's remarkable, too, in light of its assertions about the perfidy and immorality of American intelligence activities, that it could have been made and released (much less have been such a hit at Radio City Music

Hall) just after the war, when national pride ran at full gallop: *Notorious* is a film that subverts not only the idolatry of national moral supremacy but also every assumption about authentic and false love. It has, in other words, all the ingredients of box-office failure.

The story is simple enough, but even in a brief outline form it hints at concerns just below the surface. In Miami, in April 1946, Alicia Huberman (Ingrid Bergman, never lovelier) tries to escape the tragedy of her German father's treason against America by hard drinking and easy virtue. She's approached by intelligence agent T. R. Devlin (Cary Grant, never more enigmatic) with the offer to work as a counterspy in Rio de Janeiro, uncovering enemy secrets connected with a man named Alexander Sebastian (Claude Rains), who was once in love with Alicia. She and Devlin fall in love, but he is emotionally unable to prevent her further involvement with the love-smitten Alex who, once the affair has been resumed, proposes marriage—a step which will, of course, facilitate her work for America even as she's being sold into sexual

"Won't you trust me—just a little?" asks Alicia.

enslavement ("Mata Hari," Alicia says ruefully of herself when she learns of her job. "She makes love for the papers.") Alex and his mother (Leopoldine Konstantin) discover Alicia's identity as an American agent, and Devlin rescues her from a death by slow poisoning.

The basic concern of *Notorious,* repeated in almost every scene, is a twofold redemption: a woman's need to be trusted in love, enabling her to transcend a sad, guilt-ridden life; and a man's need to overcome a commitment to mere professional-political expediency and to entrust himself to love, enabling him to overcome a life of severe emotional repression.

It's fitting that Hitchcock and screenwriter Ben Hecht chose to locate this romance about trust within the package of an espionage thriller, for spies are characterized by their exploitation of trust. Going one step further, that theme is aptly and ironically located within the theme of social drinking. Far from representing unity, toasting health and celebrating joy or prosperity, all the drinking in *Notorious* is either socially fraudulent, an escape from

Cary Grant, Louis Calhern, Ingrid Bergman.

Charming but villainous is Alex Sebastian (Claude Rains).

guilt and emotional pain or downright poisonous: thus the opening
boozy party; the several times an emotionally rejected Alicia takes
refuge in drink; the discovery of an ingredient for the bomb hidden
within a wine bottle; and the arsenic-spiked coffee. *Notorious* is
punctuated throughout with other (sometimes smaller) markers
of drink and drinking, constant reinforcements of its major motif.

Few other films, in fact, withstand as much meticulous study as
this; few were constructed according to so rigorous a design; fewer
still succeed in matching structural perfection with such a depth
of feeling. Consider, in this regard, how the opening sequences
of *Notorious* not only present all its major visual and emotional
elements, but also how they are exactly reversed by the final sequences ninety minutes later. The first scene-elements may be
marked as "A through E" and the last as "a through e"; when we
do this, a perfectly balanced "table of contents" emerges.

   In the film's first scene (A), we peer with a court usher through
an open doorway and see three men standing before one judge.

Then we see a silent and solitary Alicia (B) departing the court-room. In the next sequence (C), there is a party where Alicia liberally pours drinks for herself and her guests and announces with ironic accuracy: "The important drinking hasn't started yet!" With admirable economy, the script then simultaneously estab-lishes that Alicia is a woman whose real thirst is for love—and when that is denied her she retreats to whiskey:

> ALICIA: Do you love me, Commander?
> COMMANDER: You're a very beautiful woman.

But this is not, of course, an answer, and so:

> ALICIA: I'll have another drink to appreciate that.

After the party has broken up (D), an unsteady and drunk Alicia invites Devlin for a night ride in her open roadster. He puts a handkerchief around her bare midriff so she won't take cold, and then she leads Devlin out of her house for the wild spin. When they're stopped by a patrolman, he prevents her arrest by revealing his official function as some kind of law enforcement officer or federal agent.

Next morning (E), dreadfully hung over from too much whis-key, Alicia sees Devlin—through her blurry vision—approaching her bedroom in the blinding morning light. The offer of a job "to make up for some of your daddy's peculiarities" follows at once, and the romance-adventure begins.

At the conclusion of *Notorious,* these sequences are fulfilled by reversal:

At night (e), poisoned by arsenic, Alicia sees Devlin—through her blurry vision—approaching her dark bedroom in shadow and silhouette.

Ill and unsteady (d), she is led out of the house by Devlin, who puts a coat around her. All during these final moments, Alicia and Devlin speak of poison and of love (c). When they are mo-mentarily stopped by their enemies he leads her to safety outside the house by concealing his official position and driving her away in a closed convertible roadster; she leaves the Sebastian mansion neither silent nor friendless (b). The film's final shot (a) is of one man standing before an open door, where three "judges" await— his Nazi colleagues who now suspect him of collaborating with American agents.

This structure can be easily itemized:

Opening scenes	*Concluding scenes*
A: open door with three men before one judge	a: open door with one man before three judges
B: Alicia exits courtroom, silent and alone	b: Alicia exits, whispering with her lover
C: the party talk of drinking and the need for love	c: the talk of poison and an admission of love
D: the unsteady exit; the flimsy protection of the kerchief; the night ride in an open car; he saves her by revealing his identity	d: the unsteady exit; the protection of her coat; the night ride in a closed car; he saves her by concealing identity
E: the morning hangover in the bright bedroom, her blurry vision and his offer of a job.	e: the illness in the dark bedroom, blurry vision, and declaration of love.

As Alicia and Devlin fly down to Rio, she learns of her father's suicide by poison capsule, and Ingrid Bergman's performance here (as at every moment in the film) is unerringly superb. A haze of remembrance and of pain washes across her features, which—as usual in this film—are held in close-up by Hitchcock's adoring camera. But it's also important to note that Grant's glances toward her have been directed by Hitchcock in such a way that we see his own emerging but unacknowledged feelings.

In fact, *Notorious* is very much a film about how people conceal feelings—about how they glance aside, look down, avert a gaze to cover emotion. In this regard, dialogue is often juxtaposed with an ironic image. Before the party, for example, Alex apologizes for not trusting Alicia and goes to kiss her hands in contrition. But she *is* unworthy of trust (she is, after all, betraying her husband's devotion to her and she's just now stolen his key in an attempt to further betray him). To throw him off her track and

Hitchcock's most famous MacGuffin: the uranium in the wine bottles.

conceal the key in her hand, she throws her arms round him, using the gesture of love as a ruse. Moments later, again to throw Alex off the track outside the wine cellar, Devlin sets up a "scene" to convince Alex that he (Devlin) is in love with Alicia, which of course he is. The gesture of love (this time real) is again used as a ruse. Never have gestures been so freighted with complexity, nor the signs of commitment been so layered with meanings true and false.

The crucial cinematic device linking these two tense moments is the famous crane shot in which the camera at the Sebastian party descends without a cut from a vast overview of the grand foyer of the mansion, to a close-up of the key held tightly in Bergman's hand. This extraordinary moment is not simply technical virtuosity on Hitchcock's part. Rather it's important for him to emphasize two levels of reality within a single image. The (literal) key to something dangerous lies within this impressive and sophisticated setting; one spatial continuum, in other words, contains a double reality—just as the bottles of Pauillac contain uranium ore, just as single affectionate gestures contain multiple realities.

. . .

But *Notorious* is from first frame to last a film of startling ironies and contrasts. Promiscuity and sexual exploitation are contrasted with the desire for true love. Drunken dizziness is contrasted with arsenic poisoning. Social elegance and propriety mask a murderous savagery. Giggling small talk (between Alicia and Devlin, sipping champagne to exchange information at the party) hides collusion. A labeled bottle is emptied of fine wine and contains ore to make a deadly bomb.

In addition to Ingrid Bergman's wonderfully complex portrait, the casting of Cary Grant as an antiromantic is inspired, and his smooth, handsome features are everywhere stressed by Ted Tetzlaff's remarkable lighting and camera movement. In the justly famous daytime balcony scene, Devlin and Alicia talk of supper plans as they nibble each other's lips and ears. In a single take, the camera records them on the balcony and remains close to them as they walk together from the terrace through the living room to the front hall telephone and finally to the door. This is—like the crane shot to the key in Alicia's hand—not only brilliant cinematography, with the camera following the ever-embracing couple, with the low whispering and the casual carnality of their exchange. It's also a blunt rendering of this man's character. Confronted with Alicia's ardor, Devlin can summon only a quite chilly lovemaking that has its ultimate description on the same balcony later that evening, when he agrees to put Alicia up to become Alex's mistress. She begs him, instead, to believe in her, to trust her desire for a new life and her love for him. But his fear of her, masking as a greater sense of official duty, prevails. Her refuge is to take a hefty drink.

In the role of Mrs. Sebastian was the great German actress Leopoldine Konstantin, in her only American film. One of the premier classical actresses of her day, she was praised for her European performances as Salome, Lady Macbeth and Gertrude, and her portrait in *Notorious* remains chillingly taut. Reinhold Schunzel (Otto Renssler, called "Dr. Anderson") was a much loved stage and screen performer in exile from Hitler's Germany, too; he enacted with considerable gentleness and appeal his role as a sympathetic counterpoise to the others in the Sebastians' nest of spies.

On the set, the director with script and script blow-ups.

When Bergman says to him, "Oh, you're leaving? I'll miss you,"
she means it; he's a surrogate father for her throughout her tangled
time in Rio.

The final moments of *Notorious* are remarkable for Hitchcock's
refusal to add music, and for his ability to evoke its power simply
from camera motion and from performances. All the motifs of
the picture coalesce, and Hitchcock gives us perhaps the tenderest,
truest love scene in his entire filmography. It's straight from the
pages of a fairy tale—Prince Not-So-Charming Awakens Snow-
Beige—but it's also every romantic's ultimate fantasy: to save the
beloved from the jaws of death. That it is so breathtakingly compelling is a tribute to the talents and sentiments of the director,
his writer and his players. *Notorious* withstands multiple viewings;
the older you get, the more true—the more astonishingly true—
it becomes.

19

THE PARADINE CASE

(PRODUCED 1946–47, RELEASED 1947)

Art thou but
A dagger of the mind, a false creation,
Proceeding from the heat-oppressed brain?

MACBETH

Gregory Peck and Alida Valli.

Perhaps because it lacks the stylish verve of later Hitchcock films, and because it depends on a viewer's patience with a series of darkly intense dialogues about a man's destructive romantic fantasies, *The Paradine Case* has never had an enthusiastic following. But it may be one of the director's films most in need of reassessment and fresh appreciation, and if we take *The Paradine Case* on its own terms it rewards richly. Giving oneself up to its brilliantly lit, heavily shadowed scenes (by the great cinematographer Lee Garmes, who was responsible for lighting Marlene Dietrich in *Morocco* and *Shanghai Express*), listening to its carefully structured narrative and absorbing its obsessive texture is, admittedly, not an entirely *pleasant* experience. *The Paradine Case* may best be appreciated, in fact, by audiences who can esteem *Vertigo,* with which this shares the major concern of romantic obsession and delusion. Additionally, the performances are everywhere acute, the mood is somber but seriously mature.

The story, based on a Robert Hichens novel and written by Hitchcock, his wife Alma and producer David O. Selznick, concerns defense attorney Anthony Keane (Gregory Peck), who falls in love with his client Maddalena Paradine (the Italian actress Alida Valli, here in her American debut and listed only by her surname in the credits); she is to be tried for the murder of her blind husband. Keane's wife Gay (Ann Todd) agonizes over her inability to free her husband from his growing obsession with Mrs. Paradine, and at the same time Gay herself is the object of lecherous attention by Lord Horfield, the judge in the case (Charles Laughton). Keane then learns that Major Paradine's servant André Latour (Louis Jourdan) was Mrs. Paradine's lover, and he sets out to prove that it was Latour who killed his master. Mrs. Paradine, grief-stricken when Latour commits suicide in his cell, then admits that indeed she was the killer. But Keane, too, is guilty—of subverting the law and placing his passion above his conscience and respect for it. Keane walks out on the case, his life shattered. But his wife's steadfast love augurs well for the future.

It was clearly important for Hitchcock to establish from the outset the elegant and mysterious beauty of Mrs. Paradine, and everything about her first scene conveys her cool, distant sophistication. We are to have very ambivalent feelings indeed about this woman, whom we first find so alluring. She's presented strikingly, with her dark hair, strong features and tight-lipped, exceedingly proper manner as she plays a romantic nocturne at the piano, sips sherry before dinner and then—when the police arrive—calmly hears the charge of murder. In this regard, Garmes and Hitchcock lit Valli— in the first scene and throughout the picture—with a high key light, rendering her strong features almost masklike. Moments later, when we meet Anthony Keane and his blond wife Gay, we see immediately the contrast between the mysterious defendant and her rival: as her name implies, Gay is open, cheerful, optimistic and completely devoted to her brilliant husband.

The structure of the film at once becomes clear. There's a

rigorous alternation between sequences with Mrs. Paradine in Holloway Prison and sequences with Gay at home—not so much to show us the differences between the two women, but to illuminate the character of Anthony Keane. *The Paradine Case* is not a murder mystery at all: Mrs. Paradine looks and reacts guilty from the first scene. Rather, it's the story of a lawyer who confuses devotion with duty, who idolizes, romanticizes and falls in love with the woman he defends. Immediately after the first scene with the Keanes, we move to a daytime scene when he meets Mrs. Paradine.

Louis Jourdan and Gregory Peck.

At once, he is smitten and decides she is innocent—even before he knows anything about her or her actions:

> KEANE: We will have answers for everything. You loved [your blind husband] and he needed you.
> MRS. PARADINE: You know that?
> KEANE: Weren't you his eyes? . . . It was a voluntary service. You devoted your entire life to this fellow, freely, gladly . . .
> MRS. PARADINE (reflecting a moment): Yes, I see what you mean. (Never has an attorney so gladly handed his guilty client a means of escape.)
> KEANE: It was a sacrifice, a sublime sacrifice—and it was the more tremendous that Paradine could not understand, could not possibly understand the sacrifice you were making. He'd never seen you—he'd never, as I say, seen you.

In the next sequence, we learn from Keane's colleague Sir Simon Flaquer (Charles Coburn) and his daughter Judy (Joan Tetzel) even more about Anthony's character:

> JUDY: So you think Tony was taken with her, Father? . . . Tony may be as good a lawyer as you think he is, but how he loves anything dramatic! . . . Can't you just see Tony giving another of his great performances, riding to the rescue of beauty in distress! How he must relish this!

The presentation of Keane's character continues after the dinner at Lord Horfield's:

> HORFIELD (to Keane): You, my dear chap, have this habit of overcharging yourself with emotion when facing the jury, and I am bound to confess that it does not particularly appeal to my sense of what's proper in court.

Keane's growing passion for Mrs. Paradine is carried forth in the next sequence, when he and Gay return home. He decides their anniversary trip should be not to Switzerland but to "a more colorful place," Italy—Maddalena Paradine's native country—and

Gay senses this connection at once. From this we move to the scene at the jail wherein Mrs. Paradine wishes to speak to Keane quite freely about her "unattractive past" of easy virtue. But he sees her as the victim of abuse, not the victimizer of men she willingly admits she was in the past. (It's no wonder that Hitchcock continually intercuts to the bombed and ruined courthouse: the strength of the law is certainly being undermined—from within, by blind lawyers, thus the intercuts also to "blind justice" and the scales.)

> MRS. PARADINE: I am—what would you say?—a woman who has seen a great deal of life . . . When I was still at school in Naples, it began. I was sixteen, or so I said—actually, I was younger.
> KEANE: Tragic.
> MRS. PARADINE: Yes, perhaps, but I didn't think so then. I ran away with a man—Istanbul, Athens, Cairo.
> KEANE: He was much older, of course—rich, he took advantage of your youth.
> MRS. PARADINE: He was married, respected. *I* took advantage of *him!* Then, as suddenly as it began, it ended. He wearied of me, I wearied of him—what difference does it make?
> KEANE: There were others?
> MRS. PARADINE: Of course there were others! We cannot hide these things!

Immediately after, Sir Simon and Anthony talk about their client, and it is further established that he will not even consider the possibility that Mrs. Paradine is guilty: "We have the simple, obvious fact that Mrs. Paradine is not a murderess," Keane insists. "She's too fine a woman." But Sir Simon replies, "Really? I was of the impression that she'd been a woman of very low estate and rather easy virtue." To this Keane objects violently, and as he madly insists on the sterling character of Mrs. Paradine, Gay approaches the room with a tray of drinks for the men. She is photographed regarding her husband from behind the wooden bars separating the parlor from the dining room. His passionately unrealistic defense of Mrs. Paradine thus situates him behind "prison bars" separating him from his wife—and so the entire subjective-objective shots become a neat visualization of how Gay is a prisoner of his fantasies and an equivalent image of how Keane is already in self-imprisonment with Mrs. Paradine. "I intend that the rest of the world shall see [Mrs. Paradine] as I do," Keane insists, "as a noble, sacrificing human being any man would be proud of!" Good luck.

From this point, it's Keane's goal to implicate the valet Latour (Louis Jourdan, also in his film debut) as Colonel Paradine's murderer. Mrs. Paradine objects to this—because she is his lover, as we later learn. (Keane refuses to acknowledge the possibility of Mrs. Paradine's perfidy—not from Latour, nor even from the woman herself.)

The structural midpoint of *The Paradine Case* occurs with Gay Keane's long speech to her husband. It's one of those moments in a film largely dependent on intelligent dialogue, a moment when the lazy listener can miss the emotional point:

> GAY: "It's not easy to face the thought of losing you . . . I've lain awake night after night . . . and I've come to a conclusion, Tony. I want her to live. I want very much for her to live, and I hope she gets free . . . not for any noble reason, but because I want all this business over and done with, and an end to your being part lawyer, part frustrated lover . . . If she dies, you're lost to me forever. I know you'd go on thinking that you love her, you'd go on imagining her as your great lost love."

The introduction of the lecherous judge Lord Horfield and his simple but devoted wife Sophie (Ethel Barrymore) provides another contrasting couple in this tale of three kinds of vigilant women (Mrs. Paradine, Gay Keane, Sophie Horfield) and their men (André Latour, Anthony Keane, Tommy Horfield). As the trial progresses, Hitchcock cuts to Lady Horfield, gazing silently, anxiously at her husband. That image is followed by Mrs. Paradine, sleepless in her cell bed, watched by a matron. Finally, there's a cut to Gay Keane, also awake in bed, feigning sleep when Tony comes to the doorway and gazes at her.

Because it's really neither murder mystery nor courtroom

The formal dinner, which concludes disastrously.

drama, and because it's about a common human tendency—to romanticize to the point of madness and even death—*The Paradine Case* annoys very many viewers. But Alfred Hitchcock's films are invariably romances—variations on themes of emotional need, loss and desire—and rarely has this been so uncompromisingly treated as in *The Paradine Case,* with its languorous, darkly gothic atmosphere that never yields to an audience's demands for easy glamour. From a technical viewpoint alone, it's worth serious consideration—of the courtroom sequences, for example, during which Hitchcock and Lee Garmes positioned five cameras, the better to record the tension progressively and without constantly arranging new setups.

Finally, a word about the first-rate performances of a brilliant ensemble cast. The English actress Ann Todd was especially admired by Hitchcock, and her portrait of a neglected wife is at every moment credible and touching; she prevents nobility from seeming otherworldly or artificial. Coburn, Laughton and Barrymore give their usual effortless, convincing performances, and Alida Valli, in her first American film, was appropriately enigmatic and haunted.

All these have been appreciated by critics, but only Gregory Peck has been resented—mostly because Hitchcock was ungenerous in later comments. This was singularly unfair, for Peck was perfectly cast and performed splendidly, with his usual directness and vulnerability. It's important that Peck is regarded as an attractive, admirable and positive movie presence, for so the audience at once identifies with him—both men and women, each for complementary reasons. Just as with James Stewart in *Vertigo,* Peck is a warmly handsome and intensely likable actor—thus Hitchcock's insistence that it is precisely such appealing men who fall prey to their own worst illusions. Had we seen a harsh, crude, or unsympathetic actor in the role (or in the role of Latour) our distance would have made empathy difficult, if not impossible.

20

ROPE

(PRODUCED AND RELEASED 1948)

*Man is a rope stretched between the animal
and the Superman—a rope over an abyss.*

FRIEDRICH NIETZSCHE,
THUS SPAKE ZARATHUSTRA

James Stewart, Cedric Hardwicke and Farley Granger.

S ince 1939, producer David O. Selznick had employed his contracted director Alfred Hitchcock for only three films—*Rebecca, Spellbound* and *The Paradine Case;* for seven other pictures, Selznick loaned him out to other producers and studios, earning a huge profit. By the time the contract was to expire, Hitchcock was more than ever determined to be his own producer—to earn a producer's fee, to select his own properties, to engage a cast, to have complete creative control over every aspect of production and to dictate the form of the final cut. *Rope* and *Under Capricorn* were the first two films he produced—with business cooperation from an English colleague named Sidney Bernstein, under their company banner Transatlantic Pictures: the name derived from the intent to make a series of films alternately in London and Hollywood. These first two pictures were both made in Technicolor and released by Warner Bros., and both were box-office failures. Transatlantic then quietly folded and in 1950 Hitchcock signed to produce and direct as an independent, with Warner financing and distributing.

That Patrick Hamilton's play *Rope* should be his first choice is not surprising, for Hitchcock needed a story with a single set for the challenge he set himself—an experiment in economy in which he intended to make his first color film in uninterrupted ten-minute takes. The result is an intriguing failure that contradicts the basic nature of film itself, which is of course the cut: without the arrangement of bits of film, without crucial inserts and a prevailing viewpoint, *Rope* is afflicted with an almost fatal ennui. It is a prime example, in other words, of precisely what Hitchcock condemned in so many movies—it's merely "pictures of people talking." (He had tried to make the same limitation an asset in *Lifeboat,* restricting the camera to a raft of survivors; for other reasons, that film was more successful. Most triumphant would be *Rear Window,* which limits the viewpoint to what can be seen from a city apartment.)

Rope is the only commercial film ever planned entirely in ten-minute takes; actually, some in this film are several minutes shorter. Shots in movies ordinarily last from about five to fifteen seconds, with writers, directors and editors taking advantage of the cut to vary viewpoint, maintain interest, change setting and create tension. But in this film Hitchcock did not wish to create different setups. Almost every shot lasts ten minutes, the length of time a "magazine" of film can be exposed in the camera; it was very likely the boldest technical experiment ever attempted—and it is best not repeated. "I undertook [it] as a stunt," Hitchcock said. "That's the only way I can describe it. I got this crazy idea to do it in a single shot. It was quite nonsensical because I was breaking my own theories on the importance of cutting and montage."

As the enormous Technicolor camera was moved sinuously from living room to foyer to dining room to kitchen door and back again, walls were whisked silently up into the studio flies, grips stood just off-camera removing and redepositing chairs and accessories, and actors had marked points on the floor to indicate their precise positions for each moment of dialogue. At the end of a ten-minute take, the camera was moved close to the back of a man's jacket, or to a tabletop or other object in order to black out the action; the reel was changed and the next long take resumed with the same dark close-up. If a mistake happened (and there were many), the entire complicated take had to recommence. Camera movements and positions all had to be rigorously prearranged down to every detail.

The film follows closely Hamilton's play, which was based on the Leopold/Loeb murder case, one of the most infamous and bizarre crimes in American history. Here, all the action occurs in the New York penthouse apartment of two young gay lovers, Philip (Farley Granger) and Brandon (John Dall), who murder a friend; this they do as an experiment in thrill-seeking and as the logical outcome of an intellectual thesis with which they're intrigued—that murder is the privilege of an élite few. They then hide the corpse in a living room chest, from whose lid they calmly serve a buffet dinner to guests—among them the murdered man's father, aunt and fiancée (Cedric Hardwicke, Constance Collier and Joan Chandler), and their former college professor (James Stewart). To his horror, the truth is gradually discovered by the professor whose ideas were taken to an extreme by his students; he summons police at the finale.

After the opening credits against a New York street scene, the camera pulls back from the long shot after the last title has rolled, and there's a reverse angle to the exterior of a draped penthouse window. A man screams. The camera cuts to the interior, to a close-up of a young man who has just been strangled to death, a piece of rope still held tightly round his neck by his murderers. They dump the body into a living room chest, and soon they will, with incredible nerve, use the same piece of rope to tie the dead man's books, which they return to his father. This is highly significant, for the double use of the rope establishes an association between the act of murder and the pursuit of a sterile bookishness, a primary concern of both play and film. (The camera—and viewer—as voyeur is typically Hitchcockian: we move from out-

The professor (James Stewart), flanked by his students (Farley Granger and John Dall), realizes the corpse is in the chest.

side to an interior and become peeping Toms in, for example, *Foreign Correspondent, Notorious, I Confess, Rear Window, Psycho* and *Topaz*.)

In this shocking opening, the murder and its immediate aftermath are clearly enacted and presented as a variant of sex. Once the body is deposited in the wooden chest (soon to be a buffet table), Brandon moves to switch on a lamp. "No, not yet," urges Philip, "let's stay like this for a minute." Their exhausted, heavy breathing continues as Brandon smokes a cigarette. "Pity we couldn't have done it with the curtains open, in the bright sunlight," Brandon adds. "How did you feel during it?" Philip asks Brandon. "I don't know" is the reply. "I don't know if I felt very much of anything—until his body went limp, and I knew it was over and I felt tremendously exhilarated. How did *you* feel?" Subtle it isn't.

Nor is the denunciation of the philosophy that inspired this grisly deed. "Murder is—or should be—an art, and as such, the privilege of committing it should be reserved for those few who are really superior individuals!" says Rupert Cadell (James Stewart), former mentor to the two young men who have learned so well from him that they actualize his theories. "And the victims," continues Brandon, "are inferiors, whose lives are unimportant anyway!"—"Obviously!" says Rupert.

The action that follows—a buffet supper served from the top of the makeshift coffin—creates another dark association: contempt for human life (and its ultimate extension, murder) is defined as cannibalism. As a child, Philip strangled a chicken, and the murder of their friend David is now described in the same terms. When the meal of cold chicken is served from atop the chest, the crime is seen as one of devouring life—an idea that will be treated even more forcefully in *Frenzy*. The candles, lit for the meal and placed atop the chest/coffin, also support a funereal atmosphere. In his design of the film, in other words, Hitchcock has linked the motifs of play, sex, food, murder and ritual.

The major idea of *Rope* does not become clear until Cadell begins to suspect the truth, when his questioning of the young men leads them not only to reveal themselves but to reveal their teacher's deadly influence over them. Murder, Cadell postulates, is not opposed to his way of *thinking* ("Murder is a crime for most men, but a privilege for the few"); it is opposed merely to his way of *acting*. His students cannot understand this convenient dichotomy, and they activate what he fantasizes—much as, in *Strangers on a Train*, Bruno Anthony (Robert Walker) will activate what is merely fantasized by Guy Haines (Farley Granger). Even the apparently innocent banter spotlights this in *Rope:* Who could refrain from murder "when you have trouble getting into one of our velvet rope restaurants"—the link between killing and food once again. And torture, it is said, is justifiable if enacted against hotel clerks, bird lovers, small children and tap dancers—all should be put to a slow death.

The possibility of sterile bookishness leading to depravity is not, therefore, merely *Rope*'s subtext; it is the major concern. Learning is useless without experience—an idea brilliantly focused by Hitchcock's screenwriter Arthur Laurents—and the books given to the dead man's father, tied with the very instrument of death, link sterile learning (of the sort Rupert Cadell offered) with destruction.

But the complex of hypotheses—both those condemned and those (obliquely) espoused by the picture are almost drowned by its annoying prolixity. Furthermore, conventions of moviemaking in 1948 required a stern moral to the finale of such a story, and in the final moments Cadell delivers a long and unconvincing monologue in which—entirely out of character with what he has taught for years—he condemns the young men's murder of their schoolmate: "There must have been something evil in you that would take it seriously!" How neatly he exonerates himself from responsibility. Despite the moralizing, there has been no progress in this story, and that is its ultimate horror. Hitchcock chose Poulenc's first "Mouvement Perpetuel" as his musical motif for the opening titles, and again for the piano piece Philip plays: it's appropriate, perhaps, not only because the camera is in perpetual

Hitchcock rehearses Farley Granger and
Constance Collier for the palm-reading sequence.

motion throughout *Rope,* but because, ironically, the inner state of the principal characters is an endless cycle of only apparent movement which is itself spiritual stasis.

21

UNDER CAPRICORN

(PRODUCED 1948, RELEASED 1949)

If I were to make another picture set in Australia, I'd have a policeman hop into the pocket of a kangaroo and yell, "Follow that car!"

ALFRED HITCHCOCK

Michael Wilding, Joseph Cotten and Ingrid Bergman.

In 1974, the actor, writer and director Hume Cronyn (who had appeared in *Shadow of a Doubt* and *Lifeboat* and who collaborated on the adaptation for the screenplays of *Rope* and *Under Capricorn*) spoke to the author of this book about his work with Alfred Hitchcock: "I hope this will be written down somewhere: I owe an awful lot to Alfred Hitchcock. He gave me not only his friendship but a very valuable education in filmmaking. I learned a lot from him and I have enormous admiration for him. He put together *Under Capricorn* image by image, and with all due respect, I think this method sometimes led him astray. He became so fascinated by these images that sometimes the direct line of the narrative would get lost or be bent, or there would be an awk-

wardness telling the story. He had of course been very revolu-
tionary in the way he approached *Rope,* and it had been written
to be shot in tremendously long takes. But when he came to his
next film, it was to cover the vast panorama of colonial life in
Australia. The difference in the quality of the two stories was the
difference between a miniature and an enormous landscape. Yet
he decided to use the same approach, and I feel that was a mistake
and got him into trouble.''

And trouble there was—not only during production, but ever
since, for *Under Capricorn* has never had very many admirers. The
impressive long takes that sometimes move from floor to floor,
through lengthy corridors and several rooms make this a sporad-
ically beautiful movie, but the obsession for this technique also
inspired lengthy monologues and dialogues that become perilously
arid. Too often motionless, the camera seems indifferent, as if
actors had to keep talking until the film ran out.

Based on a novel by Helen Simpson, the film tells the sus-
penseless tale of Charles Adare (Michael Wilding), nephew of the

Michael Wilding and Ingrid Bergman.

governor of Australia, who on a visit "under Capricorn" in 1840 meets an embittered ex-convict named Sam Flusky (Joseph Cotten). Exiled to Australia for a murder, Flusky is married to the wealthy Lady Henrietta (Ingrid Bergman), who has become a pathetic alcoholic. Adare takes an interest in their strange household, which is dominated by the nasty and jealous housekeeper Milly (Margaret Leighton), and while attempting to reform Henrietta he falls in love with her. This he must suppress in order to free her from neurotic guilt. Provoked by the intrigue of Milly, who is in love with Flusky, the jealous husband shoots Adare, and then Henrietta's guilt reaches a breaking point. She admits to Charles that it was she—not her husband—who was guilty of the death of her brother—and that Sam assumed the crime and suffered for it. Before Adare renounces his love for Henrietta and returns her to Sam (whose deep if strange devotion is at last reciprocated by his wife), he discovers that Milly has been slowly poisoning her. Adare exposes Milly, then bids farewell to the Fluskys.

A number of French critics have a high regard for *Under Capricorn,* perhaps because of the luxuriantly morbid atmosphere in which characters' duty is presented as their glory: there's a Racinian sense of perverse, doom-laden pain about all this that remains peculiarly Gallic. But their enthusiasm has helped tint Anglo-American diffidence about the film.

Like *Rope,* it's certainly an unusual picture. With the equally disappointing *Jamaica Inn* and the earlier *Waltzes from Vienna,* this is one of Hitchcock's trio of period pictures, a style with which he never felt comfortable. Set in nineteenth century New South Wales, it continued his fascination for the long, sustained take which he had begun in *Rope*—a technique that was supposed to be swifter and therefore more economical. But long, fluid takes turned out to be devilish to photograph and exasperating for actors. Ingrid Bergman was miserable during the production of *Under Capricorn:* "Tables were slipped away by grips, chairs pushed into view just as the camera came near you, walls were whipped up into the air—and all the time, you were just supposed to go on saying your lines. I was very upset about it, but Hitchcock calmed me down—'Ingrid, it's only a movie.' "

Nevertheless, three very long takes are especially noteworthy

The discovery of Milly's perfidy. (Margaret Leighton, Joseph Cotten, Ingrid Bergman.)

in this film. When Adare arrives at the mansion of his cousin the new governor (Cecil Parker, the swinish solicitor Todhunter from *The Lady Vanishes*), the camera follows him along a second-story corridor, striding through several rooms until he finally reaches his destination, the governor's hip-bath. There, still without a cut, a long dialogue between the two men occurs.

The second long take occurs when Adare arrives at the Flusky home next evening: there's no cut for almost nine minutes, from the moment he appears outside the house. He steps into the dining room, moves into the main foyer to meet other guests, proceeds into the drawing room with Flusky and then returns with them all to the dining room, where Henrietta makes her unshod, tipsy appearance—and only then is there the first cut of the sequence. It's fascinating camera work, but as with *Rope,* this results in very talky picture-making without a prevalent viewpoint. The conversation simply isn't engaging or suspenseful, and the lack of cutting short-circuits tension and the necessary visual-narrative rhythm.

But the third of the longest takes is the most interesting, precisely because of content and style. In her long confessional monologue, Ingrid Bergman begins to speak quietly and calmly, and—without a cut—gradually increases volume and intensity until she concludes in mild hysteria, all the while pacing the room. "I was given the Oscar for *Murder on the Orient Express* because they thought it was so wonderful that I did a long speech in a single take," she said in 1975. "Well, that really wasn't so grand—I'd done it for Hitchcock twenty-five years earlier!"

Under Capricorn stresses the Gothic-Romantic elements of Helen Simpson's rather damp novel, and Hitchcock and his writers stressed several motifs recognizable from *Rebecca:* the guilty secret; a displaced and lonely heroine; a gloomy country estate (in this case, even the name of the place is ominous: it translates as "Why Weepest Thou?") and a prevailing mood of abnormal psychology. Milly is a close relative of *Rebecca*'s Mrs. Danvers, a kind of female Iago figure who, like Adare for Henrietta, has to renounce her passion for Flusky. But she and Adare have different ways of dealing with renunciation: he frees Henrietta from the poison of alcoholic oblivion and restores her to her husband; Milly tries to steal Henrietta's husband and then gives her poison—*Rebecca*'s Mrs. Danvers unites with *Notorious*'s Madame Sebastian, as it were.

To enjoy *Under Capricorn,* one has to feel a basic psychological affinity for the heavy theme of onerous fidelity, and for the nineteenth-century conceit of remorse freed by confession. Precisely because Flusky has assumed the punishment for Henrietta's guilt, their life has been poisoned by a romantic collusion. This has never been a popular narrative tradition in America, although it has a powerful variant in Edith Wharton's terrifying novella *Ethan Frome*.

But if you can see *Under Capricorn* in a clear print that preserves its original Technicolor definitions, there's one redeeming reward. In a way, this picture is the story of a face—Ingrid Bergman's. After her first appearance—a close-up of her bare feet (a neat marker of the condition of enslavement as well as the film's motif of the abandonment of polite manners)—the camera concentrates on her tortured, confused but ever-lovely features.

22

STAGE FRIGHT

(PRODUCED 1949, RELEASED 1950)

I hold the world but as the world, Gratiano;
A stage, where every man must play a part,
And mine a sad one.

THE MERCHANT OF VENICE

Jane Wyman, Richard Todd, Alastair Sim
and Dame Sybil Thorndike.

"The aspect that intrigued me is that it was a story about the theater," Hitchcock once said. Produced in England just after *Under Capricorn* from a novel by Selwyn Jepson called *Man Running,* the screenplay by Whitfield Cook concerns Eve Gill (Jane Wyman), an aspiring actress at the Royal Academy of Dramatic Art, whose boyfriend Jonathan Cooper (Richard Todd) seeks her aid in establishing his innocence. He insists he is being framed for murdering the husband of actress Charlotte Inwood (Marlene Dietrich), who took advantage of his infatuation for her. Eve disguises herself as a maid, gains Charlotte's confidence and with the help of Inspector Wilfred Smith (Michael Wilding), nearly proves Charlotte was the murderer. But she finally plays her role so well that

Jonathan is in fact revealed to be the killer. By this time Eve has transferred her affections to Wilfred Smith, and when Jonathan is killed trying to escape, the final frames suggest she may at last find a true relationship with the inspector.

One of Hitchcock's least appreciated works, *Stage Fright* annoys some viewers because of its complex plot, its surprises, twists, double twists—and, most of all, by its bold use of an opening false flashback, an account told by a murderer (and seen by us as he tells it to another) and therefore finally revealed as a lie. There's no doubt that this is a film demanding the most careful attention— but Hitchcock always deserves that attention, and our enrichment derives proportionately. *Stage Fright* is in fact a major comic work, entirely worthy of the various significant talents who contributed to it.

The safety curtain of an English theater slowly rises under the credits, revealing not a stage set, but real-life London in full mo-

"I bought this dress just for today, Madam."
"Don't confide in me, dear—just pour the tea!"

tion; when the curtain is fully raised, we're pitched at once into the action of the story. Immediately, then, the distinctions between appearance and reality, between theater life and street life, begin to blur. Everything that follows is an interconnected series of ruses, costumes, lies and artifices, and everyone of the theater people in the story plays a variety of real-life roles—a favorite Hitchcock motif, spun as early as *The 39 Steps*. As in Hitchcock's darker romances, appearances and identities slip and slide. Nothing is certain in the world of disguises, performances, matinées and theatrical garden parties.

The opening scene of flight from the police—in the racing open roadster of Eve Gill—establishes the film's tripartite structure, a series of ever-slower journeys until the final stasis. The film is built, in fact, like a rallentando—a gradual slowing down—from that first chase to the midpoint of the more leisurely ride in a taxi (the love scene between Eve and Wilfred), to the final immobile "ride" of Eve and Jonathan in the unused eighteenth-century stage-prop carriage. Within this framework, Eve, a young novice actress, is disabused of her belief in the glamour of theater life and—precisely by successful multiple role-playing—first endangers herself and at last confronts the shifting and specious nature of her own romantic illusions.

In this regard, it's crucial that at the end Eve must go *under* the stage, to confront a more paralyzing fear and to invent an ingenious acting ploy whereby she disarms a pathological killer and saves herself. Real stage fright, in other words, is something beneath the stage, deeper than mere onstage panic. Thus the melodramatic play in which Eve is first seen rehearsing at the Royal Academy of Dramatic Art (and in which she seems to be egregiously incompetent indeed) at last becomes a "thriller" from which she must extricate herself by a superlative performance.

Besides Eve, Charlotte too is a performer, her demented lover Cooper is a performer, and everyone in the story plays roles. "You're an actress. You're playing a part. No nerves when you're on," Jonathan tells Charlotte (although in the lying flashback), just after she begs him to "draw the curtains, Johnny!" The scene points forward to the final horrific moment, when a stagehand is asked to "lower the iron curtain," effectively cutting off Jonathan's escape (and by implication his head).

Marlene Dietrich sings "I'm the Laziest Gal in Town."

Eve's father is also a role-player, in a portrait charmingly created by scenarist Whitfield Cook and engagingly rendered by the
incomparable Scottish actor Alastair Sim (whose first name is curiously misspelled on both opening and closing credits).

"You're just dying to get into a part in this and you know you
are," Eve tells him.

"A part in this melodramatic play, you mean," he replies, in
a triumphant comic scene in his cottage. "That's the way you're
treating it, Eve—as if it were a play you were acting in at the
Academy. Everything seems a fine acting role when you're stage-
struck, doesn't it, my dear? Here you have a plot, an interesting
cast, even a costume [the blood-soaked dress]. Unfortunately,
Eve, in this real and earnest life we must face the situation in all
its bearings . . . [or else] you'll spend a few years in Holloway
prison, meditating on the folly of transmuting melodrama into
real life."

Eve, we should note, is different things to different people.
To Jonathan she's a patient and helpful friend whose love for him
he conveniently exploits. To her father she's an apprentice actress
("You're my audience, Father! I wish you'd give me a little ap-

The fright beneath the stage. (Richard Todd and Jane Wyman.)

plause now and then"—which he later does, after Charlotte is unmasked by Eve). To Wilfred, she's an innocent actress. To Nellie Good (Kay Walsh), she's a newspaper reporter wishing to disguise herself as the dresser's cousin, to gain access to Charlotte. And to Charlotte she's Nellie's cousin Doris—whose name Charlotte can't quite seem to get right (she calls her Phyllis, Mavis and Elsie).

Charlotte is a performer on a deeper level, too—her widowhood, especially, becomes her most pointed attempt at self-glamorizing ("Couldn't we work in a little color?" she asks about the funereal black outfit. "Or let it plunge just a little in front?"). And she directs others—Eve especially—in their forms of address, their tones of voice, and their wardrobes.

Quite early, we learn the truth about Jonathan, which Charlotte tells the police and which Eve overhears. Charlotte is trying to exonerate herself from involvement in the crime, but what she says of Jonathan is true:

"I suppose I shouldn't have seen him as often as I did, but I didn't realize how madly infatuated he was with me. I just didn't realize. You'll never know how much I blame myself for all this. When my husband came back from New York last week and I told Johnny I couldn't see him, he kept on phoning me. He wouldn't let me alone. Oh, maybe if I'd agreed to see him he wouldn't have done this dreadful thing."

Dietrich's focused rendition of the Cole Porter song "The Laziest Gal in Town" is the film's clearest tip-off to the resolution of the plot; Hitchcock never, after all, merely inserts a song into a film without a powerful structural reason: "It's not that I shouldn't, it's not that I wouldn't, and you know it's not that I couldn't—it's simply because I'm the laziest gal in town," she sings in a triumphant proclamation with multiple meanings. Our first thought about the lyrics is obvious, but later we realize they're also a pointed reference to what she did with Jonathan, exploiting his fanatical devotion to the extreme that he killed her husband.

But on its most serious level, this leisurely comic tale is but another Hitchcockian reflection on romantic illusion. In this case, Eve's refusal to believe the guilt of the man she's in love with (in spite of overwhelming evidence) makes this film a kind of comic version of *The Paradine Case*. The crucial moment in this regard occurs when Eve's affections begin to shift from Jonathan to Wilfred, and this happens when Jonathan, seeking lodging with the Gills, embraces Eve. Convinced of (what she thinks is) the ineradicable bond between Jonathan and Charlotte, she gazes at the piano and we (with her, from her viewpoint) remember the romantic piano melody played by Wilfred (shades of *The Paradine Case* again). It's additionally important, therefore, that this sequence is at once followed by Eve's ride in the taxi with Wilfred, accompanied by the same music; it's one of the gentlest and sweetest love scenes in the Hitchcock canon.

The taxi ride is also psychologically acute, although audiences forty years later find it a little arch and coy. Wilfred and Eve are more interested in one another than in the logic of their own remarks, and finally they are so locked in the collusion of their romantic gaze that their words meld and become senseless interphrases. Hitchcock is, at this point, one up on the sophisticates, for this is the gentlest puncture of the romantic fallacy. It's the director's quiet, compassionate little joke, a grace note to the richness of this undeservedly neglected comic masterpiece.

23

STRANGERS ON A TRAIN

(PRODUCED 1950, RELEASED 1951)

This were a fine reign:
To do ill and not hear of it again.

DEKKER AND FORD,

THE WITCH OF EDMONTON

Farley Granger and Robert Walker.

After the unfavorably received *Under Capricorn* and *Stage Fright* (whose virtues were entirely ignored for many years), Hitchcock returned to Hollywood and produced *Strangers on a Train,* a film that at once reestablished him in the high esteem of critics and the public; for over forty years, it has remained one of the most discussed and analyzed thrillers in the medium and one of the director's most frequently screened films. Raymond Chandler first worked on the script, but practically nothing of his contributions remain; the work as we have it derives entirely from Hitchcock's notes and outlines, while much of the dialogue was provided by the uncredited Ben Hecht, his protégée Czenzi Ormonde and the Hitchcocks themselves. *Strangers on a Train* is based on the Patricia

Highsmith novel of that name, but very much was changed and
those changes reflect some of Hitchcock's most pointed concerns.
From the book he took the double murders and the subtheme of
the homosexual courtship, but the major visual metaphors of doubles and of crossings, the tennis, the lighter, the setting in Washington, the dark backgrounds are all significant changes or
additions. In the novel, Guy is an architect who has designed a
hospital and a country club; in the film, his role as a tennis pro
carries forward the element of crisscrossing, of "matched doubles." In the novel, Bruno's father is indeed finally murdered, and
Guy must stand trial for his part. The film's cigarette lighter with

"You've got to keep your part of the bargain, Guy."

its crossed racquets—telling the whole story in a single early image—is in the novel simply a volume of Plato, a prop to reunite the two men after their initial meeting.

The story is straightforward. On a journey from Washington, D.C. to Long Island, tennis pro Guy Haines (Farley Granger) and idle playboy Bruno Anthony (Robert Walker) meet accidentally, as strangers on a train. Bruno seems to know all the details of Guy's public and private life—most of all, that he is a champion tennis player whose desire to marry a famous senator's daughter is being thwarted by his wife's refusal to divorce him. Bruno proposes an exchange of murders: he will kill Guy's wife if Guy will kill Bruno's hated father—crimes which, Bruno insists, can be accomplished with impunity because the police will be unable to establish motives or suspects. He has the entire scheme worked out.

Predictably, Guy regards the whole thing as outrageous—but Bruno fulfills his part, following Guy's wife Miriam (Laura Elliott) to an amusement park one night and calmly strangling her. He then contacts his "friend" Guy, demanding that he keep his side of the deal. When Guy refuses, recognizing Bruno as an authentic psychopath, Bruno decides to implicate him in Miriam's murder by placing at the scene of the crime Guy's cigarette lighter, left behind after luncheon on the train. After a race against time to win an important tennis match, Guy hurries to the amusement park to stop Bruno. The two men fight on a carousel that breaks down and kills Bruno, whose hand clutches the incriminating lighter. Guy's account of the facts is finally accepted and he is free to marry the senator's daughter, Ann Morton (Ruth Roman).

An obsessively structured film, *Strangers on a Train* is as tough and chilly as *Young and Innocent* and *Stage Fright* were warm, and *Notorious* full of passionate longing. In the tradition of *Shadow of a Doubt,* the form of this film is the direct clue to its meaning— the *manner* of its structure is its *matter,* as a literary critic might put it: doubles and pairs, accumulated, intercut and linked in an almost endless series, establish the affinity between Bruno and Guy. Two men who are apparently polar opposites (as the two Charlies in *Shadow of a Doubt* seemed mutually exclusive person- alities) are in fact shown to share the same common humanity; the world of light, order and vitality is everywhere associated with

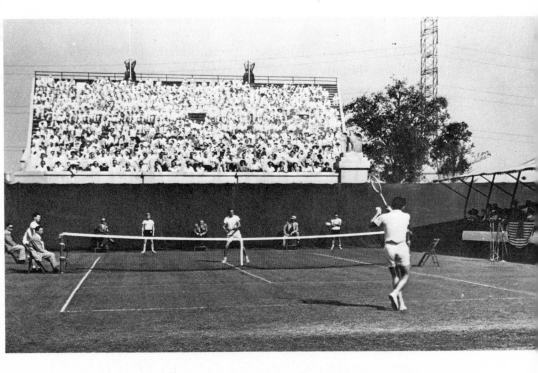

The famous crosscutting, from the bright tennis game
. . . to the dark sewer.

the world of darkness, chaos, lunacy and death. None of this is to be found in the novel.

The structure is established from the film's first frames. A taxi pulls up at Union Station, Washington, to discharge a passenger. We see only a man's trousers and a pair of snappy two-toned brogans before we cut to a second cab and another traveler—this man more conservatively dressed, with plain brown oxfords. As each approaches the train from opposite directions, we follow alternately and then cut to the train's departure, the rails ahead, then another pair of rails branching off, then another. Inside the parlor car, the two strangers—still shown only from the knees down—approach a lounge table, where their shoes accidentally touch as they cross their legs. After this significant montage, the film continues on a breathless rush. "Isn't it a fascinating design?" Hitchcock liked to ask proudly. "You could study it forever."

"I suppose you're going to Southampton for the doubles," Bruno says knowingly to Guy, and then turns to order from a passing waiter "a pair of drinks—doubles." From this moment, the picture pursues its "fascinating design" of these doubles. There are, to name only a sampling: two tennis sequences of matched doubles; two respectable, influential but distant fathers (Senator Morton and Mr. Anthony), two sequences aboard a carousel, two women with eyeglasses (Miriam Haines and Barbara Morton), two double drinks of whiskey, two boys accompanying Miriam on her date, two sets of private eyes in two cities, two small boys and two old men at two trips to the fairgrounds, two rich matrons at the Morton's formal party (each fascinated with methods of killing), two members of the Hitchcock family in the film—and Hitchcock chose to make his cameo appearance with a double of his own form, a double bass fiddle.

All this doubling has no precedent in the Highsmith novel; it was all deliberately added by Hitchcock and is the key to his intention. In this regard, the motif of the Guy-Bruno homosexual courtship is more than merely bold for its time: it serves the narrative's wider reference of the theme of dual aspects of a single personality.

The two men, in other words, represent complementary aspects of human nature. Guy is apparently the hero, inhabiting the world of light that is represented by bright tennis games, light-colored attire, formal Washington dinner parties and the aspiration toward political and social respectability—the world of "the right people." Bruno, on the other hand, is everywhere associated with the world of darkness, the gothic gloominess of his Arlington mansion and the boat—aptly the *Pluto* (god of the underworld) that he takes to commit murder, associating him with the household of the dead. Shadows constantly crisscross his face, and he is referred to as Guy's "shadow"; he activates what Guy desires, evokes Guy's hidden longings. When Guy tells Ann he is angry with Miriam for refusing to divorce him, he shouts, "I could strangle her! I could break her foul, useless little neck!" Hitchcock then cuts at once to a close-up of Bruno's hands in a strangling gesture, and when the deed is done he goes to Guy and rightly says, "But Guy—it's what you wanted!" In one stunning, terrifying shot, Bruno is seen from Guy's viewpoint, standing on the white marble steps of the Jefferson Memorial—a dark, malignant stain, a poisonous blot on the order of things. At least twice, Guy checks his wristwatch and there is a matched cut to Bruno in the same gesture. Similarly, Bruno asks a fairground attendant "what time it gets dark around here," he gazes at the setting sun—and the scene cuts to Guy on the train, turning round to look at the setting sun, too.

From Jonson's *Bartholomew Fair,* Thackeray's *Vanity Fair,* Bunyan's *Pilgrim's Progress,* Goethe's *Faust* and from the German expressionist movie classic *The Cabinet of Dr. Caligari,* Hitchcock drew on the tradition of the fairground as the place where the demented aspects of life are concentrated and expressed, where all the Dionysian riots and the repressions of the year are set free. This is the place—as it had been more gently and comically in *The Ring, Murder!, Saboteur* and *Stage Fright*—where the grotesque is enjoyed but where Bruno actualizes the metaphorical and the surrogate, unleashing the forces of madness and death. And at the finale, the same amusement park is the place where the cycle of lunacy is broken, the whirling carousel destroyed so that normality may be restored. In this regard, it is noteworthy that both killer

Bruno's death after the carousel breakdown:
an image of sex as death.

and victim are associated with the destruction of circles—burst
balloons, carousels set out of control, broken gongs, shattered
eyeglasses and bitter fights at a record shop—images of order
disrupted, of harmony destroyed.

All this was available to Hitchcock within the concomitant

STRANGERS ON A TRAIN

motif of the double. From E. T. A. Hoffmann's first novel *The Devil's Elixirs* and his tale "The Doubles," Hitchcock took the device of the *doppelgänger,* the ghostly double of a living person who simultaneously haunts and illuminates him. "I imagine my ego," Hoffmann wrote, "as being viewed through a lens: all the forms which move around me are egos; and whatever they do, or leave undone, vexes me." This is virtually an epigraph for *Strangers on a Train.*

Similarly, from Heinrich Heine's *Ratcliff,* Hitchcock knew the dramatic value of describing two persons drawn together by fate, by love and by dark impulses (precisely the operative motif in *Shadow of a Doubt*). From Poe's "William Wilson" and Dosto-yevski's "The Double" he had taken the same motif. Robert Louis Stevenson's novella *The Strange Case of Dr. Jekyll and Mr. Hyde* Hitchcock knew intimately, not to mention H. G. Wells's "Love and Mr. Lewisham," Kipling's "At the End of the Passage" and *The Picture of Dorian Gray,* by Oscar Wilde. Guy de Maupassant has dealt quite frankly with his own psychological dilemmas in "The Horla" and "Peter and John," and there were numerous examples in the tales of Hans Christian Andersen and Alfred de Musset.

Strangers on a Train stands as the second in a Hitchcock quartet of films on the theme of the double—the final two will be *Psycho* and *Frenzy.* In the Romantic and Victorian precedents, the double always reflects strong inner conflict, a clash of wills, of the reach toward integration and the peril of disintegration. Familiar with these sources, Hitchcock could exploit the double as the messenger of death. He required no training in psychology to be aware of this common creative currency and its imagery: it was one of the major recurring motifs in the art and literature of his time, and inevitably the cinema, *his* cinema, capitalized on the forms and patterns of this device.

All this artistry comes together in a single moment of the film, in the one shot that reveals the director's great care and originality: the murder scene. Bruno, having pursued Miriam to the fair-ground island, flicks open her cigarette lighter. Her face, filling the frame as she looks directly into the camera—out at us—is suddenly blocked as Bruno steps into the frame and his hands grip her throat. Her eyeglasses fall to the ground and then, in one of the most unexpected, aesthetically justified moments in film, the camera observes the strangling and the final collapse of the woman as a huge reflection in one of the broken eyeglass lenses, the shadowy distortion marking at once something gruesome and infernal, a moment sprung to life from a terrible nightmare.

To achieve this startling effect, Hitchcock designed an enormous distorting lens, then photographed his two actors reflected in it at a ninety-degree angle. Like such later sequences as the shower murder in *Psycho,* the final attack of *The Birds* and the collapse of the dying Cuban woman in *Topaz,* this brief moment (and the care Hitchcock took in planning it) vindicates François Truffaut's observation that Hitchcock filmed scenes of murder as if they were love scenes, and love scenes as if they were murders. In the oddly appealing visual originality there is a stark fusion of the grotesque and the beautiful, a merger celebrated in aesthetic theory by Baudelaire, Joyce, Cocteau and others. The aestheticizing of the horror somehow enables the audience to contemplate more fully its reality; instead of turning away from the image, repulsed, we gaze, and so are forced to assess feelings, reactions and moral judgments about the very acts perceived.

At the conclusion of *Strangers on a Train* we seem to see Guy—innocent of an actual murder but not of the *desire* to be rid of his wife—with all his fantasies fulfilled, with Bruno gone and with Ann at his side on a train as they head toward marriage. "I think it's wonderful to have a man love you so much he'd *kill* for you!" said Ann's sister Barbara (Patricia Hitchcock) in words intended to be ironic but that were as true for Bruno's attraction to Guy. But the final image suggests that things may not turn out quite so well. Guy and Ann sit lovingly on a train, side by side, hands clasped—they could be at an altar, at their wedding ceremony. A passenger across the aisle leans forward and repeats Bruno's opening line in the film: "Excuse me, but aren't you Guy Haines?" Guy and Ann look at each other and without replying quickly move away from this new stranger on a train. But the questioner is a minister, and this carries an omen beneath the humor. This couple should be moving toward the minister, not away from him, willing to reply to crucial questions of identity and intention. And if *Strangers on a Train* is also the courtship of a latent homosexual by a demonic psychopath, then this fearful drawing back from marriage makes perfect sense. Throughout, Guy has not been given up wholly to his relationship with Ann. The life of order and quiet dignity to which he aspires is in grave doubt indeed.

24

I CONFESS

(PRODUCED 1952, RELEASED 1953)

*I confess to Almighty God and to you, Father,
that I have sinned.*

FROM THE CATHOLIC RITUAL

OF CONFESSION

Montgomery Clift and O. E. Hasse.

Based on a 1902 play by Paul Anthelme called *Nos Deux Consciences,* the screenplay for *I Confess* (by George Tabori, William
Archibald and Hitchcock himself) bases its dramatic tension on a
specific point of Catholic law: a priest is forbidden ever to reveal
to anyone (for any reason) what he has heard from a penitent
during a ritual confession in the sacrament of Penance. This pro-
hibition includes both public crime and private sin; additionally—
and this is of especial importance for *I Confess*—a priest may never
allude thereafter even to the penitent himself what he was once
told. In church canons, this is called the seal of confession.

In the city of Quebec, a lawyer named Villette is robbed and
killed by Otto Keller (O. E. Hasse), the caretaker of a local Cath-

olic parish. Returning to the church late that night and removing the bloodstained cassock (the priest's black robe) he filched and wore as a disguise, Keller confesses his crime to his friend and employer Father Michael Logan (Montgomery Clift). As it happens, Villette was blackmailing a woman named Ruth Grandfort (Anne Baxter), who is now married to a prominent politician but who was romantically involved with Father Logan before he was ordained but (and Logan didn't know this) after her marriage; any public awareness of such prior intimacy would tarnish the relationship of the Grandforts and of the priest in sternly Catholic Quebec.

After two children come forward to report that they saw a man in priest's garb leaving Villette's house the night of the murder, and since Father Logan can provide no adequate alibi, the evidence is strong against him. Bound by his priestly commitment not to reveal the killer's identity and unwilling to embarrass his former love, Logan maintains his silence at the trial. He is acquitted on a technicality of reasonable doubt but reviled by the judge and the citizenry, who charge him as guilty nonetheless. The truth is implied by Keller's wife (Dolly Haas), and amid a crowd outside the court Keller shoots her; after a chase, he himself confesses and is brought down by police in the ballroom of the Château Frontenac Hotel. Keller's final public confession to Father Logan exonerates the priest.

I Confess, it must be admitted, is not a very popular Hitchcock film. Tangled and tenebrous, it has a certain gravid humorlessness uncharacteristic of the director. There is no reason, however, why he should not have been permitted to vary his style—he would do so with astonishing breadth all through the decade 1953–1963—and taken on its own terms this film is at once mainstream in several of its virtues and concerns and quite successful as an idiosyncratic (and personal) document.

As so often in Hitchcock's films, the design of the images and the choice of soundtrack beneath the opening credits are significant. From the viewpoint of a boat or ferry, we move slowly toward the city of Quebec, dominated by the outline of the great Château Frontenac Hotel, looming like a fortress in the twilight, while on the soundtrack we hear a soprano singing a romantic song about the night, about love, about romantic memories. The film that follows—firmly in the tradition of *Suspicion* and *The Paradine Case*—explores precisely the kind of unreal romantic fantasy represented in these first moments.

We then see the empty streets of Quebec at night and finally we move to one building, then toward an open window of that building (just as at the openings of *Shadow of a Doubt* and *Psycho,* among others) and inside we glimpse the body of a man. The confession of Keller, which follows soon after, is later structurally balanced by the conclusion: the first confession and gesture of priestly forgiveness are set in the privacy of the church's dark, curtained booth, where the sole light is a pointed shaft falling across Father Logan's impassive features. The confession and gesture of forgiveness at the end occur publicly in broad daylight, before the hotel ballroom's grand stage.

Between these two moments we have been witnessing, as we shall see, a dramatic spectacle—or more accurately, a play within a play, comprised of a series of confessions. These include (but are not restricted to) Keller's confession to Father Logan; Keller's to his wife Alma; Ruth's to her husband Pierre (Roger Dann) and to Inspector Larrue (Karl Malden); Ruth's to Logan; Logan's to Larrue; Alma's to Logan; and cyclically, Keller's to Logan.

I Confess is first of all another Hitchcock film about the betrayal of friendship and confidence (a recurring concern since the silent days). "I have abused your kindness," Keller admits to Logan. "You who gave my wife and me a home—even friendship, so wonderful a thing for a refugee, a German, a man without a home." The priest has hired the immigrant and appointed him in the privileged position of sacristan—caretaker of altar and sanctuary. But Keller not only exploits this goodness: he attempts to assign guilt for his own crime of murder to his friend Logan— just as later (to name only two examples) Gavin Elster will exploit his old college friend John Ferguson in *Vertigo* and Bob Rusk will exploit his buddy Richard Blaney in *Frenzy*.

When Logan goes to Villette's house to meet with him regarding the blackmail, the priest is bluntly told by a detective, "Good morning, Father. Monsieur Villette is dead." Logan's immediate reply is "Good morning," hardly the response one would expect. Of course he had indeed already known (from Keller), but the detective doesn't *know* he knows, and Logan would perhaps naturally have offered some other reaction. This calm statement ironically states the truth: Villette's death *does* make it a good morning for Logan and Ruth. A moment later, when Ruth arrives and Logan tells her the news, she smiles and whispers to him, "Michael, we're free!" (Her remark is overheard by Inspector Larrue and at once the conflict is set in motion.)

In a sense, then, *I Confess* examines a variation on the theme explored in Hitchcock's previous film, *Strangers on a Train*. Just as Bruno Anthony activated what Guy Haines desires, just so Keller effectively rids Logan and Ruth of the burden of Villette's blackmail. Keller did not know how much Logan and Ruth could secretly have wanted Villette dead—a wish that explains Logan's constantly disturbed features and distracted gaze.

Ruth then proceeds happily to her husband in court chambers and announces, "Pierre, take me to lunch!" (In Hitchcock's films, people who are suddenly let off the hook usually become hungry: when Uncle Charlie [to cite just one example] learns on Sunday afternoon that another man has been arrested for his crimes, he rubs his hands and exults, "Yessir, I could eat a good dinner today!") At the end, after Keller is cornered in the hotel ballroom, Ruth again turns to her husband: "Pierre, take me home!" Pierre, it must be admitted, never balks at these sudden commands to attend Ruth as escort, despite the evidently loveless marriage he has sustained for the sake of professional advancement. Somewhat unconvincingly, he loves her despite the knowledge that his wife is still obsessed with a man who turned from her to the priesthood.

At the center of the story is Ruth's lifetime of romantic obsession with Michael Logan, a man she once loved, who was never hers and who decided after he returned from the war to become a priest. (Inaccessible objects of desire are, of course, often the most cherished.) She has contracted a secure and respectable marriage with a man who loves her, but over the years she has harbored the unreal fantasy of her memories that Michael still returns that love. Like Lina McLaidlaw (Joan Fontaine) in *Suspicion* and Anthony Keane (Gregory Peck) in *The Paradine Case,* Ruth Grandfort clings

Montgomery Clift and Anne Baxter.

to an impossible dream. Thus as she tells Inspector Larrue the history of her relationship with Michael, the account is shown to us *from the viewpoint of her imagination* and through the haze of her amorous fixation. The impossibly romantic theme song is repeated from the opening credits and the camera describes for us not the objective reality but the subjectivity of her feelings as she describes the past. "Have you ever been young, Inspector?" she asks improbably, and what follows is shown in slow motion, with soft focus and unbalanced angles suggesting both the artificial sweetness of unrealizable fantasy and hinting at a slightly unhinged mind.

Accordingly, we see *Ruth's* vision of it all as in memory she slowly descends a spiral staircase to the arms of the young soldier Logan, and there the camera revolves round them in Hitchcock's favorite cinematic gesture for lovers. In this regard, Hitchcock is again more sophisticated than the sophisticates who see him simply yielding to the conventions of romantic moviemaking (as, some insisted, Hitchcock did in the taxi scene between Jane Wyman and Michael Wilding in *Stage Fright*). On the contrary, Hitchcock, as always, subverts every such absurd romantic convention. The hazy, gauzy, impossibly adolescent aura of Ruth's memories are not endorsed, they are shown for what they are. This woman lives in a world of storybook fiction complete with soap-opera dialogue and hopelessly antiquated greeting-card sentiment.

I Confess is not, then, merely a straightforward and gloomy narrative based on an arcane ecclesiastical code. It is rather a subtly acted examination of three sets of couples, balanced precisely in terms of plot and theme: the Kellers, the Grandforts, and Logan and Larrue.

The counterpart to Keller is his frightened, beleaguered wife (significantly named Alma), one of the most lovingly rendered supporting roles in Hitchcock's films (and reminiscent of the crofter's wife in *The 39 Steps*). Forced to complicity by her husband and thus bound to cooperate with Logan's indictment for murder, she cannot, finally, see the priest reviled by the community. When she blurts out the implication of her husband's guilt and is shot by him, she too makes a dying confession and is forgiven by Logan. At the midpoint of this first relationship is the astonishing shot when Keller confronts the priest, taunting him with the reminder of the confessional's inviolability and the consequent safety of himself and his wife. In a stunningly realized, long and swift reverse tracking shot, the two men walk through several rooms, round corners and up a flight of stairs. During this, Keller absentmindedly drops—one at a time—an armful of flowers he had intended to bring to the church; the gesture suggests simultaneously his failure at his job, the death he has caused, his loss of grace and his own inevitable funeral.

The second set of characters is the Grandforts. Where Keller shows little emotion, Ruth constantly demonstrates too much. In this regard, *I Confess* does not ultimately compare the murderer with the priest but the murderer and his former girlfriend. Both are destructive influences on Logan's life in the present, both exploit his sincerity and good will. The complement to Ruth, of course—and the parallel to the faithful and slightly pathetic Alma Keller—is Pierre Grandfort, who must also endure the pain of knowing the truth about a spouse. He is the man of the noble gesture, the martyr who hears his wife's admission that she has never loved him. He is the only man who can temper her hyperactive imagination, and her recognition of this is perhaps why Ruth leaves Logan before the final outcome and departs (smiling) with her husband.

The final structurally balanced set of couples is Father Logan and Inspector Larrue. Logan's detachment, calmness and assurance about his past and present feelings for Ruth need purifying and humbling precisely because of his unacknowledged desire to be rid of Villette, even if we grant his admirable fidelity to his priesthood. That chastening is, ironically, brought about through Logan's confession of his former affection for Ruth. And his balance in the film is provided not by Keller but by the inspector, to whom Hitchcock points by making Larrue the questioning priest during the inquiry at headquarters, where Logan is the taciturn penitent. A curtained washbasin behind the inspector's desk recalls the priest's curtained confessional and is prominent throughout the scene. There, Larrue prods and pries Logan like a priestly confessor with an adolescent boy before him. (If there is anything in *I Confess* that reflects Hitchcock's Jesuit schooling it is this confrontation.)

The title of this demanding but rewarding film is, therefore, multivalent. Everyone in the story makes a confession of feeling if not of guilt—Logan perhaps most of all. He overcomes both his own stolid personality and the dignity of his role to admit that he is a man with real sentiments and has always been so—specifically, he confesses that he was once in love with Ruth. This may be another reason why she can depart happy at the finale, knowing that Logan did, after all, once love her.

And therein lies the most pointed irony of this dark tale. The priest's fundamental humanity must be established by confronting Ruth's unfounded romantic fantasies. Logan does not confess that he once had an affair, but that he is at least capable of it—something his manner belies. Both the people and the priest learn, at the end, that there must be a humanity beneath the priestly garb (at the time, a point not officially taken for granted—much less encouraged—either in Quebec or Hollywood). In this context, it is interesting to note that the other young priest in Logan's rectory is far more relaxed, witty, even playful: he has a mania for bicycle riding, which leads to humorous punctuations of rectory scenes by the bicycle's clash and clatter.

Finally, the last scene of *I Confess* supports the motif of multiple confessions. Everything we have seen has been a play, and the final setting must therefore be theatrical—the double-curtained stage of the hotel ballroom completes both the confessional and the theater motifs. Every character in *I Confess* has depended on a public role or image to define his or her life, but reality lies deeper. Even if we grant that there is a temporary reversal of chaos by a final meting out of justice in Keller's death and the restoration of Logan's standing in the community, it remains that everyone has been divested of his role or part, and no one can ever be the same. The final image on the screen—a backtracking from the ballroom stage—is not religious but frankly theatrical, and in the last analysis we can say that *I Confess* is not really a religious movie at all—this Hitchcock left to showmen like De Mille—but rather a film about recognizably human emotions and frailties. Quietly, soberly, earnestly, it explores the contours of a woman's sealed fantasy life, and in so doing it offers the alternative of confessional humility, by which anyone can—and everyone at some time must—advance in the progress toward a healthy spiritual life.

25

DIAL M FOR MURDER

(PRODUCED 1953, RELEASED 1954)

The best way to do it is with scissors.

ALFRED HITCHCOCK

Anthony Dawson and Grace Kelly.

Frederick Knott's thriller *Dial M for Murder* was a great success in London and New York in 1952, and because he had abandoned another project, Hitchcock decided to film this play in fulfillment of his contractual obligations. The task was accomplished in little more than a month: the single set made production simple, and there was little to do with the text except tighten and focus a ready-made script. Warner Bros. required him to shoot the picture in the fad of the day—3-D, one of the industry's tricks to woo audiences away from the postwar television boom. Perhaps suspecting that this was a passing fancy, Hitchcock elected not to exploit the usual pranks of three-dimensional filmmaking, and so there are no knives or fists hurled at the audience, nor does anyone fall from a great height into our laps.

The story concerns a retired tennis champion, Tony Wendice (Ray Milland). Anxious to inherit the fortune of his wife Margot (Grace Kelly) and resentful of her attentions to the dull young novelist Mark Halliday (Robert Cummings), he ingeniously plans her murder. Arranging what appears to be the perfect crime, Tony blackmails a man named Lesgate (Anthony Dawson), a former classmate with a criminal record, into committing the deed. But the plans are foiled when Margot resists her attacker, reaches for a pair of scissors and stabs him to death. Undaunted, Tony now decides to take his scheme in a different direction, trying to convince canny Inspector Hubbard (John Williams) that his wife killed Lesgate because *he* was blackmailing *her*. The inspector, however, begins to reason otherwise, and with the help of Margot and Mark a situation is arranged which reveals Tony as the villain.

As with previously filmed plays (*Juno and the Paycock, Rope*), Hitchcock compressed the text and added significant emotional resonances. Keeping his camera at a low angle (except for one overhead God's-eye view as the plans for murder are finalized), he also used close-ups, silences, colors and props to create and sustain tension.

A good example of the film's economy is the opening. We see Tony kiss Margot and then watch as they breakfast silently. But then, with her, we read the newspaper announcement of the *Queen Mary*'s arrival. Cut to another (more passionate) kiss, this one between Margot and Tony. The first quarter of the film then proceeds at a leisurely pace, with several fluid takes in the single set. But the interior darkness begins to prevail and the room seems increasingly claustrophobic. Close-ups intensify our association with Tony and Margot, with Mark and Margot, and with Inspector Hubbard as he tries to relate to that trio.

Margot's trial (nowhere in the play) is brilliantly and simply rendered by the director in a series of close-ups of her face, as colored lights revolve round her against a natural background. These colors—synesthetic, hallucinatory, dreamlike—repeat the colors of her wardrobe as the story unfolds (from white to red to brick to gray to black).

Most memorable is the attempted murder and Margot's subsequent stabbing of Lesgate in self-defense—a sequence that took one of the four weeks of shooting. In a daring exploitation of

Ray Milland dials M for murder.

audience identification, Hitchcock planned the crosscutting:
Tony's watch stops, and he dials the telephone number of his
home from his club at a few moments past the agreed time with

the killer. Lesgate is about to leave—and so we become edgy, impatient because, after all, we came to this movie theater expecting a good thrill; we *want* the killer to await the call that will summon the wife from the bedroom to the place where she can be killed by the intruder. This is viewer manipulation at its most perverse—much as, later, we want Marion Crane (Janet Leigh) to escape the pursuing trooper in *Psycho* and then for Norman Bates (Anthony Perkins) to get away with her car sinking in the

John Williams, Grace Kelly, Ray Milland.

swamp; and just as we want *Marnie* (Tippi Hedren) to get away with her theft of money from the Rutland safe and not be found out by a nearby cleaning woman. To further raise the ante, Hitchcock here intercuts the inner mechanisms of the telephone call; this is, of course, a fine example of film time, stretching out a few seconds of real time to emphasize its importance and thus the tension involved in delay.

At the living room desk, the camera then pans round Margot as she finally answers the ringing telephone. Implicating and involving his audience throughout, the director controls the viewpoint to Lesgate's position behind the curtains. We emerge with him, and the strangulation begins. Reflections from the fireplace blaze from the wall, the musical soundtrack becomes frenzied, and we seem in fact to feel both Margot's agony and terror and the killer's strength. The ordeal finally ends as she reaches behind her for the scissors she earlier placed on the desk and stabs him in the back. Lesgate whirls up and around, then falls to the floor on his back, so that the scissor blades are more deeply pushed into his body. With the accidental impaling of a boy in the dream-remembrance of *Spellbound,* the shower murder of *Psycho* and the rape-strangling of *Frenzy,* this is one of the few viscerally shocking moments in the entire Hitchcock filmography.

From this point, *Dial M for Murder* relies solely on dialogue for its interest and effect, and there is a marked civility about everyone involved. Inspector Hubbard is smoothly confident, and the handsome and charming husband is far more likable than the lover—indeed, it's hard to imagine Grace Kelly preferring Robert Cummings to Ray Milland, but there you are. Admirable for pacing, performances and its refusal to capitulate to the eccentricities of 3-D gimmickry, the film is spare and meticulously precut, with not an extraneous frame. Hitchcock was right about cinematic planning and economy: the best way to do it is with scissors.

26

REAR WINDOW

(PRODUCED 1953, RELEASED 1954)

Live with a lame man and you will learn to limp.

PLUTARCH, *MORALS*

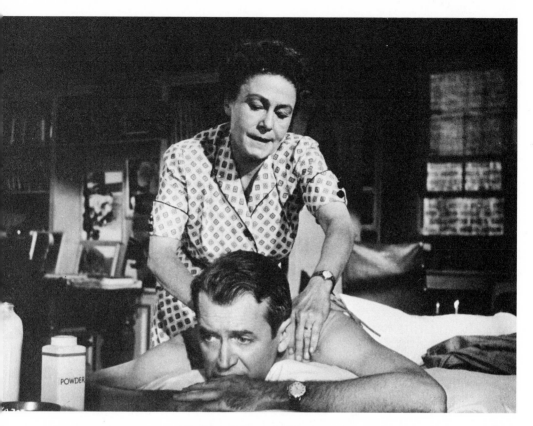

Thelma Ritter and James Stewart.

"I was feeling very creative at the time," Alfred Hitchcock said about *Rear Window*. "The batteries were well charged." So well charged, it seems, that he was able to produce a motion picture to satisfy even the most bored, cynical and detached spectator—someone like the hero himself.

The rear window looks out from a small apartment in crowded Greenwich Village, New York City. There a freelance traveling photographer named L. B. Jeffries (James Stewart)—called Jeff by friends—is confined to a wheelchair, his leg immobilized in a heavy plaster cast after a serious injury sustained while on assignment. With little to distract him from acute boredom and from the challenge to his maturity and commitment presented by his longtime girlfriend Lisa Fremont (Grace Kelly), he spies on all the neighbors in apartments nearby. These observations lead him to suspect that a traveling salesman named Lars Thorwald (Raymond

"We've become a race of Peeping Toms . . ."

Burr) has murdered his invalid wife. At first the evidence is so sketchy that Jeff can convince neither Lisa nor his detective friend Tom Doyle (Wendell Corey). But at last Jeff is helped by Lisa and by his visiting nurse Stella (Thelma Ritter), who become his "legs." They discover sufficient material evidence to bring in the police—and at the same time Jeff is mightily impressed by Lisa's pluck and daring. But Jeff is nearly killed when Thorwald learns about the spying, enters Jeff's apartment and tries to kill him by tossing him out his own rear window. The final frames show Jeff, attended by Lisa, with both his legs now immobilized in casts.

Rear Window certainly succeeds as a light comedy-thriller, and anyone asking only for that level of entertainment is certainly supremely rewarded. But the script by John Michael Hayes (based on a short story by Cornell Woolrich) is multileveled, with nearly every line of dialogue and each episode containing several rich aspects for consideration. To approach the film *only* as a light diversion may in fact (Hitchcock implies) indict a viewer, along with Jeff, as one who merely peers at the lives of others from a distance and leaves unexamined his own inner life.

That Hitchcock is frankly unconcerned with the killer and his wife is obvious when we keep in mind (1) that we don't see the actual crime; (2) that we know nothing about this man and woman, nor about their histories, their life together or the nature of her "illness" (she seems quite hale and lovely); and (3) that they are always shown from afar, and that Thorwald's ultimate entrance into Jeff's apartment (as suspenseful a moment as it is) has the quality of a sudden nightmare. There is something indefinable, even slightly unreal about the Thorwalds. In any case, from first frame to last, Hitchcock shows cavalier disinterest in the private life of the killer; he's more concerned with the reactions of the watchers—both those on-screen and those in the audience. The Thorwald murder is the MacGuffin, merely a pretext to examine the movie's central concern, the affective relationship of Jeff to Lisa. The killing is rather like the bottled uranium ore (in *Notorious*)—it gets the real story going, allowing its more important aspects to flourish.

The movie begins as the credits appear over a slowly ascending bamboo shade (recalling the opening of *Stage Fright,* another seriocomic exploration of role-playing and role-directing). The view

Raymond Burr as Lars Thorwald.

we finally see beyond the shade is the panorama of the largest indoor set ever built at Paramount Studios up to the end of 1953—the array of apartments in the buildings surrounding Jeff. For the record, Hitchcock and his crew did their homework: Thorwald's apartment, we're told, is at 125 West Ninth Street. But West Ninth Street ends at Sixth Avenue (Avenue of the Americas) in Manhattan; thenceforward, West Ninth is called Christopher Street. In 1953, moviemakers had to refrain from using actual addresses for murderers, but at number 125 *Christopher Street* (at the corner of Hudson Street; it was, of course, originally 125 West Ninth) is the building that exactly inspired the design of the Thorwald apartment. A courtyard separates that building from Jeff's, which is on Tenth Street, just east of Hudson. This explains why, when they're summoned, the police arrive after only a few seconds: the Sixth Precinct of Manhattan's Police Department is right there on Tenth, directly across from Jeff's flat. It also explains the business

about the Hotel Albert (now rehabbed as apartments), at Tenth
Street and University Place, a short walk away.

Whereas other Hitchcock films (*Foreign Correspondent, Shadow
of a Doubt, The Paradine Case, Rope, I Confess, Psycho, Topaz*) take
us at the opening from outside to inside, from the larger to the
smaller viewpoint, we're led here from inside to outside, and the
implication is clear as we move to an outer-directed, subjective
vision. It's not that *we* are admitted to something hidden and
private, but that what we see is what *Jeff* looks at: his viewpoint
limits ours.

The film may profitably be studied from several angles. First, Jeff
and we watch, through his rear window, the projections of his
and our minds as the possibilities of a serious relationship develop
with Lisa. In this regard, the entire first third of the film (almost
forty minutes) concerns that relationship, which is then explored

Each apartment Jeffries sees represents
a possibility for his own life with Lisa.

with each male-female couple they and we see in the other apartments. Second, there is the subtheme of the indictment of voyeurism and the suspicion that prying into others' lives (except when they're murderers, of course) corrupts the ideal of neighborly love. Third—and this is *Rear Window*'s most subtle theme—there is the issue of the moral responsibilities incumbent on a man devoted to picture-taking: photographers first of all but, by logical extension, filmmakers too. "Jeff" is in fact a surrogate for "Hitch" in this regard: chair-bound, he takes up a camera with a telephoto lens and then field glasses, through which he peers into the rectangular windows of his neighbors and sees people, gives them names, makes up stories about them, tells others these stories and then directs a "crew" (Lisa, Stella, Doyle) he sends forth onto the "set." *Rear Window* is, on this level, nothing so much as a movie about moviemaking Hitchcock-style. And fourth, there is a compassionate but distinctly antiromantic treatment of erotic intimacy in *Rear Window*—something necessary for some people, Hitchcock seems to say (here as elsewhere), but a human reality freighted with danger, dread and uncertainty.

In each of these four levels of the picture, the Lisa-Jeff relationship is explored. In each of them the claustrophobic atmosphere of Jeff's bachelor apartment contributes to the tension: it's a stifling setting from which both we and the hero make a final ambiguous exit when he falls from the window ledge. To each of the levels, finally, Hitchcock gives a strange, dreamlike quality, established through an unusual number of fade-outs (elsewhere used sparingly). Just how he worked out each of these levels deserves careful assessment.

Each of his neighbors offers Jeff a kind of correlative for the future. In the first scenes, he says to a friend on the telephone that he regards the possibility of marriage as fearful, boring and oppressive. "Can't you just see me, coming home from work to a nagging wife?" And as he says this, he and we gaze across at Thorwald arriving home from work to attend a nagging wife—who, as we discover when Lisa arrives moments later, bears an astonishing resemblance to her. They're both attractive blondes, and Lisa's first appearance—in half-darkness at night, rousing Jeff from sleep and coming into his world as if from a sensuous romantic dream—

suggests that it's Mrs. Thorwald who has entered his apartment.

But each of the female neighbors is a variant on what Lisa could become in the future: one lives with her befuddled, balding husband but lavishes all her affection on their small dog; another is a shapely dancer entertaining many men at a party but rebuffing their advances and faithfully awaiting the return of her boyfriend from the army ("You said it reminded you of my apartment," Lisa tells Jeff); another is a dumpy sculptress fashioning an abstraction of "Hunger"; another is a sexually voracious young bride who is soon furious with her disaffected groom. Most of all—and most related to Lisa—is the pathetic "Miss Lonelyhearts," the desperate spinster saved from suicide by a neighbor's haunting piano-playing. For much of the film Lisa wears a pale green suit; Miss Lonelyhearts is shown in a brilliant green dress the night she picks up a young stranger, brings him to her apartment and then becomes hysterical when he does exactly what she thinks she wanted but clearly does not.

One often hears that Hitchcock was the most misogynistic of filmmakers, the man with contempt for women's dignity—a view apparently derived from the observation that often terrible things happen to women in his films (*Notorious, Strangers on a Train, Vertigo, Psycho, The Birds* and *Frenzy*). But this is a bit like saying that a Holocaust story has contempt for its victims because they're shown to be so badly treated. In fact the highly moralistic Hitchcock describes the devastating effect of crime *on the victim;* his real contempt is for the victimizer, in every case a man. In most Hitchcock romances, the woman is courageous precisely because she is willing to risk so much for love—something alien to the manipulative, ungrownup man. *Notorious* and *Rear Window* (and in an odd way, *Vertigo* as well) are the best examples, and in *Rear Window* Lisa is shown to be resourceful, brave and self-giving.

Jeff, however, regards her merely as something to be *watched* but not touched—just as he watches his neighbors. In this regard, one of the movie's two signature tunes is significant: on a neighbor's radio, Bing Crosby croons "To See You Is to Love You" (from Paramount's 1953 movie *The Road to Bali*), and this is literally true for Jeff, who is satisfied with merely gazing (". . . to know you at all is to know you by heart . . . I'll see you in the same old dream tonight," sings Crosby; it's the ultimate romantic fantasy). Lisa models a dress for him and later a peignoir, but the implication of lovemaking is genuinely off-putting to him. Intimacy frightens Jeff, and he exploits every opportunity to reject Lisa. He complains to Stella that Lisa is the kind of girl concerned only for a new dress and a lobster dinner, and later she arrives with a new dress and a lobster dinner catered from the 21 Club. She's a woman who fulfills fantasies, but because she offers love and loyalty along with beauty and brains, it's apparently too much for Jeff's need for supremacy, and in this supper scene with her he's downright cruel. (If we attend Grace Kelly's acting toward the end of this sequence with the lobster dinner and observe how Hitchcock photographed her, we see irrefutable proof of where his personal sympathies are and where ours are meant to be.)

When she gamely climbs into Thorwald's apartment, she finds his wife's wedding ring and slips it on her finger, proudly displaying it to Jeff as he watches through binoculars. But this gesture gives her away and endangers Jeff, for Thorwald notices what she's doing and glances from her finger to Jeff watching—that is, straight out at us—and this is the single most chilling moment of the film (at this point, a collective murmur is heard from the audience when *Rear Window* is screened). With this scene, therefore, Hitchcock closes the circle of his intention: Lisa has seen the entire adventure as a way of showing Jeff what a good wife she'd be; she slips on the ring not only to prove their suspicions about the fate of Mrs. Thorwald but also as a kind of proposal to Jeff.

It is this that links the Jeff-Lisa relationship to the subtheme of voyeurism, for Jeff places his own life and that of others in peril precisely because he has been an observer and not a participant in life—in a way, then, this photographer is the ultimate moviegoer as well as moviemaker. "Do you think it's ethical," Lisa asks him, "to go around the world taking pictures of people—just taking pictures of people?" Confined to his wheelchair, Jeff can no longer travel; but he still gazes out and takes pictures—once, literally (snapshots of the garden) and constantly records and describes a series of mental images reflecting his own frightened, lonely emotional condition. (The casting of James Stewart was inspired, for he was so often the "regular guy" in American films. But how could James Stewart, after all, make such an effort to avoid someone like Grace Kelly?!) Furthering the theme of voyeurism is the richly comic mother figure of Stella (in a rendering of pure gold by Thelma Ritter). "We've become a race of Peeping Toms," she says with homey wisdom. "What people ought to do is get outside their own house and look in for a change!" Jeff is urged to look into his own house—into himself— and not to make psychological projections onto other people. To put the matter plainly, *Rear Window* endorses introspection rather than voyeurism. Stella calls Jeff a "window-shopper" when he stares at the shapely dancer in her apartment: Jeff does his shopping in a chair, much as Hitchcock did in his director's seat and the moviegoer does in his place.

"Whatever happened to that old adage, 'Love thy neighbor'?" Lisa asks Jeff. And a neighbor, discovering her dog has been poisoned (by Thorwald, of course, because the dog was sniffing around evidence) shouts for all to hear, 'None of you know the meaning of the word neighbor! Neighbors like each other. Speak to each other. Care if anybody lives or dies. But none of you do." This theme of caring, neighborly compassion is finally located not only in the crisis faced by Miss Lonelyhearts but also in *Rear Window*'s concern for the moral responsibility of those who take pictures—filmmakers included, we must presume—and herein the film moves from an indictment of uninvolved voyeurism to an analysis of its relationship with "going from place to place taking pictures" and merely watching a companion (as Jeff watches Lisa). "I wonder if it's ethical to watch a man with binoculars and a long-focus lens," Jeff says to Lisa. "Do you suppose it's ethical even if you prove he *didn't* commit a crime?" Lisa's reply is straightforward: "I'm not much on rear-window ethics. But look at you and me, plunged into despair because we find out a man *didn't* kill his wife. We're two of the most frightening ghouls I've ever known." But of course Thorwald *is* a murderer, as they will soon confirm, and this fact is more than simple dramatic irony. A terrible, longed-for fantasy—the desire for murderous excitement Jeff expressed on the phone in the film's opening moments— can indeed become a terrible reality.

The coda of the film is not just a comic respite after so much spiraling tension. Jeff's final fall is a kind of retribution, and the last scene shows him with two broken legs. He will have to relive

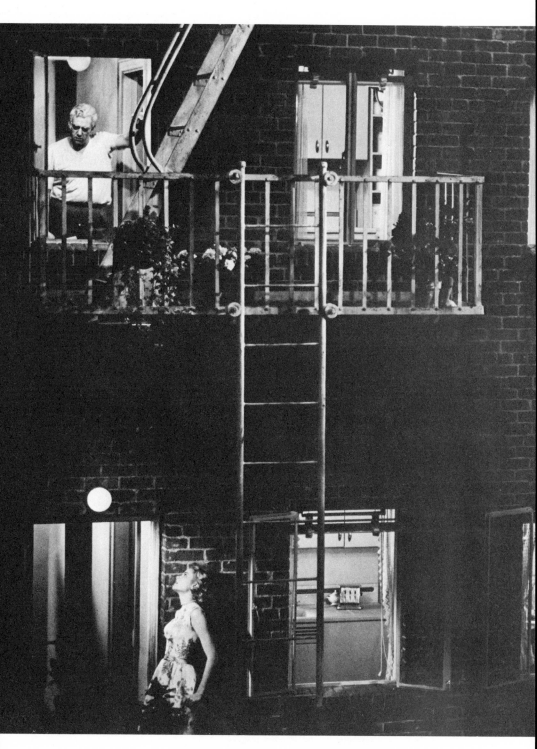

Lisa hides after leaving the letter under Thorwald's door.

the enclosed situation, but with Lisa instead of Stella as his companion, and with his wheelchair significantly facing *away* from the rear window. While he is still immobilized and sleeping, the vigilant Lisa slyly puts aside a book designed to further win his confidence (*Beyond the High Himalayas,* an example of the remote places Jeff routinely visits on assignment) and takes up her current issue of *Harper's Bazaar.* Just as the Jeff-Lisa relationship is still in progress, so the situations of the other neighbors change, too. The couple who lost their dog have an adorable new puppy; Miss Lonelyhearts has met up with the lonely composer of the song that stopped her suicide; the dancer's boyfriend Stanley comes home from the army; the sculptress has finished "Hunger" and is sleeping peacefully, sated; the Thorwald apartment is being repainted, readied for new tenants; and the randy newlyweds, no longer in bed, have struck the first sour note in marital harmony: "If you'd told me you'd quit your job," whines the bride, "we never would've gotten married!"

"Rear Window," Hitchcock once told the author of this book, "was structurally satisfactory because it is the epitome of the subjective treatment. A man looks; he sees; he reacts. Thus you construct a mental process. *Rear Window* is entirely a mental process, done by use of the visual." Hitchcock has, then, shown the deepest truth of Stella's remark, "What people ought to do is get outside their own house and look in for a change."

27

TO CATCH A THIEF

(PRODUCED 1954, RELEASED 1955)

Set a thief to catch a thief.

H. G. BOHN,

''A HAND-BOOK

OF PROVERBS''

Grace Kelly, Cary Grant, Jessie Royce Landis, John Williams.

Hitchcock's brilliant *Rear Window*—intense, claustrophobic, and obsessive—was followed by "a lightweight story," as he called it. From the facsimile of a crowded New York block and work on a studio-bound picture, he traveled to the bright openness of the French Riviera. For his second project with writer John Michael Hayes, they turned David Dodge's novel *To Catch a Thief* into a rambling, relaxed comic caper. Robert Burks won an Academy Award for his luminous color cinematography for it, and Grace Kelly (in her third feature for Hitchcock) was gently poised between stylish elegance and a kind of cool, poignant isolation. The picture is ravishingly pretty, intermittently funny, surprising (for 1955) in its risqué dialogue, and in the final analysis a sweetish confection, the relaxed work of a man on holiday. This is not to damn with faint praise; it is merely to indicate that the picture should perhaps not be taken with very much gravity.

To Catch a Thief concerns John Robie (Cary Grant), a former jewel thief and collaborator with the Resistance during the Nazi occupation of France. The police suspect he's returned to his former job and is responsible for a series of burglaries among the Riviera's rich. To prove his innocence, Robie embarks on his own investigation to catch the thief. He engages the help of an insurance agent named Hughson (John Williams), and soon meets the rich young American Frances Stevens, called Francie (Grace Kelly) and her mother (Jessie Royce Landis). Francie is fascinated by the man's reputation as a thief, falls in love with him and, although she at first believes him guilty, finally helps him catch the real cat burglar.

On location, the French Riviera.

This turns out to be Danielle Foussard (Brigitte Auber), a woman he thought was a friend, the daughter of a former Resistance colleague who is himself a thief and who exploits Robie's friendship and attempts to pin on Robie the blame for the crimes.

The film's title, drawn from the famous proverb, is of course double-edged. Robie is indeed a former thief who must catch a thief. But Francie also tries to catch Robie—first when she thinks he's the villain (and this excites her somewhat more than it should), then as a husband. Her sexual desire is in fact indistinguishable from her fascination for his criminal record. ("I've never caught a real thief before. This is quite stimulating!")

This complex of ideas makes *To Catch a Thief* a kind of outline for later (and superior) works—specifically, *Psycho, Marnie* and *Family Plot.* The classic Freudian notion of sex as larcenous is here located in Francie, the ice-cool blonde who tempts and traps. She whispers alluringly of her jewels, and the double entendre—especially since she wears a strapless gown in her dimly lit hotel suite—is not exactly subtle: "Here, hold them. They're the most

Grace Kelly, dressed for the ball sequence.

beautiful thing in the world, and the one thing you can't resist." She seduces him by exploiting his taste for fine jewels—turning off the lights one by one for the love scene, as in *Rear Window* the same actress's first scene showed her switching the lamps on one by one. So what else could Hitchcock do but intercut a montage of colorful fireworks bursting in the sky as the love scene continues: it's robbery-as-sex (and vice versa) pushed to the limits of a cinematic joke. The sheer arrogance of the cliché is more amusing than its content.

For Francie—as later for Mark Rutland (Sean Connery) in *Marnie* ("I've really trapped a wild animal this time—a thief!" he gloats to poor Marnie)—an unacknowledged possessiveness counterbalances the larceny of which the love object was or is guilty. The infatuation, therefore, is more than slightly pathological. And between these two films is the much darker *Psycho,* which aligns even more closely the everyday nature of risk, theft, sex and death. In *To Catch a Thief* the motifs are linked comically and casually, whereas the targets are hit squarely in *Psycho.* In the later film, the ultimate happens: personality itself is robbed, annihilated, swallowed up in death—an idea only obliquely suggested by the masked ball in *To Catch a Thief.*

Francie, then, is the *moral* thief; Danielle is merely the material burglar—and this explains the narrative's basic indifference toward her and her motivation. The robberies, the jewelry and the thief herself—all elements of the ubiquitous MacGuffin, simply allowing the romance to gleam more brightly. We may not be prepared for the final revelation of Danielle as the culprit, but it hardly matters. That the real thief is in fact a woman *is* crucial, however, since there is a link by association with Francie. Danielle, too, knows how to engage in emotional bribery: she proposes early on that Robie flee to South America with her to escape the police, and when she thinks she can't compete with Francie for Robie's romantic attention, she vaguely threatens to expose him to the police. In this way, the postadolescent brunette is half sister to the beautiful blonde. In her jealousy, her sneaky pushiness and her capacity for emotional blackmail, she is very like Lil Mainwaring (Diane Baker), the brunette opposite the blonde *Marnie* (Tippi Hedren).

Hitchcock's birthday (August 13) was celebrated by cast
and crew during a break in shooting the ball sequence.

. . .

The instinctive understanding that all this remarkably expensive
jewelry is morally worthless is ironically located in the rich Mrs.
Stevens herself, in a glowingly funny and warm performance from
Jessie Royce Landis. "I'd rather have a hundred Jeremiahs," she
says longingly, referring to a comparison of her jewels with her
late husband. "You can't cuddle up to diamonds." And her daughter isn't, after all, irredeemably spoiled: "Palaces are for royalty,"
Francie tells Robie as they stroll past the great mansions. "We're
just common folk with a bank account."

The usual Hitchcock markers appear aplenty in *To Catch a
Thief*. Birds flutter in a cage next to Robie on a bus as he flees the
police. The biplane pursuing him in Danielle's motorboat recalls
a scene in *The 39 Steps* and anticipates *North by Northwest*. A
chicken leisurely crosses the road, causing the police to swerve
and smash up their car—a wreck which the bird survives with
strutting indifference, although his cousins are moments later eaten
for lunch by Robie and Francie. The teasing, the empty accusa-
tions, and denials at this picnic—and the accumulation of sexy
double entendres—lead of course to the inevitable kiss, as Robie

presses Francie down so that she's in fact the lunch, her head in the open food basket!

The picture has considerable charm and the performances are unerringly right. *To Catch a Thief* is in the genre of *The Lady Vanishes*— a creampuff of what is sometimes called a movie-movie, with just a little suspense at the end. Here, it's Danielle's last-minute clinging to the rooftop. The film is a comedy, and she's saved, of course— ultimately luckier than *Saboteur*'s Fry or *North by Northwest*'s Leonard and Valerian or poor Judy Barton in *Vertigo*—because Danielle is . . . well, only a thief, after all.

28

THE TROUBLE WITH HARRY

(PRODUCED 1954, RELEASED 1955)

I love Vermont because of her hills and valleys, her scenery and invigorating climate, but most of all because of her indomitable people.

CALVIN COOLIDGE, IN BENNINGTON, VERMONT, 1928

"What seems to be the trouble, Captain?"
(Mildred Natwick and Edmund Gwenn.)

"Understatement is important to me," Alfred Hitchcock once said. "*The Trouble with Harry* is an approach to a strictly British genre, the humor of the macabre. I made that picture to prove that the American public could appreciate British humor." The picture, Hitchcock's third with writer John Michael Hayes, was based on a short novel by J. Trevor Story to which it closely adheres. Parisian audiences and critics were quite enthusiastic when it was first released there, but in fact British and American audiences reacted less warmly to this visually beautiful but static and finally unsettling little movie.

It opens on a small boy, Arnie (Jerry Mathers), playing in the Vermont hillside on a splendid autumn day. He comes on the dead

Arnie (Jerry Mathers), unperturbed by Harry's corpse.

body of a man—Harry Worp, as it happens. Elderly Captain Wiles (Edmund Gwenn), a retired sea merchant, believes his hunting rifle dispatched Harry. But Harry's widow Jennifer (Shirley MacLaine, in her film debut), a local old maid, Miss Gravely (Mildred Natwick), the town doctor and others also think they might have been responsible for Harry's death. The corpse is secretly buried by committee—and then disinterred at least three times until it is determined that death in fact was due to natural causes: Harry was, we learn, a rather nasty, heavy-drinking lout. When no one need fear recrimination, a joint decision is made by the group to put Harry back in full light of day. The boy will discover the corpse again, as if no trouble had intervened. Now that the slightly dim deputy sheriff Calvin Wiggs (Royal Dano) has been sufficiently intimidated, the authorities can be notified, the customary rituals may be performed and normal life may be resumed. The film ends as the local abstract painter, Sam Marlowe (John Forsythe), who had tried to impose order on all the confusion, proposes to Jennifer.

"With *Harry*," Hitchcock added, "I took melodrama out of the pitch-black night and brought it out into the sunshine. It's as if I had set up a murder alongside a rustling brook and spilled a drop of blood in the clear water. These contrasts establish a counterpart; they elevate the commonplace in life to a higher level." This is an interesting comment, but like many of the director's remarks to interviewers, it is something of a red herring, an evasion of what seems the film's ambiguous tone and stance. For although Robert Burks's glorious cinematography gives it a vivid splendor, there is an almost palpable undercurrent of a dark and grotesque Puritanism in this picture. But whether the film affirms or satirically mocks that Puritanism is difficult to determine. Audiences who remember *The Trouble with Harry* as a disarmingly funny comedy

Mildred Natwick and Shirley MacLaine.

may in fact have something of a discontinuous memory; in fact it is uncharacteristically talky and despite its grim humor and casual tone there is a nasty set of subtexts.

In a countryside aglow with the golds, russets, and oranges of New England's loveliest season, most of the action is set in that archetypal locus of evil, the forest; here autumn may be beautiful, but it also announces the death of nature. If the trouble with Harry was that no one liked him, and if the trouble with Harry is that he can't stay buried, the characters who knew and dealt with him react with marvelous detachment to his death and the necessity of disposing of his remains. They speak nonchalantly about him, but they also speak nonchalantly about sex. Those who do not so speak of sex—Miss Gravely, for instance—respond defensively to the suggestion that their private lives, like their innocent presence in the forest, may cover up something. Death in the countryside may be covered up; sex in the countryside may be covered up. Puritan New England, the film seems to say (and the film's first image is a Congregational New England church) is remarkable in its consistency. Sex and death—the two great American obscenities—are taken matter-of-factly by this film, which directly supports Hitchcock's own assertion that "understatement is important." Just so, the characters understate their various fears, their reactions, hopes, hatreds and passions.

One of the oddly intriguing aspects of this picture is that it is a kind of double-edged sword which elaborates two viewpoints simultaneously. The first, supported by a quiet wit, affirms the idea that death is part of life, that it should be taken with a calmly stoic detachment. "Suppose it was written in the Book of Heaven," says Sam to Captain Wiles, "that this man was to die at this particular time at this particular place." If Wiles hadn't shot him (which he didn't), "why, then, a thunderbolt or something would have knocked him off!" No one really becomes very upset about Harry's demise, nor about the need (for a variety of reasons) to disinter him and then reinter him. The film implies that there are worse things in life than death, and that real maturity lies in accepting that, like everything else in nature "we all have to go sometime" (thus Mark Rutland in *Marnie*). Such acceptance leads to a life without whimpering.

The casual and (for 1956) frank sex talk in *Harry* supports this

understanding of the film, for there are a surprising number of
sexual allusions and double entendres. This language—indeed, sex
is very nearly an obsession of everyone in the story—is linked by
association with Harry's corpse: dates are made over it. (Miss
Gravely nervously invites Captain Wiles for blueberry muffins,
then steps lightly over the corpse as if it were a child's sandcastle
she'd rather not disturb.)

The film may, then, endorse that mature healthy-mindedness
which simply does not take sex or death as realities to be considered
with ultimate gravity. In so doing, it then overturns the popular
understanding of the Puritan ethos by recommending that sex and
death be viewed without hysteria. Bernard Herrmann's score (the
first of eight for Hitchcock) contributes very much to this aspect,
for it's as fresh and hummable as a country tune. Like the gorgeous
color, it urges an exorcism of precisely the fear and trembling that
surround the two traditional American obscenities. *The Trouble
with Harry,* seen in this light, rids us of their obsceneness (or, more
accurately, the obsceneness of exaggerating their importance) by
the detached nonchalance of laughter. Sex and death are thus accepted like the seasons.

But there is another viewpoint the film may advocate: a con-
firmation rather than a condemnation of that decadent Puritanism
which sees sex as undesirable and death as fearsome—thus exaggerating the significance of each. In this regard, both sex and
death emerge as realities to be mocked in *The Trouble with Harry.*
The dead man looks slightly ridiculous, after all, especially when
despoiled of shoes. More offensive still is the sniggering attitude
toward Miss Gravely and Captain Wiles which begins with the
condescension of Sam toward the possibility that senior citizens
could possibly have an affective (much less an erotic) life. Laughing
at death is thus like laughing at sex: it hides true feelings, and the
laughter really betokens nervousness. The frank sex talk—and the
subdued laughter behind cupped hands at the end, when Jennifer's
earlier request for a double bed is at last revealed to the others—
provides the only surprise in the film. The secret about the double
bed, revealed as the two couples crouch behind a fallen tree to
await the boy's rediscovery of the corpse, makes the final absurdist
connection between sex and death. Such a view of the film would
see a nasty attitude about sex and a squeamishness about death in

every understatement and low joke. It, too, seems a wholly tenable position to take on the picture.

Since Hitchcock so often referred to *Shadow of a Doubt* and *The Trouble with Harry* among his personal favorites, we might seek a link between them. And this may lie in the identical problem each presents—that of balancing (1) Gnostic-Puritan ethic on one side of life, and (2) a Judaeo-Christian optimism on the other. The first affirms the coexistence of evil and good as basic to the world; takes seriously the infinite capacities for criminal activity that lie within everyone; distrusts relationships and, in its schizoid attempt to deny the reality of the flesh, warns about the poisonous nature of sex. Consequently, Gnostic Puritanism urges as complete a withdrawal as possible from social and sexual intercourse.

But the second way asserts the primacy of God's self-disclosure *within* the world and man's ability to respond to that revelation—and most radical of all religious convictions, affirms that one is saved from meaninglessness in this life and guaranteed another to follow. The path to salvation is within the present economy, which is seen as good but capable of being abused and disordered. Only a filmmaker steeped in the Anglo-American cultural and literary tradition could evoke the emotional resonances of our Gnostic-Puritan heritage. And only one familiar with the doctrines of Christianity and its Western literary tradition could offer that hope for equal reflection. Perhaps that's why it may be better not to opt for a single vision in this film; its cool stance and ambiguities may be deliberate, just the right means of presenting the two ethics for balanced consideration.

A word must be said, however, about the view of some European critics that *The Trouble with Harry* is really a filmed parable on the death and resurrection of Christ, presented ironically. For them, the sketch Sam makes of the corpse recalls a Rouault *Christus*. Moreover, these critics see the continual physical "resurrections" of Harry as pointing to the issue of a more significant, unique resurrection. They make much of the remark of Captain Wiles and Miss Gravely, who say they must bury Harry "with hasty reverence," seeing it and similar remarks as reflecting the New Testament account of Christ's burial.

None of this is very persuasive. It may well be legitimate to point knowingly to images or a complex of ideas drawn from Christian art and iconography, but to say these images point a film in a specific theological direction—or to extract from them a significant theological statement (or even a personal faith) seems misguided. (Also, such critics have not taken into account the unsavory character of Harry himself.) This methodology does a disservice to Hitchcock's wit and to his function as storyteller rather than evangelist; he may be a moralist, but he is no homilist. An equal disservice may also be done to Christian tradition, which surely does not need to be made boringly "relevant" by seeing dubious references to it in a film that emerges quite well on its own merit.

The single memorable line from *The Trouble with Harry* occurs when Miss Gravely meets Captain Wiles as he drags the corpse for burial. She looks down at the body without so much as fluttering an eyelash, then asks, "What seems to be the trouble, Captain?" No matter how one regards this strange and static motion picture, this is a gloriously perverse line of dialogue. "That's the spirit of the whole story," Hitchcock said. That's also the spirit of a supremely gifted and confident director who cares little about the trouble taken by critics. We can almost hear Hitchcock speaking in Sam's response to a prospective art buyer: "Don't think I'm rude, but it doesn't matter to me what a critic says."

29

THE MAN WHO KNEW TOO MUCH

(PRODUCED 1955, RELEASED 1956)

Free will does not mean one will,
but many wills conflicting in one man.
FLANNERY O'CONNOR,
PREFACE TO SECOND EDITION
OF *WISE BLOOD*

Doris Day and James Stewart.

"Let's say that the first version was the work of a talented amateur and the second was made by a professional," said Alfred Hitchcock, comparing his two filmings of *The Man Who Knew Too Much* (henceforth they will be designated here as Man-1 and Man-2). Even a single viewing of each supports the director's own estimation. Where Man-1 had an easy wit and a kind of grimy nonchalance, Man-2 is everywhere a richer film—not only in technical execution, but also in the complexity of its characters and themes and, most of all, in the depth and directness of its emotion. The fourth and final collaboration with the gifted screenwriter John Michael Hayes, this is one of Hitchcock's masterworks, impeccably photographed by Robert Burks, with a brilliant Bernard

Herrmann score and flawless performances from principals and supporting players. It also seems to this writer Hitchcock's warmest film—lacking a major wicked character or situation, and really full of love.

Credits appear over a formally dressed orchestra in the Royal Albert Hall, London, playing a selection from the first part of the "Storm Cloud Cantata" which accompanies the climactic scene later. The camera cranes down from a vast overview of the musicians—without a cut—to a close-up of the percussionist who impassively strikes the cymbals together and holds them toward us as we read: "A single crash of Cymbals and how it rocked the lives of an American family." This is a curious epigraph, frankly inaccurate in light of the events to follow: it is not at all a crash of cymbals that causes all the trouble—in fact, the people most in danger know nothing about the crucial timing of a cymbal crash. Rather, it's a kidnapping that rocks them. (With the additional inaccuracy of capitalizing the word "cymbals," it's tempting to see the epigraph as offering a pun on "symbols.")

The plot outline for Man-2 is the same as for Man-1, although the kidnapped child is now a boy, and the original characters of Abbott and his nurse (Peter Lorre and Cicely Oates) have become the far more complex Mr. and Mrs. Drayton (Bernard Miles and Brenda de Banzie). The story now opens on a bus, with a close-up of young Hank McKenna (Christopher Olsen) seated between his parents, Dr. Ben McKenna (James Stewart) and Jo Conway McKenna (Doris Day), an internationally famous singer who has abandoned her Broadway career in favor of her husband, whose medical practice is in Indianapolis. The opening image synthesizes a contradiction, for Hank is a link between the parents; his absence will threaten their stability by dividing them and yet enables them to rediscover their interdependence as they struggle to recover him. In fact the central issue in this picture is neither the political situation at the core of Louis Bernard's murder and the child's kidnapping (that crisis, whomever it involves and whatever is at stake, comprises Hitchcock's MacGuffin), nor is it the safety of the child (somehow never really an issue). No, the problem most explored here is the relationship between Ben and Jo, the delicate state of her emotional health, and how a man who thinks he knows

Doris Day, Christopher Olsen, James Stewart and Daniel Gélin.

so much (Ben) must learn the contours of his own interdependence
with others.

This average American family is on extended holiday in North
Africa, following Ben's attendance at a Paris medical convention.
"We saw the same scenery last summer driving to Las Vegas,"
remarks Jo somewhat distractedly, as Hank glances out to see only
a dull expanse of rock. As a refuge from his boredom, the child
walks down the center aisle of the bus, which suddenly lurches
and throws him off balance. He accidentally tears off an Arab
woman's veil, and at once there is a noisy and embarrassing social
predicament when her husband causes a minor riot. From this
point on, the McKennas will be (like Richard Hannay in *The 39
Steps* and Roger Thornhill in *North by Northwest*) no longer bored,
passive spectators but rather active participants, and the chief excitement in the unfolding drama will derive from the possibility
of their dissolution as a family. In light of this, the concert later
takes on new meaning as a sign and climax of the *struggle together*

(the root meaning of the word "concert") which the family must endure for the sake of unity. (Boredom, leisure time or forced retirement provide protagonists with similar motivation for excitement in *The 39 Steps, Shadow of a Doubt, Under Capricorn, Rear Window, To Catch a Thief, Vertigo* and *Torn Curtain.*)

To the social rescue comes a darkly handsome Frenchman, Louis Bernard (Daniel Gélin), who speaks the native language. He calms the offended Arab, introduces himself to the American family and asks a series of pointed questions about them. At once Jo is suspicious of his inquiries but charmed by his manner. "There are moments in life when we all need a little help," Bernard says pointedly.

The moment is significant, for an interruption has occurred in a hitherto unexciting journey, and the entire film that follows is structured on a series of such interruptions. That evening, they are interrupted in their hotel room by a man (soon revealed as the hired assassin) who has apparently come to the wrong door. Then the McKennas are interrupted at the restaurant by the Draytons,

The dying Frenchman tells Ben about an assassination plot.

who happen to be seated at an adjacent table. In London, Ben and Jo are then interrupted by friends who come to their hotel suite just when they hope to continue their search for Hank. And the film's two great moments of suspense—Jo's reaction to the news of the kidnapping and her response to the possibility of assassination at Albert Hall—are interrupted, the first by a sedative that stifles her scream and the second by her scream. That scream recalls Bernard's comment about Jo's early singing in the hotel room: "Your wife has a beautiful voice—too bad it [her singing] was interrupted." Her scream at Albert Hall is the mother's cry in childbirth, a liberating cry of anguish and a triumph over death— and it literally brings their son back to them. (It serves likewise as the audience's release from mounting tension.)

These interruptions are thematically significant in the film and exteriorize (as so often in Hitchcock's films) the capricious, hostile emergence of *accident*. "It was only an accident," Jo says, defending Hank on the bus. So is the family's presence at the market next day: the McKennas' entire involvement in the plot to kill a foreign dignitary hinges on the accident of Ben's physical proximity to the disguised and dying Bernard. (Hitchcock's narrative world is interlaced with accident, which can be identified as the single crucial element in virtually every one of his films.)

The process by which the McKennas find and retrieve their child becomes in fact a second birth for a tired family. "When are we going to have another child?" Jo asks her husband in the crowded Arabian market, moments before Bernard's murder. "You're the doctor, you have all the answers." Ben is indeed the man who knows too much, and another irony of the story is that he will be disabused of this presumption when their son is in fact saved—not by his knowledge or superiority but by the reemergence of his wife's capacity as a singer (in the embassy sequence). Throughout, Ben is the man of science, a benevolent family superior who knows too much for the good of his loved ones. At three important points in the film, Jo says he has "all the answers," and he constantly insists on the ancient prerogatives of supremacy connected with his roles as father, husband and physician. As if to italicize this, Stewart's height is everywhere emphasized; others are dominated or intimidated by his height, and his personal attitude is an extension of his feeling that he is "above" others. But as we see, his height is also his weakness, for it makes him vulnerable, susceptible to both social embarrassment (in the Arabian restaurant) and to danger (his height makes him instantly recognizable to the dying Bernard).

The song written for Man-2 and sung by Doris Day—"Que Sera, Sera"—was no mere concession to popular taste; again more sophisticated than the sophisticates, Hitchcock offered a clear pointer to a complex of meanings in this extraordinary film. First, as Jo helps Hank prepare for bed, they sing together—and he whistles, which of course will reveal his whereabouts later when he's locked upstairs at the embassy. (In the hotel, Hitchcock avoided the Hollywood cliché and insisted that Day and Olsen sing without invisible orchestral accompaniment; another reason is that Hitchcock refuses to stress musicians until the great concert sequence.) But the song itself has enormous significance in context: accepting the future's possibilities, it counterpoises a certain Italian fatalism with faith in the power of love to sustain the unknown: "Whatever will be, will be—the future's not ours to see . . ." Like the concert music later (appropriately, the "Storm Cloud Cantata"), which builds inexorably to the crash of cymbals meant to cover the fatal gunshot, destiny is uncontrollable. The burst of a storm cloud, the workings of fate, the chaos in a hostile world—all these will occur, no matter what precautions are taken. And thus Jo's grief on hearing that her son has been kidnapped—temporarily postponed because Ben has administered sedation—will be released in her scream at Albert Hall. Que sera, sera.

When Ben finally tells Jo the news that their son has been taken away, she turns from a happy wife talking cheerfully about conceiving a second child into a near-hysteric. Very much of the touching effect of this scene (and that which follows) derives from Doris Day's perfectly modulated performance as a tortured mother. Words and cries change to stifled sobs and choked whispers in her throat; the effect of the sedation gives her the appearance of a woman virtually dead with grief and confusion, yet with sufficient presence of mind to feel the quick knife of agony.

In this regard, it is also important to note how Hitchcock carries forward his lifelong theme of the impotence of *manners* to provide security. A breach of manners causes the crucial opening tearing of a woman's veil; at dinner, Ben and Jo are upset by Bernard's rude manner in abandoning them for a dinner companion, and Ben forgets his manners, eating the chicken with all ten fingers rather than in the prescribed local custom shown by the Draytons; the McKennas rudely abandon their friends four times in the London hotel; Jo rudely screams at Albert Hall and sings too loudly and (deliberately, of course, to attract Hank's attention in hiding) without style or nuance at the embassy, causing the guests to exchange shocked glances at her apparent vulgarity. Traditional manners, Hitchcock insists, must often be jettisoned so that lives may be saved or at least lived more fully. For Hitchcock, manners may be a mark of civilization, but they can also give a false sense of security.

This theme of manners is related to a primary concern in the Hitchcock canon: the gulf often separating appearance from reality; things simply are often not what they seem. Louis Bernard at first seems suspicious; asking personal questions, talking and laughing with irate Arabs outside the bus immediately after meeting the McKennas. He is also recognized by the assassin (Reggie Nalder) who comes to the McKenna hotel room. He then leaves them after a curious telephone conversation (in French) and seems to talk about them at the restaurant (but really he murmurs to his companion about the Draytons, whom he—working for the "right side," as we later learn—has tracked as the dangerous couple); he has, it turns out, befriended the McKennas, after the accident of meeting them, in an effort to enlist their aid in preventing a political assassination.

The character of Mrs. Drayton embodies even much more poignantly this theme of people being other than what they seem. At first glance, outside the hotel, she appears to be a suspicious character. Then she appears friendly at the restaurant—so much that Jo can entrust Hank to her care. Henceforth she is a sinister accomplice and kidnapper—until at the finale she is both generous, compassionate and self-sacrificing. In fact Mrs. Drayton is the richest single character in the story, the mother manqué who longs for a child but gives him up to his natural mother rather than endanger his life: thus her tearstained encouragement to the boy to "Whistle! Whistle as loud as you can!" so that he will be revealed and saved. This conveys the meaning of Mr. Drayton's strange remark to his superior at the embassy: unaware that the target of the assassination attempt has been only wounded and the hit man killed, Drayton—his wife by his side—says, "Excuse me, sir, but something very unusual has happened." The reference is now clear: Mrs. Drayton has taken the child to her heart and longs to keep him for her own. That she will be forced to abdicate these hopes, and that she will witness the loss of her husband, is a situation not without poignancy, and Hitchcock takes the especial care to *show* us Mrs. Drayton, alone on the embassy staircase, after her husband's death. She is a keenly touching character in the final analysis, an unfulfilled mother, the only person left alone at the finale. (Notice, too, how throughout the ordeal Mrs. Drayton insists that the boy be well treated, given treats, never be abused: "It doesn't hurt to be kind," she says to her bespectacled accomplice as she pats the boy's head tenderly—as so often—and throughout her dealings with Hank, we see her troubled features whenever Hank's safety is involved. Now we appreciate just how far the character of the nurse in Man-1 has been deepened and humanized.) As always, Alfred Hitchcock constantly overturns our judgments about others.

Related to this is Ben's occupation. As a doctor, he is supposedly concerned with the sufferings of others. But actually he benefits from their pains, providing Jo with a catalogue of how various human ills have improved the McKenna family: Mrs. Campbell's gallstones pay for the three days in North Africa; Bill Edwards's tonsils bought Jo a new dress in Paris; Johnny Matthews's appendix paid for Ben's new suit; the boat trip to Europe was bought by multiple births and Mrs. Morgan's hives; the journey home is underwritten by Herbie Taylor's ulcers and Alida Markle's asthma. But Ben will presently share in the pain of others, not merely benefit from them.

Once the action moves to London, there is much less emphasis on the villains than in Man-1. The sympathetic humor and easygoing wit of Abbott and his preparations for the concert have been omitted from the original precisely because the relationship between the parents receives the emphasis in Man-2. In Man-1, the parents were rarely together throughout this final phase of their ordeal: Bob Lawrence went to Ambrose Chapel with his brother-in-law, after the sinister dentist sequence that did little to advance the plot. In Man-2, the McKennas proceed together to the chapel, and the dentist sequence was wisely dropped in favor of the incident at the taxidermy shop that carries forward the mistaken-identity motif and allows Jo to realize the meaning of Ambrose Chapel: "It's not a person, it's a place!"

The great sequence at Albert Hall is a perfect summary of Hitchcock's method and one of the most astonishing episodes in film. (The theater is of course a typical locus for the eruption of chaos, as we know from *The 39 Steps, Sabotage, Saboteur, Stage Fright* and *Torn Curtain*.) A wordless, twelve-minute, 124-shot sequence, it gives full scope to what Hitchcock called "pure cinema." To create and sustain tension, he employed all the counterpoints, balances and juxtapositions at his disposal.

The elegant setting, the situation of concert and harmony, become the ironic locus for the emergence of perfidy, chaos and

At the taxidermist.

murder. Will Jo cry out and save the prime minister's life? Or will she remain silent and save her son's life? This is where the suspense lies—not first in the external order, but in the will. The American author Flannery O'Connor (1925–1964) wrote compellingly of this tension in the preface to the second edition of her novel *Wise Blood* (1962): "Free will does not mean one will, but many wills conflicting in one man. Freedom cannot be conceived simply. It is a mystery, and one which a novel, even a comic novel, can only be asked to deepen." That is exactly the scope of the moral tension in Man-2: many wills conflict in one woman.

Hitchcock achieved his brilliant success through the rhythm of crosscutting and through a careful balancing of separate sets of *triads*. There are first of all the conductor, the chorus and the orchestra—all engaged calmly and collectively in the presentation of beautiful music. Then there are the impassive cymbalist, the assassin and his woman companion—all following the score and preparing for the clash of cymbals. Finally there are Jo, Ben and the prime minister—the innocent targets.

Each shot in this sequence has been carefully arranged. The audience in the hall is shown in ordered sections—stalls, grand tier, balconies. Then we see the choir and orchestra—center group, lower right section, upper right and so forth, just as we were shown the vast audience. From a view of the entire orchestra we then move to the single chair on which the cymbals rest, harmless until the assigned moment. The sequence not only reveals the minimal importance of dialogue in advancing both emotional tension and theme; the order and harmony of the music, reproduced in orderly shots of playing musicians and attentive audience, are also a forceful counterpoint to the imminent chaos. And presiding over the entirety is the conductor—Bernard Herrmann, who acts on the podium as alter ego for Hitchcock himself.

As the cantata reaches its climax, the expressionless percussionist picks up his "weapons." He grasps the second cymbal in his right hand—and the film cuts at once to the assassin removing the gun with *his* right hand, thus linking the two in an inexorable movement toward the climax. Outside, Ben tries to persuade the police to act and we cut at least twelve times to Jo, whose tear-stained face shows the agony of her decision.

At Albert Hall.

The idea of "wills clashing" in one person may be schematized in relation to the title of this movie:

Those who know too little	*Those who know too much*
Two percussionists:	
The cymbalist .... linked to .... the assassin	
Two authority figures:	
The police .... linked to .... Ben	

Thus the clash is finally expressed by the one caught in the middle—Jo—who becomes the resonating force in the confrontation between opposites.

The elements and the characters are linked further by Hitchcock's use of color. Red chairs hold the cymbals, red curtains hang over the stage and in the boxes of the assassin and prime minister. Jo stands to the right and the assassin to the left of a red curtain. Black-and-white further link them: we see the formal attire of both musician and killer, Jo's black hat and white gloves. Mr.

The escape from Ambrose Chapel.

Drayton was earlier disguised in black-and-white, as a minister preaching clichés at Ambrose Chapel. And in the embassy sequence, Mrs. Drayton wears black-and-white. Jo's scream, seen in close-up, anticipates by a fraction of a second the clash of cymbals and causes the prime minister to move slightly in his place—thus sparing his life. Ben breaks into the assassin's box, and in his attempt to escape, the man falls to the floor below and is killed.

The Albert Hall sequence is perfectly balanced and in fact fulfilled by the episode at the embassy which follows immediately; in Man-1, the concert was followed by an annoyingly anticlimactic shoot-out. Here, Hank is locked in an upstairs room with red curtains and rich wood paneling—a kind of mini–Albert Hall box, in which the child is a recapitulation of the endangered prime minister. Now Jo is the musician, accompanying herself on piano as she sings "Que Sera, Sera." And the mother figure is now Mrs. Drayton, tearful, compassionate, anxious and pacing back and forth—all the characteristics of Jo at Albert Hall. Ben here repeats the actions at Albert Hall, dashing up the stairs and breaking into the room—and Mrs. Drayton screams as Jo did before, thus saving the life of the boy as Jo had saved the life of the prime minister. Mr. Drayton at once appears, gun in hand, and now *he* is the potential assassin. But like the gunman at the concert, he too falls, this time downstairs (the assassin had fallen to a floor below) as he is killed by the gun intended for his protection.

Before the kidnapping, Ben and Jo took their son somewhat for granted, but now the family structure has taken on new meaning for them. The linear journey from America to Europe to Africa to London has ended in a double fall, and during Ben and Hank's final descent on the staircase Jo sings "We'll Love Again." The final frames return us to the hotel where the abandoned friends still await, dozing from the combined effect of cocktails and boredom. They awake happily and Ben announces calmly, "Sorry we were gone so long—we had to go over and pick up Hank."

Rich in character, plot, theme and feeling, the later version of *The Man Who Knew Too Much* remains one of America's great films. The clash of "Cymbals" referred to at the outset is really a clash of symbols: a song becomes a scream—the cry of anguish, the cry to be saved, to be reborn; a concert becomes a struggle to decide in favor of life; a man's height becomes an image of his dominance and vulnerability; and a journey to exotic ports has become an inward journey. Finally, a man who has gloried in knowing so much is disabused of his self-importance. A family has been revived by a mother's quiet courage, and there is Hank, safely repositioned between his parents in the film's final image that exactly reverses and thus fulfills its first. The lyrics of "Que Sera, Sera" have rightly become the sentiments of "We'll Love Again."

30

THE WRONG MAN

(PRODUCED AND RELEASED 1956)

Only our concept of time makes it possible for us
to speak of the Day of Judgment by that name;
in reality, it is a summary court in perpetual motion.

FRANZ KAFKA, *THE TRIAL*

Henry Fonda in the title role.

T*he Wrong Man* is based on a true story, as Hitchcock himself announces in a brief pre-credit sequence, and because it has the texture of cinema verité, lacking the color, humor and style of his preceding pictures, it's been a much unappreciated and unfairly neglected film. Uncompromising it certainly is, humorless and relentlessly grim, too. It is also a magnificently structured work— very close to true classical tragedy—and it's Hitchcock's ultimate excursion into the twilight world of Kafka.

In January 1953, a musician at New York's Stork Club named Christopher Emmanuel Balestrero (Henry Fonda) arrives home from work late one night. He looks in on two sleeping young sons, then chats briefly with his wife Rose (Vera Miles) whose expensive dental work is the latest drain on their finances. Manny (as he is always called by his family) decides to borrow money against Rose's life insurance policy. At the insurance office next day, three office workers claim that Manny is the one who recently committed armed robbery in their presence but is still at large in the community. They notify authorities, and next evening Manny is arrested as he arrives home.

Taken through the neighborhood by police detectives frantic to charge him and close the case, Manny is subjected to the capricious judgments of local merchants who have also been robbed. Most witnesses are not quite sure Manny is the right man, but— well, what the hell, he *probably* is, and people will feel so much *better* if someone's caught. The similarity of Manny's appearance and handwriting to those of the thief lead to his arrest and imprisonment on a charge of armed robbery, and he spends a harrowing night behind bars. Relatives post bail, and next day Manny is released to prepare for trial.

While being defended by a young lawyer named Frank O'Connor (Anthony Quayle), Manny watches helplessly as Rose withdraws into severe paranoia, suffers a mental breakdown, and finally must be placed in an asylum. Alone and desperate, he is encouraged by his mother (Esther Minciotti) to pray for strength. At the same time, the criminal responsible for Manny's "crimes" attempts another robbery and is captured, and Manny—the wrong man—is freed. Rose, however, must remain hospitalized.[1]

Because the scenario (written in several difficult stages by Angus MacPhail and Maxwell Anderson) was based on the facts of the case and the narrative was filmed mostly at the actual sites in Manhattan and Queens, New York, many critics and viewers have dismissed The Wrong Man as an anomaly, a simplistic distraction in the increasing complexity of Hitchcock's films from 1954. But it seems in fact a perfectly logical development, for the director

[1]The film's final shot (of a family strolling in a tropical setting) and on-screen words (that Rose was released two years later completely cured and the family lived happily ever after) were added by the studio, over Hitchcock's loud objections. In fact the Balestreros never recovered from the lived nightmare, but the truth was not permitted to interfere with Hollywood's need for a traditional happy ending in 1956.

was ever fascinated by the motif of a man trying to establish his innocence of a crime (as in *The 39 Steps, Young and Innocent, Saboteur, Spellbound,* and *To Catch a Thief*—and later, in *North by Northwest* and *Frenzy*). Whereas *The Man Who Knew Too Much* delineated the threat to family stability abroad and examined the tenuous emotional stability of a wife under pressure, *The Wrong Man* offers an urban treatment of exactly the same theme; identical dangers—not from spies but from the chaos and compression of modern living and a diseased legal machinery—lurk right at home, and once again the emotions of a loving wife and mother are very much at the center of concern. In a way, *The Wrong Man* is the logical link between the films preceding (*The Man Who Knew Too Much*) and following (*Vertigo*), for the nature of knowledge and identity is more deeply investigated in each, and breakdown, loss of control, the fear of madness, and mental illness itself are very real elements (as they will be in *Psycho* and *The Birds*).

Robert Burks's black-and-white cinematography everywhere subverts balance and objective viewpoint—indeed, this is nothing like cinema verité (much less is it documentary filmmaking): little is shown at eye level; high and low angles of vision predominate. We see what Manny sees, and we feel both his impotence in coping with a flawed police system and his growing despair for himself and his wife. As the story progresses, we are in a world increasingly off center. One false accusation wrecks his home and precipitates his wife's breakdown, and the entire cinematic movement of the picture upsets every social and psychic "balance" the camera observes. If nothing is what it appears to be, and if the judicial system is itself unstable and untrustworthy, susceptible to corruption by the police determination to "get a man at any cost" and by the careless observation of uncaring citizens, then the modern world is mired in chaos indeed. You needn't go to Morocco or to Albert Hall for trouble; stay right at home and it'll find you.

There are two acts or narrative movements in the film. The first involves the details of arrest and imprisonment, and Hitchcock's style is terrifyingly calm and straightforward. Manny is arrested on the doorstep of his home just before entering, and as he is driven away he glances back to see his wife cheerfully preparing dinner in the kitchen. She is so near and yet so far away and (since it is 1953, before laws regarding summary arrest were changed), he is not even permitted to telephone her. He then endures a grueling and humiliating police interrogation, and we watch the details of fingerprinting and his incarceration in a cell. Reduced to the status of a helpless child as the police systematically strip him of dignity, Manny's eyes (in Henry Fonda's brilliantly blank gaze of moral outrage) behold the contours of nightmare. Even when he is released on bail next morning, the experience has taken an enormous psychic toll. This is innocence (even naïveté) captured, tortured and forever bruised.

This leads to the film's second narrative movement. After attorney O'Connor is hired, we move from the physical enclosure of prison to the world of mental enclosure, as Rose's paranoia results in her total emotional collapse. As Manny and Rose travel to the countryside and to distant parts of the city in search of witnesses to testify on his behalf, and as these efforts are variously frustrated by the relocation or death of the witnesses, Rose becomes progressively more unstable, nervous and finally steeped

Rose's gradual withdrawal from reality. (Vera Miles, Henry Fonda and Anthony Quayle.)

in despair. Then, convinced that the entire tragedy was her fault, precipitated by the need to borrow money for her dental treatments, she withdraws into a world of remorse, her reason threatened.

The key scene signifying her withdrawal from reality remains one of the most frightening and poignant in the entire Hitchcock filmography. It's set in O'Connor's office, where—as the attorney and Manny discuss witnesses—we see Rose's anguished withdrawal, her sad, distant, affectless gaze. At home that night, Rose warns Manny that the only way they can conquer this nightmare is to "lock all the doors and windows, and shut everyone out. We won't ever let anyone in. No one will ever be able to find us." When he suggests she needs a doctor, she reacts violently, grabs a hairbrush and strikes a blow on his forehead. We see a split image of Fonda, reflected in a broken mirror—the refraction of his shattered image in her own broken mind—and henceforth the imperfect legal situation is tragically balanced by a more agonizing personal nightmare. The imprisonment theme is now carried over to Rose. Worst of all, when Manny is finally cleared of all charges and goes to tell Rose—in the hope of restoring her to emotional health—the final tragedy is revealed:

MANNY: I'm free now, Rose. They caught the real criminal. We can go back home now.

ROSE: That's fine for you—fine.

MANNY: Doesn't it help you, too?

ROSE: No.

MANNY: Have I done something wrong?

ROSE: No. It's nothing you've done. Nothing can help me. No one. You can go now.

MANNY: Don't you want to come with me?

ROSE: It doesn't matter where I am. Or where anybody is. It's fine for you. You can go now.

The pathos of this dialogue certainly derives from the acutely sensitive performance by Vera Miles, her expression a wash of drained and confused innocence and lost faith in everything—most of all, herself.

The shattering of an image.

. . .

Both the situation and the emotional landscape of *The Wrong Man*
recall Franz Kafka's *The Trial,* for the sense of urban compression,
impersonality and decay are dramatized in both by the proximity
of loud elevated trains and the contiguity of the attorney's office
and insurance office. Kafka and Hitchcock also share a sense of
ineluctable tragedy which depends for its effects on the use of
dialogue and setting which are intentionally banal; the human
dimensions they describe have the tone of poetic tragedy. In this
regard, perhaps the single most heartbreaking line in the film
occurs when Manny comes face-to-face with the real criminal:
they gaze at each other and Manny says with a stifled, outraged
sob in his voice, "Don't you realize what you've done to my wife?"

But the ironies don't stop here. When Manny's double is ap-
prehended, he shouts, "I haven't done anything! I have a wife and
kids waiting for me at home!" These were the words Manny used
at the beginning, and when the "right man" is sent before the
police lineup to be identified by the insurance office workers, their
sincere, certain identification of him is repeated in exactly the same

tones as when Manny was brought in. There's no guarantee, in
other words, that the "right man" is indeed so. We know nothing
of this new suspect except that he attempts one armed robbery at
the end; whether he is guilty of the *other* robberies—or that with
which Manny was charged—is not established. It's possible, therefore, that the entire tragedy may be repeated with another cast.
Who, after all, *is* the right or wrong man? and in what social or
spiritual dimension? For Hitchcock, as for Manny and Rose, the
answers are not so simple as the police would have us believe.

31

VERTIGO

(PRODUCED 1957, RELEASED 1958)

We die with the dying:
See, they depart, and we go with them.
We are born with the dead:
See, they return, and bring us with them.

T. S. ELIOT, *FOUR QUARTETS*

Judy, disguised as Madeleine, pretending suicide.

Often critics speak and write as if their interpretations were the last word, presuming that their insights, like bridges from artists to audiences, close the door to meaning, and thenceforth no dog should bark. But that should be very far indeed from the function of the interpreter. Obviously, the ardor a critic brings to the study and discussion of certain works reveals much about the critic himself, and in setting forth particular themes, images, ideas and concerns in the art of Alfred Hitchcock—works everywhere full of passion—there is no escaping a certain self-discovery and self-revelation. To such dangers the act of interpretation is always prey. But it is precisely the act of interpretation—of disclosing possibilities of meaning not only for the work itself but, more important, for the work's resonance in the viewer—that interprets the interpreter to himself. And if the interpreter does his task well, then the very interpretation may open up the work—and the viewer—to himself. By such connections art lives, not merely as a static, self-contained entity, but as a reality that furthers the humanizing process, that survives the specifics of its own time and place, that enables a viewer to feel yes, some of life is like that. Some of *my* life is like that—or could be—and yes, at its darkest and most fragile, life is in danger of *becoming* like that. The task of criticism, then, should only bring us back to the beginning, to the work of art itself. Here is offered, then, a schematized treatment of what this author considers Alfred Hitchcock's great masterpiece, *Vertigo*.

San Francisco detective John "Scottie" Ferguson (James Stewart) discovers his acrophobia—a pathological dread of heights—when a police colleague falls to his death during a rooftop chase after a suspect. The condition leads to vertigo, a psychosomatic illness which produces dizziness and a sensation of spinning in space—a frightening but strangely pleasurable experience.

Forced because of this condition to resign from work, Scottie is asked by his old schoolmate Gavin Elster (Tom Helmore) to follow his wife Madeleine (Kim Novak) who, Elster says, believes that she is possessed by the spirit of a long-dead relative who is driving her to repeat the dead woman's suicide. At first reluctantly, but then willingly, because of the woman's great beauty, Scottie takes on the assignment; after he saves her from drowning when she throws herself into San Francisco Bay, it is clear that they are falling in love. Then, because of his terror of heights, he cannot climb a church tower to save her when she hurls herself to death. Overwhelmed by the loss of his beloved and by insupportable guilt, Scottie suffers a complete mental breakdown and must be put in an asylum—an illness which even his close friend and former fiancée Midge Wood (Barbara Bel Geddes) is powerless to prevent or to help.

After his recovery, Scottie accidentally meets a San Francisco shopgirl who bears a striking resemblance to the elegant blond

Madeleine Elster: the redhead Judy Barton, however, is a store clerk who lives in a Post Street hotel. Fascinated by her resemblance to the dead woman, Scottie becomes obsessed with her, and she seems responsive to his attention and generosity. He then begins to change her into the image of Madeleine, dressing her in Madeleine's wardrobe and asking that she alter her hair color. Desperate for Scottie's love, Judy reluctantly agrees to the transformation.

But then in a flashback we learn—before Scottie suspects—that Judy was in fact the girl who played the role of Madeleine Elster. She was really Gavin's mistress, a participant in a carefully contrived plot to kill his wife by strangling her, then throwing her body from a church tower while Judy, trained and dressed as her double, ran to the spot. Scottie had been set up as a witness to Madeleine's "suicide," which masked her murder; his vertigo prevented his climb to the tower.[1]

Scottie finally guesses the truth when Judy inadvertently wears a necklace that had belonged to Madeleine, a copy of one worn in a portrait of a long-dead ancestor. Humiliated, enraged and unbalanced by the realization that his great love was a great illusion, he forces Judy back to the church tower and forces her to admit the truth. There, the girl, frightened by footsteps in the dark, trips and falls from the tower to her death.

Based on the novel *D'entre les morts* (reprinted as *Sueurs froides,* or *Vertigo*) by Pierre Boileau and Thomas Narcejac, *Vertigo* was originally called by its French title, *From Amongst the Dead;* its final designation came from Hitchcock, despite executives' coolness to what they considered a fancy word. The project was enormously difficult from conception to final cut (details of which may be found in this author's biography of Hitchcock, *The Dark Side of Genius*), and at least two drafts of the screenplay—by Maxwell Anderson and Alec Coppel—were found to be unshootable until playwright Samuel Taylor was engaged. His collaboration with Hitchcock resulted in a scenario of great beauty and subtlety.

[1] Although Judy-as-Madeleine is indeed not the *real* Madeleine Elster—whom we never see—I shall refer to her assumed identity by Judy simply as Madeleine, without the awkward quotation marks otherwise necessary to indicate that the Madeleine we see is of course not the real Madeleine at all.

James Stewart and Barbara Bel Geddes.

"When I arrived," Taylor recalled years later,

I deliberately did not read the original novel or screenplay. The story had already been worked out by Hitchcock, and I wanted to concentrate on what he wanted, not what the book had. He had already determined what he wanted to do, and he and James Stewart were ready to go—all they needed was a script. The metaphysical implications of the story, which were discussed to a great extent, were more in Hitchcock's mind than in Coppel's treatment, and I said that in order to realize them we would have to personalize the characters. So I rewrote the screenplay completely. I invented the character of Midge because I realized that we needed her to get the story going, and I tried to make Scottie a human being. Hitchcock and I did a

lot of location-scouting together, and I spent two or three days
at San Juan Bautista, exploring the countryside and the mission
and absorbing the spirit of the place. I sat down every day
with Hitchcock and worked it out step-by-step. I suggested
to him the drive under Fort Point, but most of the scenes—
the graveyard sequence, for example—were already in Hitchcock's mind. The long silences are his, the camera movements
are his. He was always the focal point and the motivating factor
in the production. Working with him meant writing with him.
He never claims to be a writer, but he does write. A screenplay
for Hitchcock is a collaboration, and that is extremely rare. He
is the quintessence of what the French call the *auteur*. I gave
him the characters and the dialogue he needed and developed
the story, but *Vertigo* was from first frame to last his film.
There was no moment he wasn't there. And anyone who saw
him during the making of the film could see, as I did, that he
felt it very deeply indeed.

Vertigo continues to impress moviegoers, students and filmmakers,
Taylor felt, "because it's really a very human story—bizarre, but
really human. It takes place in the mind of the viewer and very
quickly becomes more than merely a good yarn."

Often (and ungallantly) Hitchcock spoke of his dissatisfaction with
Kim Novak's performance—primarily because his first choice,
Vera Miles, became pregnant when production was so long delayed—and the Hitchcock-Novak collaboration was difficult because of what he called her "preconceived notions." And the
author of this book had numerous friendly arguments with Hitchcock, who refused to see that Novak was in fact ideal for the role,
as Taylor elaborated: "If we'd had a brilliant and famous actress
who really created two distinctly different people for Madeleine
and Judy, it would not have been as good"—nor in fact as credible,
since Judy is supposed to be a simple, transplanted Kansas shopgirl,
not a brilliant charlatan who can so easily and convincingly alter
her entire personality. "She seemed so naive in the part," Taylor
concluded, "and that was good. She was always believable. There
was no 'art' about it, and that's why it worked so well."

James Stewart's appearance was set from the start, and not

The pursuit: first to the flower shop . . . then to the cemetery garden.

Scottie peers at Carlotta Valdes' headstone.

only because he and Alfred Hitchcock had the same agent and shared the production's profits; he was perfectly cast as the sympathetic but profoundly troubled romantic who at once has the audience's sympathies but whose image suggests a kind of dark earnestness and naïveté rather than slick glamour. Tom Helmore had been a distinguished actor in British and American films and plays, and in fact his work with Hitchcock dated back to *The Ring* (1927), in which he played a challenger to the hero. Later, Helmore made two brief appearances as a young officer in *Secret Agent* (1936), and perhaps because of his recent stage success in Los Angeles as the manipulative misogynist Henry Higgins in *My Fair Lady,* Hitchcock cast him as the elegant Gavin Elster. This character is the latest in the tradition of Hitchcock's smooth, handsome villains (a long list that includes Godfrey Tearle in *The 39 Steps,* Paul Lukas in *The Lady Vanishes,* Herbert Marshall in *Foreign Correspondent,* Joseph Cotten in *Shadow of a Doubt,* Leo G. Carroll in *Spellbound,* Robert Walker in *Strangers on a Train* and Ray Milland in *Dial M for Murder*).

The recollections of people involved in the 1957 filming of *Vertigo* reveal Hitchcock's meticulous concern for detail. At the florist Podesta Baldocchi (then at 224 Grant Avenue, San Francisco), Kenneth Clopine worked with the director on the design of the nosegay and the arrangement of all the flowers in the window; an interior sequence was also filmed there. On an autumn Sunday in 1957, Clopine recalled, the actors, crew and director assembled.

> Hitchcock was very particular about the customers in the store and about the traffic outside. He spoke with the police and then picked out each car and truck that passed outside—the color, the size, he selected each one. The mirrors in the store had to be hung with black drapes to prevent reflections, and the lights caused such intense heat that the sprinkler system went on. An artificial door was constructed at the rear of the store, through which Stewart could look in at Novak, as if from a rear alley—which the real store did not have. That artificial door was not used after all, because the production designer (Henry Bumstead) determined it was too large. That moment was recreated back in Hollywood. And the alley be-

hind Sloane's, on Claude Street, was used to suggest the back entrance to the store. Everyone worked for twelve hours that day—for a minute of final film.

The dress salon at Ransohoff's, an elegant department store then at 259 Post Street, was recreated back at Paramount Studios; there the director and his cast spent three days, according to Ruth Sinclair and Bobbie Rutledge, longtime employees. Minute room measurements and designs of salons were taken, and the store lighting was carefully noted. Similar visits were made to the Empire Hotel on Post Street (later the York Hotel), where the character Judy Barton lived: corridors and rooms were measured, photographed and meticulously recreated later. And at the California Palace of the Legion of Honor, a guard remembered that Hitchcock took a week to shoot the brief, wordless scenes there, and that he consulted the museum's curator while the crew waited for the proper light, entering the translucent glass ceiling, to com-

The rescue at Fort Point.

bine with electric lighting for the final perfect effect. California's State Park authority has published a brochure on San Juan Bautista mission and it historic park and buildings ("the setting for Alfred Hitchcock's movie *Vertigo,*" it proclaims). The church was completed in 1812, but the original steeple was demolished after a fire. When Hitchcock arrived, there was no bell tower, so the interior had to be constructed in Hollywood, and for the exterior a trick matte shot was created, carefully painted in.

Many critics and admirers of Hitchcock have written about *Vertigo,* with varying degrees of success. Robin Wood's early essay (in his provocative little book *Hitchcock's Films*), despite some minor errors of continuity, was gracefully provocative and every enthusiast owes him gratitude for his pioneering appreciation of this director. Representative of the more common and sloppier kind of writing about movies was Raymond Durgnat's essay on *Vertigo* in his confused and confusing book *The Strange Case of Alfred Hitchcock*. Durgnat sets the story in Los Angeles, which is more than a mere geographical gaffe and loses a great deal of the film's significance. He also makes the crucial error that Madeleine's

The first meeting.

Tom Helmore and James Stewart.

suicide attempt occurs at an advanced stage of her affair with Scottie: in fact, of course, it happens before they meet or exchange a word. He also concocted the odd idea that the real Madeleine Elster was confined to a mental institution, but here he is wrong again: we are simply told that "she lives in the country and rarely comes to town." Durgnat also criticizes *Vertigo* for major implausibility in the fact that Gavin Elster could remember Scottie's vertigo affliction after twenty years. But in the film Elster tells Scottie that he has just read all about the recent tragedy and Scottie's *recently discovered* vertigo in the local newspapers. It's hard to take seriously any film analysis (and impossible to call it "scholarship") which deals so carelessly with the content of the picture itself.

The transformation from the French novel to the American film reveals many significant and deliberate developments, all of them serving Hitchcock's intentions. The book's Paul Gévigne—an un-

Amid the sequoias.

attractive, greasy villain—has become the elegant and successful Gavin Elster. The brunette Madeleine has become the typically blond Hitchcock doll. Pauline Lagerlac has been renamed Carlotta Valdes and given Spanish-American ancestry. Also in *D'entre les morts,* detective Roger Flavières, fully aware of his vertigo at the outset, fails to apprehend a criminal and sends an assistant to his death. In *Vertigo,* however, Scottie's discovery of his condition is an accident, simultaneous with the moment of crisis. Hitchcock thus obliterates Scottie's guilt and makes him more sympathetic than Flavières. The book has no equivalent for the film's forest sequence, for its spiritual theme of "wandering," or for the crucial theme that Madeleine is an unrealized aspect of Judy's own personality. The novel dwells on the World War II ambience (which Hitchcock has completely excised) and contains no final retributive fall, no return to a church tower. Flavières simply strangles Renée (Judy) on a sofa and the novel ends with the crazed man promising somehow to wait for her.

Hitchcock's treatment of the story has, among its roots, the ancient legend of Pygmalion and Galatea. According to the Roman poet Ovid, Pygmalion was a gifted young sculptor who (like Scottie) never married because he detested the blemishes and faults nature gave women. He resolved to fashion the image of a perfect woman to show other men the deficiencies they must endure. But poor Pygmalion went too far with his statue and discovered that he had fallen in love with his own creation.

The legend of Tristan and Isolde is also relevant. When Isolde marries King Mark, the heartbroken Tristan weds another woman named Isolde to keep alive the memory of his former love. The end is tragic, climaxing in Tristan's death and the first Isolde's suicide. The link between love and death—echoed in legend, literature and art—is apposite to *Vertigo;* and Bernard Herrmann's lush, symphonic score for the film—arguably one of the finest musical contributions to the medium—more than once recalls the "Liebestod" from Wagner's *Tristan und Isolde.*

Vertigo opens to the strains of Herrmann's haunting prelude, as the camera draws in to a close-up of a woman's face, moving from her lips to her eyes as she glances anxiously from left to right. The face is oddly characterless, and the camera moves to a tight shot of her right eye. Then Saul Bass's psychedelic patterns— prophetic of popular designs to come in the 1960s—emerge as the camera seems to enter the woman's pupil. This image, which will reoccur in *Psycho* after the shower murder, is especially important in *Vertigo*. During the credits, the screen is gradually filled with multicolored spirals of red, purple, blue, lavender, aqua, green, indigo, puce, gold, red, yellow, and, finally, a blazing red as the shapes fade back into the pupil.

The image of the spiral is more than an innovative and arresting design suggesting the dizziness of vertigo: it is the basic image on which the entire structure and design of the picture are based. The winding staircase of the bell tower at the mission, the twists and turns of the cemetery walk, the spiraling dark hair in the portrait of Carlotta Valdes (and, in imitation of that, Madeleine's and Judy's hair); the spiraling downward journey of the two cars on San Francisco's hilly, vertiginous streets, the rings of the tree in the forest, the camera's encircling Judy during the letter-writing scene—all these swirling motions create and sustain the halluci- natory, dreamlike effect of the film, the condition of vertigo with

One of Hitchcock's famous trick shots: the simultaneous forward zoom and reverse tracking shot of the miniature of the stairwell, doubled with a shot of Stewart descending a short flight of steps.

which Scottie is afflicted. The geometry of the film is itself vertiginous: set in America's most vertical city, the manner of the film entirely threatens verticality itself. The condition, after all, is described as the fear of falling and the desire to fall; the longing for risk and the fear of loss; the desire to die and the terror of death; the fear of losing balance and control and the concomitant desire to swoon, to pass away, to lose life itself in the pursuit of love. The technique of moving from outside the face to within the eye—the ultimate of Hitchcock's preferred opening, from a city overview to a single room—sets a pattern for every sequence in the film that follows. The camera invariably moves from exteriors to interiors, night scenes alternate with daylight sequences.

The structure of *Vertigo,* in other words, is vertiginous circularity itself. And in this regard, the city of steep hills, of sudden rises and falls, of high climbs and dizzying drops, is appropriate for this story in another sense: it is the city most obviously poised between a romantic-Victorian past and the rush of present-day life. Aptly, Hitchcock has drenched his film in atmosphere and has exploited all the mysterious, dreamlike settings of the city: old Fort Point, directly under the southern end of Golden Gate Bridge; the Legion of Honor Palace; the Palace of Fine Arts; an old house at Eddy and Gough Streets; the old Mission Dolores. In *Vertigo* these old settings seem precariously balanced with modern technology, and although the full effects of its collective past are felt there is an unavoidable sense of things decaying, with no sure center for the future.

After the last title, a single horizontal line appears against an indefinite background. The camera pulls back, showing it to be an iron bar, the top rung of a ladder on a fire escape, which a man's hand at once seizes. He leaps onto a roof and a chase follows: a policeman fires a revolver and a plainclothes detective (Scottie) follows in swift pursuit. This opening shot in fact establishes the entire premise of the film—the pursuit of an unknown person we never see again. (Interestingly, that is also the motif of the next two Hitchcock films, *North by Northwest* and *Psycho,* both of which have at their center a nonexistent person.) In the background, across the rooftops, blink the red and green lights which are soon to assume significance—not only as the film's two primary and constantly recurring colors but also as markers of the stop-and-go, cyclic, hallucinatory, romantic dreamworld of the story. Suddenly, an accident occurs: the detective misses a broad jump between buildings to an adjacent roof and clings to a gutter hanging from a Spanish-tiled roof. Hanging tentatively high above a noisy street, he (and we) are at once pitched into the film's first terror.

Scottie looks down, and the first of Hitchcock's extraordinary combination of forward zoom and reverse-tracking shots conveys at once a sense of vertigo. (The camera movement will occur again when Scottie tries to overcome his vertigo by practicing with a stepladder in Midge's apartment, and of course at the time of Madeleine's death.) "Give me your hand!" urges the policeman, straining to reach the paralyzed Scottie. There follows the first of three falls and three piercing screams as the policeman plunges to his death, leaving Scottie clinging to the weakening gutter.[2] *Vertigo* postulates the precarious verticality of human existence and experience.

This opening pursuit of an unknown person begins a film that is henceforth a slow, dreamlike pursuit that accelerates at two points—at the seashore (when Madeleine runs away from Scottie) and at the mission (her rush to the tower). The movement of the camera in the first half of the film, as established in the rooftop prologue, is from right to left; the camera pans in that direction in Midge's apartment, at Ernie's Restaurant and in the downhill journeys of Scottie's and Madeleine's cars. In the second half of the film, that direction is reversed, establishing a new pattern of movement. Immediately following the death of Madeleine, the scene opens on the mission church's arcade, and the camera moves from left to right across to the Plaza Courthouse. Later, the left-right pattern is maintained in the sweep across the city skyline

---

[2]Leonard South, a longtime member of Hitchcock's technical crew and director of photography for *Family Plot*, recalled that the policeman's fall, like that of Fry at the end of *Saboteur* and Jeffries in *Rear Window*, was achieved by double printing: first, an actor was dropped from a height onto mattresses and rubber padding. Then in the laboratory, miniatures of the background were painted in and the second take was made (alternatively, an actor could be positioned in a swiveling chair and the camera swung up and away from him, with the additional painting done as described). This use of the so-called "traveling matte shot" was perfected by Albert Whitlock, an artist who worked with Hitchcock in London, came to work for Disney, and then contributed very much to Hitchcock's films.

after Scottie's mental collapse and in his pursuit and transformation of Judy.

The first part of the story opens in Midge's apartment, where she and Scottie are photographed in mostly separate shots—he in a chair, she at her easel. In this sequence, the dialogue is not merely expository: Scottie, we note, tends to end each question with the word "Remember?" He's a man drawn ineluctably into the past—a man (as Hitchcock's careful close-ups of Midge's reactions testify) who has been afraid of intimacy and commitment, who broke off his engagement with Midge. Most significant is Midge's conclusion to the discussion of a possible cure for his vertigo: " You're not going to go diving off another rooftop to find out!" He will do just that in his dream after losing Madeleine, and the final shot of the film suggests death as the only cure. In this same sequence, Hitchcock demonstrated one of the most carefully prepared aspects of his films: every sound effect had a cue, nothing was left to

Henry Jones in the courtroom sequence.

chance or a sound editor, every item was marked in the script. In this regard, it's important to remember that *Vertigo* has long periods without dialogue, with only Herrmann's brilliant score and Hitchcock's ambient sound effects. The film is, after all, like a dream, an oxymoronic "slow chase," with all the aural evocations of memory, desire, obsession and loss.

If one seeks a single word to describe the world of the Hitchcock films of this time it might indeed be "loss": the loss of a good reputation in a straitlaced town (*The Trouble with Harry*); the loss of family security (*The Man Who Knew Too Much*); the loss of innocence and sanity (*The Wrong Man*); the loss of identity itself (*Vertigo* and *North by Northwest*); the annihilation of personality (*Psycho*); the fear of abandonment and the concomitant loss of love (*The Birds*); and finally, all of these taken together (*Marnie*).

Into his film score for *Vertigo,* Herrmann inserted a selection from Mozart—the second movement of the thirty-fourth symphony, played on a phonograph in an attempt to help Scottie's recovery at the asylum (the script calls for a bit of Mozart, "the broom that sweeps the cobwebs away"). Elsewhere the score evokes a lost world of California's Spanish past, variations on the Magic Fire music from *Die Walküre* and on the "Liebestod" from *Tristan und Isolde.* Memories and dreams and fragments of hope float like lily pads in *Vertigo;* aptly, then, the sounds of the film, beginning in the sequence in Midge's apartment, are elusive, lonely sounds, fragile and ghostly sounds—a ship's horn, echoing mournfully in the San Francisco fog; whispers and muffled conversations in public places like restaurants and stores; hollow footsteps on a cemetery garden path.

In the next sequence (and after an exterior establishing shot of the shipbuilders' offices at the Embarcadero, where Hitchcock makes his ritual cameo as a pedestrian with a trumpet case), Scottie meets Gavin Elster, who is certainly not "on the bum," as Midge suspected. He is a man, he says, who has assumed responsibilities—just as Scottie later tells Madeleine that, having saved her life, he is responsible for it. "The things that spell San Francisco to me are disappearing fast," Elster complains quietly and, referring to the old maps and woodcuts in his office, he continues, "I should have liked to have lived here then—color, excitement, power, freedom." The words "power" and "freedom" will be repeated twice later at critical junctures in this film: Pop Liebl, at the Argosy Bookstore, refers to the man who used and discarded Carlotta Valdes (as Elster uses and discards Judy Barton) by saying: "Men could do that in those days—they had the power and the freedom." And in the last sequence of the film, Scottie refers to Gavin's abuse of Judy by saying, "Oh, Judy, with all his wife's money, and all that freedom and power, he ditched you." As once used by the father of Carlotta's child, as exploited by Elster and as exerted by Scottie over Judy, power invariably precipitates trag-edy and subverts freedom. And the sadness of the old things "dis-appearing past" is deliberately introduced to effect in Scottie (and in us who are urged to identify with him) a nostalgia for a bygone era.

Speaking of his concern for his wife, Elster asks Scottie, "Do you believe that someone out of the past, someone dead, can enter and take possession of a living being?" This refers not only to Carlotta Valdes's apparent possession of Madeleine Elster, but also to the effect the dead Madeleine has on Scottie, as well as on Judy as Scottie transforms her. It also foreshadows the last seconds of the film, when the figure of the ghostly nun rising as if from the past or the grave suggests the avenging Carlotta or Madeleine. Perhaps most of all, the question looks forward to Hitchcock's *Psycho,* when "someone out of the past, someone dead" will indeed "enter and take possession of a living being."

When Elster describes his wife's mental state, he says signifi-cantly, "And she wanders—God knows where she wanders." This introduces a major theme of the film, the idea of "wandering" mentioned many times later by both Scottie and Madeleine. It describes their inner as well as their outer lives, their physical restlessness and their spiritual rootlessness. Scottie pursues an elu-sive romantic ideal that turns out to be a fraud; Judy, seeking a new life in California after an unhappy home life in Kansas, is exploited twice by men who, seeing her, are reminded of others— men with power and freedom. These two are archetypal wan-derers, each of them primed for disappointment, set up for grief. Never before or since has Hitchcock so insisted on the tragic— yet recognizably human—nature of his characters.

. . .

After an exterior nighttime establishing shot at Ernie's Restaurant—a lovely Victorian landmark—we move inside. Night is, of course, the right time for the first dreamlike, wordless appearance of Madeleine—the new Isolde, the new Galatea, the new Queen of the Night. (Scottie, however, will see only a new Juliet.) We see him seated at the bar, and he turns round to glance at Elster and Madeleine. In one of the most rapturous camera movements in Hitchcock's films, accompanied by Herrmann's voluptuous score, the camera pans leisurely along the paneled and red walls of the dining room, from right to left, finally stopping and tracking toward a lovely blond woman, her back to us and her profile slightly turned. At once, we're totally involved. There is something statuesque about her, something eminently desirable and yet infinitely remote, the quintessence of the mystery of Woman. Red and white flowers decorate the dining room (they will be the colors of the nosegay Madeleine buys in imitation of the flowers in the portrait of Carlotta, and they will be in the plaster decoration in Judy Barton's hotel room). As the couple prepare to depart, Madeleine moves forward toward us, seeming to glide rather than walk, out of a rich background into a haze of light, stopping just long enough for Scottie to see her exquisite profile; a matched profile shot of *him* concludes the scene.

The color coordinates in this scene are of considerable significance, each of them worked out carefully by Hitchcock and included in his notes and final shooting script. Madeleine wears a black evening gown with a lustrous green stole in a room with red walls. Later, in Scottie's apartment, he wears a green sweater and she wears his red robe; the appointments of the room are also red (the front door, the cushions, the draperies) and green (the ice bucket, other cushions). Afterward, his walk through Union Square is punctuated by the blinking red and green traffic lights; Judy will appear with dyed red hair and wear a green dress; Madeleine's car is green; and Hitchcock (as he confirmed) selected the Empire Hotel because of its green neon sign, which he reflected in the rooms and on the characters—green being, in stage tradition, the color for the appearance of ghosts. The reiteration and transference of these two colors link the two characters and suggest the up/down, stop/go bipolarity which is itself vertiginous.

The scene in Ernie's immediately rouses the audience's expectation of romance. There is something sensuous yet aloof about this woman, and we (with Scottie) want to pursue her. Yet something prevents us, something says she is unattainable, perhaps even slightly unreal. That is precisely the vertigo—the desire to let go, to fall, to float through space, combined with the fear of falling. The real world (indicated by constant background voices at Ernie's, the sounds of dinnerware and of glasses clinking) tries to press in on Scottie's accelerating fantasy.

Just as the film opened with a fast chase, there now begins the first long, fluid, slow and silent pursuit of Madeleine by Scottie around the city as his work of "detecting" takes on another dimension. The silence and Herrmann's mysteriously provocative "search" music create an atmosphere of hushed romanticism. The sequence occurs entirely in broad daylight as Scottie follows Madeleine (dressed in a gray suit, Hitchcock insisted, so that she would look "as if she just stepped out of the San Francisco fog") as she drives from her apartment (the Brocklebank, Nob Hill). The journey is downhill, left, right, left, a descending spiral, until she arrives at the rear door of a florist, where—still from his viewpoint, since the entire pursuit is meant to identify us with Scottie— we behold her in the shop, surrounded by flowers and by piles of green boxes. Purchasing a red and white nosegay and carrying her black coat, she departs.

The pursuit continues, to Mission Dolores (founded in 1776) and its cemetery garden where, in soft, washed-out colors of an almost surreal loveliness, Scottie follows Madeleine and sees that she has visited the grave of Carlotta Valdes (whose dates are 1831–1857). Of this sequence Hitchcock was particularly proud, as he told the author: "I diffused it, you know. I gave it a kind of undefined outline. I wanted to put a feeling onto it." The walled cemetery garden separates Scottie and Madeleine from the world, and this daylight sequence is something of a retreat into the past, a kind of tryst with death. In a carefully composed shot of great beauty, we see (still from Scottie's viewpoint) Madeleine standing before a gravestone, surrounded by a bank of red flowers and clutching to her heart the small nosegay—the gesture will be repeated (without the flowers) in the redwood forest and in the stable at San Juan Bautista.

With only the music and sound effects, the pursuit continues, as Scottie follows Madeleine to the Palace of the Legion of Honor, where she sits before the portrait of Carlotta as if hypnotized. From there we go on to the McKittrick Hotel, where there occurs perhaps the strangest moment in the film, for it appears that Madeleine has never been there at all. Any logical explanation—that the two women were in collusion or that Madeleine escaped through a rear door—is not supported by the script or the atmosphere up to this point. Hitchcock called this "icebox talk"— the point suddenly occurring to people when they returned home from a movie and were rummaging through the refrigerator for a snack. At this point in *Vertigo,* it is enough that Madeleine is in fact something of a phantom, a ghost—indeed, she is a fraud.

From these dreamy sequences we move back to the world of solid reality—Midge's apartment, where she suggests that a good authority on old San Francisco lore is Pop Liebl at the Argosy Bookstore. There, Liebl (Konstantin Shayne) tells the story of Carlotta Valdes. "The beautiful Carlotta, the sad Carlotta," from the area around San Juan Bautista, taken by a rich and powerful man who built for her the great house (now the McKittrick Hotel). He fathered her child, then tossed her aside and kept the child; as a result, she became a poor, wandering madwoman who eventually died by her own hand. "Poor thing," Midge says with feeling (the same comment spoken after Madeleine's death, by the woman Scottie later meets outside Elster's apartment; the phrase "poor thing," applied to a woman in distress, occurs some two hundred times in Hitchcock's films).

When Scottie returns Midge to her apartment, she mocks the idea that Carlotta has returned from the dead to possess Elster's beautiful wife, and in a splendid example of audience manipulation we resent her rejection of this idea. So insistently and with such irresistible romanticism has the idea been proposed to us—and so much do we want Scottie to be Madeleine's savior (and lover)— that we have accepted the fantastic theory and dismiss Midge's logical positivism. For Scottie and for us, the dream is taking over, gaining acceptance as reality. "Anyone," as Scottie says to Elster in the following sequence at Elster's club, "could become obsessed with the past with a background like that!" This is, of course, precisely what is happening to Scottie himself.

The next sequence shows Scottie following Madeleine again to the Legion of Honor Palace, and then there occurs the "suicide attempt" and his rescue of her. (It may occur to readers already familiar with Hitchcock's work that women who throw themselves into water are an oddly recurring motif from the suicide attempt Hitchcock added to *The Skin Game* in 1931 to the rumor about Melanie Daniels and the fountains of Rome in *The Birds* and *Marnie*'s suicide attempt in the swimming pool aboard ship.)

The first conversation between Scottie and Madeleine occurs in his apartment when she awakens, and it's a dialogue of great poignancy—especially in light of our later knowledge that this is really Judy Barton. Her talk about living alone, her loneliness ("One shouldn't live alone, it's wrong") and her great sad gazes take on considerable gravity after we know the truth. There is also much talk about wandering—their mutual occupation—and then, just as she did at the McKittrick Hotel, Madeleine mysteriously vanishes.

Next day, Scottie follows her again—but this time she leads him straight back to his own apartment (at the corner of Lombard and Jones). She has come to leave a note of thanks, they again discuss wandering around, and then agree to wander together. Their journey takes them to the giant redwood forest at Big Basin:

> SCOTTIE: Their true name is *Sequoia sempervirens*—always green, ever living . . . What are you thinking?
> MADELEINE: Of all the people who've been born and who died while the trees went on living . . . I don't like it, knowing I have to die.

They approach a felled cross section of an ancient tree, the rings marked at key times of history from the birth of Christ to the twentieth century. "Somewhere in here I was born," she says, tracing her glove finger across the span of an earlier century, "and there I died. It was only a moment for you, you took no notice." Is she speaking as Madeleine or Judy? Or pretending to be Carlotta speaking to her lover? Or Judy speaking to Gavin? This entire sequence must be doubly reevaluated later in light of the revealed truth, for since we learn that Judy Barton is falling in love with Scottie Ferguson, she at this point hesitates to continue with the scheme that will not only exploit him but lead to her "death," for once Madeleine is gone there will be no more use for Judy in Scottie's life.

Good detective that he is, he pries her with questions: "Tell me," he urges as she leans against a tree, struggling for breath and clutching her heart in the gesture familiar from the cemetery garden. "When were you born? Where? Tell me! Why did you jump?" But she hesitates to answer (and later we learn why): "I can't tell you. Please don't ask me any more questions. Take me away from here, somewhere in the light. Promise me you won't ask me again, please promise me!"

The first kiss at the seashore follows at once, after Scottie expresses his commitment of responsibility for her life and she recounts her dream: "It's as though I were walking down a long corridor that was mirrored, and fragments of that mirror still hang there. When I come to the end of the corridor, there's nothing but darkness. And I know that when I walk into the darkness, I'll die. I've never come to the end. I've always come back before then. And a room. I remember a room. I sit there alone, always alone—and a grave, an open grave. I stand by the gravestone looking down into it. It's new and clean and waiting." She rushes toward the shore but Scottie catches her; sobbing, she claims she's *not* mad, and he kisses her passionately. "Keep me safe," she begs. "I'm here," he replies. "I've got you." The impossible dream is now ineluctable fact, as both they and we seem satisfied that love will redeem them from whatever powers of destruction threaten.

The scene in Midge's apartment follows, in which she takes the extreme measure of trying to shock her friend from his romantic illusions by drawing a caricature of the portrait of Carlotta with her own grinning, bespectacled face. But her attempt strikes too close to his nerve; with Madeleine the world of reality retreats, and Scottie departs. At his home very late that night Madeleine arrives and continues with her dream: "I saw a tower, a bell, an old Spanish village, a square, a green with trees and an old whitewashed Spanish church with a cloister. Across the green there was a big gray wooden house with a porch and shutters, a balcony, a small garden and next to it a livery stable with carriages lined up inside. At the end of the green there was a lovely whitewashed stone house with a pepper tree." Scottie interrupts exultantly: this is no dream, she has just described the perfectly preserved old Spanish-American mission San Juan Bautista, ninety miles south of San Francisco. "It's no dream, Madeleine! You've been there!" He will take her there next day and her bad dreams will cease, he insists.

On a clear beautiful morning, they drive south in Scottie's car. (On Madeleine's gray suit is pinned a gold mockingbird, for which the German word is *Elster*. Not only is this apt for Hitchcock's lifelong theme of the birds of chaos, but of course this Madeleine *is* a "mocking bird," one woman imitating another.) Once they are inside the Plaza Stable, Madeleine is seated in an unused antique carriage, clutching her heart a third time and looking blankly ahead. But try though he might to break through her apparent delusions, she seems focused on some distant goal. "Try, Madeleine," he begs as they kiss. "Try for me." She protests, "No, it's too late, there's something I must do"—and later we know that of course Gavin Elster is waiting atop the tower with the dead body of the real Madeleine, and she must fulfill her part of the bargain, follow through with the nefarious scheme to its bitter end. There is virtually a giveaway as she cries to Scottie, "It's too late! Look, it's not fair! It wasn't supposed to happen this way! It *shouldn't* have happened this way. Let me go! You believe I love you. Then if you lose me, you'll know I loved you and wanted to go on loving you." This entire speech has a double meaning after we know the truth. There follows her race up the tower stairs and his abortive attempt to save her.

The fade-in after her "death" begins with a long, slow pan (left to right, now) from the church colonnade to the town hall, where there concludes the inquest by the presiding official (Henry Jones). After the jury reports that Madeleine Elster "killed herself while in a state of unsound mind," Gavin approaches Scottie: "It was my responsibility. I shouldn't have got you involved . . . Good-bye, Scottie. There's no way for them to understand. You and I know who killed Madeleine."

Next day, Scottie visits Madeleine's grave and later endures a terrible nightmare precipitating complete mental breakdown from guilt and loss. The dream begins as Madeleine's nosegay turns to a crude cartoon. For a moment, Scottie's subconscious suspicion of the truth emerges in his nightmare, as he sees Elster embrace Carlotta Valdes and she turns toward Scottie. He then walks down a long corridor and enacts the dream Madeleine describes: he stares into an open grave at the Mission Dolores cemetery garden and, with arms spread open as if embracing his beloved in death (his precise gesture in the last shot of the film), he falls into the open grave. The vertigo has logically become his own attraction toward death as release, and death as union with Madeleine. Scottie is, in the final analysis, a man who has courted death and kept faith with images of a dead past which lures and intrigues him. (The complexity of this theme is classic and is found in myth and literature from Pyramus and Thisbe through Romeo and Juliet to Tristan and Isolde.)

The hospital sequence establishes Scottie's breakdown (a poignant and terrible motif in Hitchcock, recurring from *Shadow of a Doubt*

The nightmare sequence.

through *Under Capricorn, The Man Who Knew Too Much, The Wrong Man, Psycho, The Birds* and *Marnie*). As Scottie sits withdrawn, unaware of Midge's attempt to comfort and assist, she tries to be brave and amusing, and the scene is played by Barbara Bel Geddes with enormous sensitivity. After a vain attempt at small talk, she comes to embrace him: "Please try, Johnny. You're not lost—Mother's here . . . You don't even know I'm here, do you? Well, I'm here." Moments later, the doctor describes Ferguson's condition as "acute melancholia, together with a guilt complex" over the woman's death to which Midge wisely adds, "He was in love with her—and he still is." She slowly leaves the hospital, walking away from us down a dark corridor. The scene fades and we never again see the single person capable of disrupting Scottie's impossible illusions.

After a slow fade-out and fade-in, Hitchcock suggests a passage of some time. Now Scottie begins to impose his lost dream on reality, seeing every woman as Madeleine no matter how remote the similarity of dress or manner—he is living within the closed circle of an obsession, and he sees his dead beloved everywhere: outside her apartment house, at Ernie's restaurant, at the Legion of Honor Palace.

Then an odd thing happens. As he gazes at flowers in the window of Podesta Baldocchi, he glances to see a girl walking and chatting with friends. She wears a tightly fitting green dress, her red hair pulled back. But there's something else: her face— and only her face—bears a striking resemblance to Madeleine. He follows her along the city streets to the Empire Hotel in Post Street, then goes to her door and announces that she reminds him of someone. "I heard that one before too," Judy Barton says sarcastically (as indeed she must have, when Gavin Elster first approached her with his plot). He questions her, and she gives some details of her family background in Kansas, her arrival in California, her job as a clerk at Magnin's. Like Carlotta, like Madeleine, like Scottie, this poor girl, too, is a wanderer: she left home, she says, because after her father died she didn't like the man her mother married. And how like Madeleine and Carlotta Judy has become: we notice in her small hotel room a small nosegay on the dressing table, a Spanish fan hanging from a fixture, red and

"You're not lost, Johnny-O. Mother's here."

white flowers painted on the headboard; bouquets of flowers painted and sewn everywhere. Carlotta and Madeleine seem to have become the embodiment of Judy's own fantasies: the desire to be loved by a rich, handsome, respectable man. Playing the role of a Madeleine-obsessed Carlotta, in other words, seem to have released within Judy Barton unrealized aspects of herself; it gave her a purpose—to make Gavin Elster love her, and to transcend her own banal life by vesting her personality, however briefly, within the image of a lovelier, more elegant and more exotic woman. At this point we begin to see that *Vertigo* is as much the tragedy of a lost and exploited woman as it is the bizarre story of an abused man (who in any case survives, while the poor woman is forever lost).

She half-willingly agrees to dine with him, and he leaves. Judy then slowly turns to us and we see the truth in a flashback. Intending to leave at once, she writes Scottie an explanatory letter:

Dearest Scottie,

And so you found me. This is the moment I dreaded and hoped for—wondering what I would say and do if I ever saw you again. I wanted so to see you again, just once. Now I'll go and you can give up your search. I want you to have peace of mind. You've nothing to blame yourself for. You were the victim. I was the tool and you were the victim of Gavin Elster's plan to murder his wife. He chose me to play the part because I looked like her, dressed and walked like her. He was quite safe because she lived in the country and rarely came to town. He chose you to be the witness to a suicide. The Carlotta story was part real, part invented to make you testify that Madeleine wanted to kill herself. He knew of your illness, he knew you'd never get up the stairs at the tower. He planned it so well, he made no mistakes. *I* made the mistake: I fell in love. But that wasn't part of the plan. I'm still in love with you and I want you so to love me. If I had the nerve I'd stay and lie, hoping I could make you love me again—as *I* am, for myself—and so forget the other, forget the past. But I don't know whether I have the nerve to try.

The letter (which she tears up in an obvious decision to stay) is heard by Judy's voice-over as she writes and the camera half-circles round her—one of the most startling moments in Hitchcock's films. This was a crucial mistake, thought many critics when the film was released. Why reveal the surprise ending now? Why not wait until the end (as in the novel, as in most such stories)? But Hitchcock chose to sacrifice surprise in order to gain suspense: from this point, we not only look *with* Scottie, we look *at* Scottie, observing his reactions, wondering how he will respond to Judy. Additionally, Hitchcock wants the audience to evaluate our own responses to this revelation, and to see how far we might go with Scottie in his deadly retribution once he knows the truth.

Now begins Scottie's attempt to recreate his past with Madeleine and to turn Judy into the image of Madeleine—the second time she has been made over into a false image. They dine at Ernie's, next day they stroll by the Palace of Fine Arts, then he buys her a corsage and takes her to Ransohoff's, intending to buy her a wardrobe identical to that worn by Madeleine. This is Hitchcock at his most brilliant, for after all *we* don't like Judy as much as Madeleine any more than does Scottie. We'd like to see the dead Madeleine come to life, that handsome, loving couple restored to us. And as Scottie begins the process, we concur—even (and especially) because we know the terrible, impossible truth.

Vertigo is the profoundest treatment Hitchcock could offer of the opposing drives that the film describes as spiritually poisonous (as do all his films about the double). Here, the clash of opposing impulses derives partly from Scottie's fear of touching the beloved, and partly from the awareness that so perfect a beauty may be illusory.

SCOTTIE: We could just see a lot of each other [the worship of gaze again, à la Jeffries in *Rear Window*].
JUDY: Why? Because I remind you of her? That's not very complimentary. And nothing else?
SCOTTIE: No.
JUDY: That's not very complimentary, either.

The impulses are sexual and domineering, but the gestures are freighted with fear. Henceforth, *Vertigo* is as much a tract on moviemaking—and Alfred Hitchcock's particular genius as a moviemaker—as it is anything else.

SCOTTIE: (selecting clothes for Judy): No, that's not it—nothing like it.

SALESWOMAN: But you said gray, sir.

SCOTTIE: Now, look, I just want an ordinary, simple gray suit.

JUDY: I like that one.

SCOTTIE: No, it's not right.

SALESWOMAN: The gentleman seems to know what he wants.

SCOTTIE: I want you to look nice. I know the kind of suit that would look well on you.

JUDY: You want me to look like her! No! I won't do it!

SCOTTIE: It can't make that much difference to you. Do this for me.

JUDY (later): Why are you doing this? What good will it do?

SCOTTIE: I don't know—no good, I guess. I don't know. But there's something in you.

He reaches to caress her face, then withdraws.

JUDY: You don't even want to touch me.

SCOTTIE: Yes, I do.

JUDY: Look, couldn't you like me—just me—the way I am? When we first started out it was so good—we had fun. And then you started in on the clothes. All right, I'll wear the darn clothes if you want me to—if you'll—just—like me.

SCOTTIE (gazing distractedly at her red hair but obviously thinking of the blonde he had adored): The color of your hair!

JUDY: Oh, no!

SCOTTIE: Please, it can't matter to you.

And at this point comes perhaps the film's most tragic and human statement, the moment in which there is highlighted the theme of romantic delusion, as we hear the desperation in the voice of a girl longing to be accepted and loved, and willing to do anything to achieve that:

> JUDY: If I let you change me, will that do it? If I do what you tell me, will you love me?
> SCOTTIE: Yes—yes.
> JUDY: All right, then, I'll do it. I don't care anymore about me.

Perhaps never have exploitation (disguised as love) and self-annihilation (disguised as self-sacrifice) been so tragically presented in film. This dialogue is a moment of searing honesty about the way people attempt to change others, which amounts virtually to a definition of false love—a passion which is narcissistic on the one hand and neurotically self-destructive on the other hand. "Do this for me" are words, Hitchcock implies, heard daily in the boardrooms, staterooms and bedrooms of the world. No matter how innocent or blithe, they contain the seeds of a fatal blossom.

And so begins the final tragic transformation, remaking Judy just as Gavin had remade Judy (as Scottie admits later). As the

"Well, you gotta nerve—followin' me right up to my room!"

The gradual, second transformation of Judy into Madeleine.

first part of the film ended with the real Madeleine's death and the death of the false Madeleine, so the second part will end with the death of the real Judy and of the recreated false Madeleine. Romantic delusion and exploitation are indeed fatal, and Scottie Ferguson resembles Gavin Elster more than one could ever have suspected.

Judy returns from the beauty salon, wearing Madeleine's gray suit, but although the color of her hair is right the style is not, and we think what Scottie says: "No, that's not right!" Here's Hitchcock's audience manipulation at its most effective, for we, too, want her hair just right, we give ourselves up to the recreation of the dream with him—even though we know what Scottie does not, that this is all a fraud. "It should be pulled back and pinned at the neck. I told her that. I told *you* that!" Anxiously, Judy acquiesces, and when she reemerges from the bathroom the metamorphosis is complete, and the haze of green light which surrounds her suggests the captured presence of a spirit, Scottie's repossession at last of his romantic ideal.

("For that hotel room set," Hitchcock told me, "I deliberately chose a hotel that had a vertical green sign outside. I wanted her to emerge from that bathroom as a ghost with a green effect, so I put a wide sliding glass in front of the camera, blurred at the top when she first appears. We raised this glass as she came toward Scottie and the camera. In other words, he saw her first as a ghost, but with her proximity she became clarified and solid.")

The Judy-Madeleine identification is now complete when, during the long kiss, Judy's room dissolves and they are back in the Plaza Stable. The confusion clouding Scottie's face is that of a man experiencing vertigo—he seems to have the illusion of movement in space or of objects moving round him. ("I had the hotel room and all the pieces of the stable made into a circular set," Hitchcock continued. "Then I had the camera taken right round the whole thing in a 360-degree turn. Then we put that on a screen, and I stood the actors on a small turntable and turned them round. So they went around, and the screen gave the appearance of your going round with them. That was in order to give him the feeling that he was back in that particular spot.") The romantic fantasy has been utterly realized, and all that can now happen is tragedy.

And so we move to the final sequences. Judy absentmindedly puts on the necklace worn by Carlotta in the painting, and at once Scottie knows the truth in a moment of illumination that must have simply brought to his conscious mind what he suspected all along. "I've got my face on," Judy says with ironic veracity. It's possible, of course, that Judy's wearing of the necklace was no accident: Scottie cannot love her as Judy and cannot "forget the other, forget the past." What's to happen next day, when Judy Barton is due at Magnin's? How long can the charade be sustained? Each time Judy became Madeleine, she willingly annihilated herself. Isn't there in this poor girl a lingering fascination with death, a vertigo to match Scottie's? She's caught in her own spell now, for a meaningful existence without the *false Madeleine* is impossible for both of them. She has become Madeleine for Scottie's sake now, not for Elster nor for his plot to murder his wife. This time she has really renounced herself and has become the double of a double, an imitation twice removed from the reality. She has allowed herself to imitate the *false* Madeleine who was herself forced to imitate the *real* Madeleine who we never see, never know. The first Madeleine was simply an Elster-concocted fraud, an impersonation by an impostor, while the second is an indulgence of Scottie's fantasy. So following the double death (the literal death of the real and the figurative death of the false Madeleine), Judy is compelled—*by her own passion*—to become a nonexistent person again, and so there occurs the death of the real and of an imitation— of the real Judy and of the false Madeleine.

The final episode occurs at dusk, as had the opening of the film, and it's simultaneously one of the most terrifying and moving in Hitchcock's catalog. The poignancy derives from our acknowledgment that these are neither ciphers nor cardboard characters but real, suffering human beings, emblematic of much that is common in human experience—and the dilemma facing a filmmaker. "You played the wife very well, Judy," Scottie says in rage as he drags her up to the San Juan Bautista tower. "He made you over, didn't he? He made you over just like I made you over— only better. Not only the clothes and the hair, but the looks and the manner and the words . . . And then what did he do? Did he train you? Did he rehearse you? Did he tell you exactly what to do and what to say?"

Throughout the scene, he calls her alternately Madeleine and Judy, and although he at last overcomes his vertigo and climbs successfully to the belfry, the victory is empty—indeed deadly.

> SCOTTIE: This is where it happened. But you were his girl. Did he ditch you? Oh, Judy, with all of his wife's money, and all that freedom and all that power—and he ditched you [shades of Carlotta]. Did he give you anything?
>
> JUDY: Money.
>
> SCOTTIE: (his voice choked with grief): And the necklace. That was where you made your mistake, Judy. You shouldn't keep souvenirs of the killing. You shouldn't have been—you shouldn't have been that sentimental. Oh, I loved you so, Madeleine!
>
> JUDY: Scottie, I was safe when you found me. There was

nothing that you could prove. When I saw you again I couldn't run away, I loved you so. I walked into danger and let you change me because I loved you and I wanted you. Oh, Scottie, you love me. Please keep me safe.

SCOTTIE: It's too late. There's no bringing her back.

Judy then sees a black-shrouded figure rise up—*is* there a "bringing back" of Madeleine Elster? "Oh, no!" Judy gasps, stepping back as the figure steps forward, saying quietly, "I heard voices." And then with a piercing scream Judy falls to her death. The voice, now clearly identifiable as that of a nun, says, "God have mercy!"—the film's last words, significantly—and she tolls the mission bell.

The last image is of Scottie standing on the roof of the mission, his arms spread out in the identical gesture as in his dream, when he plunged into Madeleine's open grave. This is an image of an utterly drained man destroyed by his own illusions.

It's of course essential that the relationship between Judy and Scottie involve fraud and a deadly plot, for the overarching theme of *Vertigo* is that a romantic fantasy is a dangerous hoax, potentially fatal for all involved. Were Hitchcock to have given us a straightforward account about a romance that ends tragically, that would indeed be a reinforcement rather than a condemnation of dangerous illusions. Here the love object is literally a fraud, and we're struck by the wasted energy spent in pursuit of what's neither attainable nor authentic. The death of Judy actualizes the feigned death of the artificial Madeleine and at last puts to rest the persona of Madeleine that had existed in Judy all along.

The emotional landscape of *Vertigo,* with its haunted and hopeless pursuit of an empty ideal, is Hitchcock's ultimate statement on the romantic fallacy. In expressing it, he resembled his countryman Ernest Dowson (1867–1900), also a sensitive artist. The one romance of Dowson's life, with a London waitress, was probably an invention of his imagination; never convinced that he could find real love, he wanted to kill off its possibilities in advance and lament the loss ever after. All the stories in his collection *Dilemmas* (1895) tell of frustrated love—the failure of a weak man and his melancholy retreat into the solitude of the disturbed romantic—

and any of them could have been transmuted into cinematic terms by Hitchcock, whose spirit they share.

But however much *Vertigo* indicts the tragic and the deadly, it remains a work of authentic beauty and grandeur, a film of astonishing purity and formal perfection in every element. Each line of dialogue, each color, each piece of decoration, each article of wardrobe, each music cue, camera angle and gesture, each glance—everything in this motion picture has an organic relationship contributing to the whole. Never has there been presented so beguilingly the struggle between the constant yearning for the ideal and the necessity of living in a world that is far from ideal, with people who are one and all frail and imperfect. *Vertigo* is a work of uncanny maturity, authorial honesty and spiritual insight, and if its characters are indeed doomed to a tragic end—not one of them able to reach the fulfillment of an earthly love—that is not due to Hitchcock's contempt. It is, in the final analysis, a work of unsentimental yet profound compassion, and a statement of transcendent faith in what cannot be and yet what must, somewhere, be true.

32

NORTH BY NORTHWEST

(PRODUCED 1958, RELEASED 1959)

O the mind, mind has mountains; cliffs of fall
Frightful, sheer, no-man-fathomed. Hold them cheap
May who ne'er hung there.

GERARD MANLEY HOPKINS,

FROM THE SO-CALLED

''TERRIBLE SONNETS''

Cary Grant, James Mason and Eva Marie Saint.

etween the brooding emotional traceries of *Vertigo* and the dark urgency of *Psycho* came *North by Northwest,* Alfred Hitchcock's great comic thriller, plotted and written by the gifted and prolific scenarist Ernest Lehman. One of the few films in the genre worthy of multiple viewings, it leavens the gravest concerns with a spiky and mature wit. Not the least aspect of its prophetically cool stance toward politics is that it calmly locates treachery equally on "our side" as on "theirs"—and this during the Eisenhower years, when American chauvinism galloped at full pace. The entire, messy danger precipitated by an early accident in *North by Northwest* is, in fact, the brainchild of Washington agents, willing to give up a life or two for secrets they consider vital. Never has the entire hierarchy of unprincipled political expediency been so ruthlessly dissected—and, mercifully, in a comedy.

It's easy to be over-solemn about so enjoyable a picture, but it's also easy to ignore, by a sort of inverse snobbism, the ever timely issues it raises. In *North by Northwest,* we watch the ordeal of a character played by Cary Grant, who was for so long our clearest exponent of high-class sex appeal and achievement, very nearly an idol image of success. We're shown the fundamental impotence of his self-confidence in the face of chaos unleashed by political intrigue. But he's somehow never alarmed by any of this, although the single moment of surprise occurs when he's told that the woman who at first seemed innocent and then perfidious has actually been a double agent all along, posing as the enemy's

"You men aren't really trying to kill my son, are you?"
(Jessie Royce Landis, Cary Grant, Adam Williams, Robert Ellenstein.)

mistress in order to work for "our side." For just a moment, Grant (as Roger O. Thornhill) flinches: "Oh, no!" he mutters, and ever so briefly we glimpse a more attractive humility and humanity long buried beneath a carefully cultivated urban sophistication and the inbred habits of sexual sparring and conquest. At the finale, he has a chance to manifest at last an unselfish heroism—if he can just hold on long enough. Literally.

The complex, carefully rendered narrative need be only outlined for our purposes here. A group of spies dealing in the discovery and exporting of high U.S. government secrets (presumably for Russia, although that country is never mentioned) is headed by Philip Vandamm (James Mason). Their target is Roger O. Thornhill (Cary Grant), whom they mistake for "George Kaplan," a nonexistent decoy created by American intelligence agents (headed by a nameless professor played by Leo G. Carroll) to throw Vandamm and his men off the scent of the *real* double agent working right under Vandamm's nose and posing as his mistress—Eve Kendall (Eva Marie Saint). Thornhill becomes involved in a bizarre journey and a web of circumstantial evidence that implicates him in a murder and forces him to "become" Kaplan; he meets and has a brief affair with Eve, only to be betrayed by her very nearly to the point of his death. The adventure takes the leading characters from New York to Mount Rushmore in Rapid City, South Dakota. After a terrifying finale, all ends happily for Thornhill and Eve.

When he began to construct the scenario for *North by Northwest,* Lehman hoped to create the ultimate Hitchcock thriller. He succeeded magnificently. First of all, the film is in a way the sequel and conclusion of *Notorious,* in which a tippling blonde was nearly sent to her death by a character played by Cary Grant after he blithely turns her over to the enemy. In *North by Northwest,* Grant seems to get his just deserts: he's the tippling businessman nearly sent to *his* death by a duplicitous blonde. And behind it all in both cases is a depraved political order, with government leaders committing mayhem in the name of necessary intelligence activities.

For years, Hitchcock had preferred the journey motif and the forced name-change to structure a seriocomic tale about a man's search for a deeper, authentic identity and the establishment of a relationship—so much had been true of films mentioned above.

In *North by Northwest,* Hitchcock and Lehman gave us the ultimate "fantasy of the absurd," as the director liked to call it. In other ways, too, the film is a virtual résumé of the Hitchcock chase thriller, with elements of *The 39 Steps* (the innocent man on a journey to clear his name of a crime he didn't commit, forced to assume multiple roles and to trust an initially fickle blonde) and of *Secret Agent, Foreign Correspondent* and *Saboteur.* Brilliantly capsuled is the concomitant theme of the hunter and the hunted, as everyone in this tale becomes both. At the center (as in *Vertigo* and *Psycho*) is a vacuum, an absurdity, a nonexistent person. Kaplan (who doesn't exist) is pursued by Thornhill, who is pursued by Vandamm who believes *him* to be Kaplan; Eve, meanwhile, pursues Vandamm, who thinks she's an ally. All this, as we'll see, is carefully presented in the motif of role-playing, false identities and the constant mention of play-acting and the theater.

The title designs for *North by Northwest* (created, as they were for *Vertigo* and *Psycho,* by Saul Bass) are a series of names careening up and down along the side of a grid which becomes a Manhattan skyscraper; the motif of identities slipping and falling is made literal, of course, in the final moments of the film, as people fall from or are saved from the faces on Mount Rushmore.

The first scenes brilliantly sketch Thornhill's character as he strides, giving orders to his secretary, dictating, arranging his love life, displacing a man from a taxi with the lie that his secretary is sick: "Maggie," he tells her (Doreen Lang), "you ought to know that in the world of advertising there's no such thing as a lie— there's only the expedient exaggeration." Washington intelligence agents couldn't have put it better, as we'll soon learn. As the advertising man in the gray flannel suit, Thornhill is never seen in his own home; he's always on the run, transplanted—still wearing the same suit—to the most unlikely and inhospitable surroundings, an irresistible, charming, utterly empty cultural idol whose middle initial "O," as he admits, "stands for nothing—it's my trademark—ROT." So much for the glamorous, lucrative world of advertising.

All the charm he can muster is no defense, and as so often, chaos is at the ready—even amid the civilities of the Plaza Hotel's Oak Bar on a sunny afternoon, or in the security of the public

One of Hitchcock's most famous sequences:
the chase in the cornfield.

"When I was a little boy, I wouldn't even let my mother undress me."
"Well, you're a big boy now."

lounge at the United Nations, or a vast, serene cornfield in the Midwest, or at Mount Rushmore, or—well, wherever it's least expected. "It's a Most Unusual Day," plays the unseen orchestra in the Plaza's Palm Court when Thornhill enters, and well they might: moments later, the simple accident of raising his hand to summon a bellboy—which coincides with the ruse of a message for the decoy Kaplan—leads Vandamm's men to mistake Thornhill for Kaplan, and a few seconds later the kidnapping is in progress. There's no preventing this kind of thing, and even Thornhill's habit of bribing, of constantly overtipping for favors, accomplishes nothing. Everyone seems to have a going rate—even his mother (Jessie Royce Landis, actually one year younger than Grant), whom he bribes to obtain a hotel key at the Plaza.

The opening scenes also establish the basic geography of the film: Thornhill exits the C.I.T. building on Madison Avenue, heads *north* and then enters a taxi heading *west* on Sixtieth Street. Henceforth the entire film moves in a northwesterly direction (except for the necessary side trip to Glen Cove, the residence of the Russian delegation in the 1950s). From New York to Mount Rushmore via Chicago, the action then remains consistently in a northwesterly direction (with, appropriately, a flight on Northwest Airlines from Chicago). The final choice for the film's title may well have been inspired, therefore, by Hamlet: "I am but mad north-northwest," for as Hitchcock insisted, this is a fantasy of the *absurd*.

Roger Thornhill is abducted to be an "actor" in a real-life drama more exciting than anything he could have been hoping to see that evening, when he had tickets for the Winter Garden Theater to see a show with his mother. The script, accordingly, is wonderfully laced with theatrical references indicating just how phony and deceptive every character is. "What a performance!" Thornhill says to the elegant lady masquerading as Mrs. Townsend (Josephine Hutchinson). Indeed, everyone is engaged or paid or bribed to perform, and this motif is synthesized at the action sequence, when Vandamm says to Thornhill:

Has anyone ever told you that you overplay your various roles rather severely, Mr. Kaplan? First you're the outraged Madison

Avenue man who claims he's been mistaken for someone else. Then you play a fugitive from justice, supposedly trying to clear his name of a crime he knows he didn't commit. And now you play the peevish lover, stung by jealousy and betrayal. Seems to me you fellows could stand a little less training from the FBI and a little more from the Actors Studio.

To which Thornhill replies: "Apparently the only performance that's going to satisfy you is when I play dead." Vandamm: "Your very next role. You'll be quite convincing, I assure you." And of course "playing dead" *is* Thornhill's very next role, and he *is* very convincing: Eve shoots him with fake bullets at the Mount Rushmore cafeteria, and he falls and plays dead—very convincingly, to everyone including Vandamm, the bystanders and the media.

At the thematic center of the film is the auction sequence, in which it is not only the pre-Columbian statue that is up for sale, concealing something (microfilm secrets—Hitchcock's MacGuffin). Eve, too, is the art object, passed back and forth from spy to spy as an object of sexual blackmail and enslavement. She's sister to Alicia Huberman (Ingrid Bergman) in *Notorious,* this seductive, deceptive and finally alarmingly sympathetic Eve, associated throughout with the dangerous number thirteen. She's in car 3901 on the Twentieth Century Limited, and in room 463 at the Ambassador East in Chicago; the structurally obsessive Hitchcock loved little jokes like this, for the digits of course add in each case to 13), and they were apparently his last-minute additions to the script, grace notes contributed to Lehman's rich symphony.

Thornhill endures a kind of moral education in this story, forced to become what he has been all along: a nonperson. Thus the man who is thrice identified as a gin-drinker finally asks for a pint of bourbon when he's confined to the Rapid City hospital—for it was bourbon that was forced on him when he was thought to be Kaplan at the Glen Cove mansion. The innocent man on the run is forced to find a deeper identity, disabused of the illusion that his tailored city life in advertising has any meaning. He's the modern prototype of the uncommitted man, twice divorced, never

Cliff-hanging at Mount Rushmore.

seen at work or in his own home, always on the run. He must,
therefore, deny his apparent identity and enter into a kind of
shadow-world of espionage, to deny himself in order to begin a
real identity and reach the point where he can cry to his would-
be killer, "Help! Help me!"—the plea that invites the final saving
shot. The distance separating Thornhill from Kaplan, is, then, the
distance hitherto separating Thornhill from himself—the abyss of
a life in moral disarray long before the adventure began and clarified for us in the opening dictation to his secretary. The accumulating images of entrapment (in limousine, jail, elevator,
hospital room, hotel room, even a cornfield and at a national
monument) express what might be called his emotional or even
his spiritual condition of entrapment.

North by Northwest finally presents us with a world in which
everything is a fake—a world dealing in deadly espionage activities, a world of phony identities and shallow values. Everyone
steals, creates and assumes double and false identities: thus the
microfilm in the statue is itself empty, meaningless and fraudulent
for Hitchcock, who hasn't a care for what it contains. This is why
the principals must be brought to a point in which they cling to

Eve, about to be saved by Thornhill's sudden escape.
(James Mason, Eva Marie Saint, Adam Williams, Martin Landau.)

the edge of an abyss—a moment comically augured at the beginning of the film with the repetition of the name of Sergeant Emile *Klinger* ("No, I don't believe it, either," Thornhill says drunkenly to his mother on the phone).

As usual, all the solid markers of stability are powerless to save in the face of human perversity; thus the United Nations and the Mount Rushmore memorial are the Hitchcock-Lehman update for the enormous god's head (*Blackmail*), Swiss country chapels and charming chocolate factories (*Secret Agent*), Westminster Cathedral and the Dutch windmills (*Foreign Correspondent*), the Statue of Liberty (*Saboteur*), a concert hall and a foreign embassy (*The Man Who Knew Too Much*) and a mission church (*Vertigo*). Just as in advertising (the crowded chaos of Madison Avenue veils deception practiced by Thornhill) and art (the statue camouflages secrets), the so-called ordered life of security is everywhere penetrated by pretense.

That these serious concerns should be clothed within scintillating comedy is the hallmark of great dramatic art from Euripides' *Alcestis* to Shakespeare's *A Midsummer Night's Dream* to Molière and Feydeau, to name only a few. *North by Northwest* remains, with superb reason, one of Hitchcock's two or three most popular films. With Ernest Lehman's astonishingly composed screenplay—a model of construction, wit and timeless high style—and with a shimmering, snappy score by Bernard Herrmann and an array of unerringly acute performances, this film retains a freshness on many levels. There's not a moment of boredom, not an extraneous shot in the picture—and it's Hitchcock's longest, too, at one hundred thirty-six minutes. Everything occurs with lightning rapidity, and no matter how often you see *North by Northwest,* it never fails to reward.

33

PSYCHO

(PRODUCED 1959–60; RELEASED 1960)

The purpose of playing . . . is to hold,
as 'twere, the mirror up to nature.

HAMLET

Janet Leigh as Marion Crane.

This is, of course, the film for which Alfred Hitchcock is most famous—a horror film, most people might call it. But to say that about *Psycho* is a little like describing *Hamlet* as a play about a confused young man who doesn't much like his family. Or that van Gogh's *Starry Night* is a distorted vision of the Dutch countryside. Or that *Oedipus* is about a neurotic royal clan. The statements are more or less true in a crude gradeschool way, but they don't begin to describe the richness and depth of each work.

In fact, *Psycho* continues to impress audiences (and filmmakers) more than thirty years after production and to spin off (one could hardly say "inspire") hundreds of poorer imitations *not* because it's a shocker but because of other, deeper themes—themes, images and *ideas* of which we're perhaps only casually or obliquely aware until after multiple viewings. For this film is really a meditation on the tyranny of past over present. It's an indictment of the viewer's capacity for voyeurism and his own potential for depravity. It's also a statement on the American dream turned nightmare, and there's a running concern for the truth that physical vision is always only partial and that our perceptions tend to play us false—thus Hitchcock's insistence, from the opening shot, on staring eyes that are finally empty, blank and dead. *Psycho* is also— and this doesn't exhaust the contents—a ruthless exposition of American Puritanism and exaggerated Mom-ism. Made in black-and-white with a television crew in six weeks at a cost of $800,000, it has earned something in excess of $40 million, which says something about economy. And success.

Based on a little novel by Robert Bloch, Hitchcock and his screenwriter Joseph Stefano fashioned *Psycho* quickly in 1959. Marion Crane (Janet Leigh) and her lover Sam Loomis (John Gavin) cannot marry because of his heavy financial responsibilities. Secretary to a real estate and insurance broker, Marion then steals forty thousand dollars in cash from her employer and his client and leaves Phoenix, planning to start a new life with Sam in California. A storm forces her to spend the night at a lonely motel, managed by Norman Bates (Anthony Perkins), who says he tends a sick, elderly and reclusive mother.

As Marion showers before retiring, a figure—apparently the old lady—enters the bathroom and stabs her to death. Moments later, Norman comes on the bloody scene and covers up for the crime, sinking Marion's car and corpse in a swamp along with the money he doesn't know is wrapped in a newspaper.

Attempting to find Marion, an insurance detective named Arbogast (Martin Balsam) is sent to the Bates motel, but he, too, is murdered, and again the mad Mrs. Bates seems to be the killer. Then Marion's sister Lila (Vera Miles) joins Sam in the search. They learn from the local sheriff (John McIntire) that Mrs. Bates has been dead for years. The couple then proceed to the Bates motel and house, where Lila is very nearly the next victim—not of Mrs. Bates, but of Norman himself, who is a homicidal maniac.

The director with Janet Leigh.

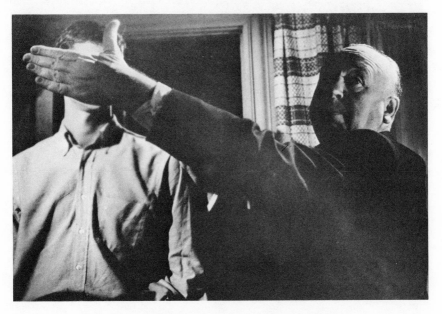

Checking a lighting cue for Anthony Perkins.

He killed his mother (and her lover), kept her corpse preserved and, in an effort to deny matricide, has assumed her identity in moments of madness. Our last view of the incarcerated Norman indicates that Mother has completely taken over his personality.

Psycho certainly accumulates the traditional window dressings of the gothic tale: in this regard you can list the forbidding gingerbread house, a dark and stormy night, a confined and demented relative, a series of bizarre murders and a hidden treasure. But the two most powerful gothic elements in the picture are the secret and the mirror.

Everyone in this story has something to hide: Sam and Marion are lunchtime lovers; Marion's coworker Caroline (Patricia Hitchcock) hid tranquilizers on her wedding day; Cassidy (Frank Albertson) hides undeclared cash to avoid taxes; Lowery (Vaughn Taylor) hides a whiskey bottle in his desk; Marion lies and steals; Norman hides the worst secret of all. Arbogast sums it up neatly when he says of the Bates Motel: "This is the first place that looks like it's hiding from the world."

"My mother—what is the phrase—isn't quite herself today."

Even more significant is the abundance of mirrors with which Hitchcock deliberately punctuated the sets, for the mirror is not only a prop suitable for the representation of a split personality. It also marks the need for introspection, as Hitchcock knew from his school readings of Tennyson's *Lady of Shalott,* Matthew Arnold's *Empedocles,* George Eliot's *Adam Bede* and *Middlemarch* and Dickens's *Our Mutual Friend*—works which presented to Victorian society the mirror as an image of self-awareness. To see the world more clearly and to partially disguise ourselves, insisted these books and Hitchcock's films, one wears eyeglasses. But for a true glimpse of our divided selves, one consults a mirror. ("I'll buy you a new mirror," says Charles to Henrietta in *Under Capricorn,* "and it'll be your conscience.")

Accordingly, Marion stands before a mirror twice in the opening hotel scene. At her office she regards herself in her compact mirror. At home she again stands thinking before a mirror—and behind her the open bathroom door and drawn shower curtain reveal the ultimately fatal locale at precisely the moment she decides to steal the money. Several times she glances at the pursuing trooper in her rearview car mirror. She counts out cash for her new car in the salesman's washroom, and the deed is shown reflected in a mirror. At the Bates Motel, she's reflected in a mirror as she checks in. There's a mirror in her room that splits her image—and so on and on. But not until one of the most jolting moments in the film does the meaning for all this mirror imagery become clear—and that's the moment when Lila is surprised by the *double* reflection of herself in Mrs. Bates's bedroom mirror. What she (and we) find frightening is the alarming impression of a split or doubled personality. This is immediately followed by Lila's discovery of an impression on Mrs. Bates's bed—an image which recalls the film's opening scene, with Marion on the hotel room bed.

The mirror is not only a traditional, disturbing gothic prop. It's also a marker of the haunted double (mainstream Hitchcock, as we know from *Shadow of a Doubt* and *Strangers on a Train*), and it effectively splits everyone's image. This splitting or cutting of the image is everywhere evident in *Psycho*'s cutting images: Saul Bass's title designs form names from horizontal bars, then violently wrench them apart; in the opening image, a construction

Norman Bates (Anthony Perkins),
victim and victimizer.

crane bisects the horizon of Phoenix; the interior of the hotel room
first reveals a standing man and a supine woman; the actors are
positioned before venetian blinds and tapes that seem to "split"
them; Marion's parked car is bisected by a telephone pole; the
wipers on Marion's windscreen are linked to the raised knife;
scythes and rakes hang overhead in Sam's hardware store—and
most of all we have the horizontal motel and the looming, vertical
Victorian house, which provide the predominant geometric form
of the film and illuminate the meaning of all the others. This is a
film that splits images in every scene, for after all (thus the psychiatrist at the finale), "When the mind houses two personalities,
there is always a conflict, a battle." And Hitchcock ensures that
every image, every personality will be split—not just Norman's.
Marion is also of two minds, wanting and not wanting to steal.

Even more important is the fact that the *viewer of the picture* is
of two minds, and this Hitchcock establishes with a relentless
exploitation of audience identification through point of view. With

The discovery of Mother's crime.

Marion, we are both repelled and fascinated by the desire to steal with impunity; we want her to escape Lowery's suspicious recognition on the Phoenix street corner; we want her to escape the pursuing patrolman (after all, he gives her deadly advice: "There are plenty of motels around here—I mean, you should've—"). Just as we have conflicting feelings about Marion (so sympathetic a creature, with her lunchtime trysts and scrubbed innocence), so we have divided, split feelings about Norman. He does such a first-rate cleanup of Mother's messy murder, doesn't he, and with him we're ever so relieved when Marion's car, which has momentarily stuck in the swamp, finally sinks with a septic gurgle. All of *Psycho* in fact becomes a series of our own schizoid feelings, our wanting to see and our wanting not to see. In the opening camera movement of the film, Hitchcock makes us aware of being voyeurs: the camera in fact does what the moviegoer has just done, as it moves from a bright exterior into a dark room, finds an empty chair, moves over, "sits" in the chair and looks up—to see half-naked lovers.

From this unseemly action we move gradually to complicity in theft, then we are led to approve the cover-up of a monstrous act of madness. No doubt about it, we have split personalities, split wills. We want Lila to get out of that spooky house at the end, but we want to find out what's below stairs, too.

The audience manipulation is more than simply perverse; it has an artistic, even a moral purpose. Involving us deeply in the half-wishes and secret desires of the characters, Hitchcock involves us *by the very act of watching*. The camera becomes the extension of the eye of the viewer, but as always, this vision is partial and illusory. In the fruit cellar, Lila's hand hits a suspended light bulb, and as we gaze at Mother's empty eye sockets the swinging bulb casts shadows that give the *illusion* of eyes darting back and forth in mockery—just as Marion's dead stare was the *illusion* of life and points to the deadliest stare of all, which is Norman's staring straight out at us at the end, smiling madly (and fulfilling the moment when Marion, driving, imagined Cassidy's threats to her and smiled, madly, out at us). This motif of the illusion of seeing and the illusions of life is synthesized in one of the picture's most enigmatically beautiful (and frightening) shots, the haunting zoom

Scenes of Perkins watching the sinking cars were shot day-for-night.
At his feet is a marker giving him his exact position.

Martin Balsam and Anthony Perkins.

to the crossed bronze hands on Mother's vanity table—the illusion
of gentle fingers in life or death.

All of this comes together in Hitchcock's theme of the empty
staring, the imperfect vision that is *Psycho,* which fulfills the overt
image of voyeurism. With Norman we spy on Marion as she
undresses for her shower: he removes a painting from the wall
and there's a convenient peephole; the camera swings round after
a close-up of Norman's eye watching, and *we* do the watching.
And so that we have no doubt about his intention, Hitchcock
makes everything clear: Norman removes from the wall a replica
of "Susanna and the Elders," the biblical story of three old men
who spied on a righteous woman as she prepared for her bath and
then, passions aflame, leaped out at her with threats of sexual
blackmail. Norman, in other words, removes the *artifact* of deadly
voyeurism and replaces it with the *act* itself. So much for "mere"
spying.

. . .

Relative to all this is *Psycho*'s self-referential character, for it's a moviemaker's movie about moviemaking, and few films have been so direct about this. "Have you ever been inside one of those places?" Norman asks Marion, referring, it seems, to a lunatic asylum—or perhaps a movie theater: "The laughter and the tears and the cruel eyes studying you." This is of course fulfilled in the film's final shot: "They're probably watching me now," Mother's voice opines. "Well, let them. As if I could do anything but just sit here and stare"—like a director in his chair, like the viewer in the theater. "I hope they are watching me! [We are, ma'am, we are!] They'll see and they'll know, and they'll say . . ." From first scene to last, the film accumulates its markers: the private eye is stabbed in the eye, for one thing. And as Lila climbs the stone steps to the Bates house there is a stunning subjective-objective cross-tracking, as we approach the house and *are* the house.

All the looking, all the eyes, all the acts of *staring* in *Psycho* finally bring us to the realization that perceptions based on visual seeing and appearances alone are inadequate, sinful, erroneous, dead and blank. This is a classic moral theme, the idea of what

The final scream. Vera Miles as Lila Crane.

constitutes authentic inner vision, and *Psycho* presents it in universal filmic terms. (The idea is explored in *Rear Window* and will be completed in *The Birds*.) Hitchcock trips us up at every turn—or more accurately, he lets our seeing—or what we *think* we see—play us false. Related to this is the untitled book in Norman's room, the volume Lila opens, and from which Hitchcock immediately cuts, after just a flicker of shocked reaction on her face: in Victorian times (and what a Victorian house this is), pornography was printed with unprinted spines.

It's precisely this kind of sinful, imperfect vision that begs the *power* that *Psycho* vilifies: familial, financial and sexual power, and the power of a diseased imagination—not family, money, sex or fantasy in themselves, but these items when hooked up to exploitation.

Family power linked to money, first of all. Sam cannot marry Marion because he must pay off his dead father's debts and his ex-wife's alimony. Cassidy overprotects his daughter ("My baby never had an unhappy day in her life. Know what I do about unhappiness? I buy it off!") Caroline's mother protected her on her wedding day (by giving her tranquilizers) and still telephones to see if Caroline's husband has called. The ultimate parental power is exercised by Mrs. Bates herself—the only survivor of the mayhem. Then there's sexual power: Mrs. Bates built this dreary place under her lover's influence, as Norman reminds. Sam and Marion's situation, their obviously desperate passion, ignites the theft. Norman's madly repressed erotic instincts lead to hysteria and murder. Most dangerous of all is the theme of imagination soured into fantasy. Marion's life, like Norman's, is destroyed by a fantasy—hers, that money will solve her problems; his, that maternal devotion cancels out the true evil. All this is described in a markedly American context very far indeed from the worlds of *The Man Who Knew Too Much* and *To Catch a Thief*—even from the cramped coziness of *Rear Window*.

All the illusions of power, due to faulty vision, lead inevitably to entrapment—thus the shower as enclosure, whence it's impossible to escape the effects of one's past. Norman sums it up for us: "I think we're all of us clamped in our private traps. We scratch and claw, but only at the air, only at each other, and for all of it we never budge an inch." There's no denying the edge of despair that envelops *Psycho* (apart from the cathartic-therapeutic effect of watching the horror enacted so we ourselves can escape it). And the entrapment is located within the film's accumulating bird imagery (nowhere found in the novel), which further supports the motif of the illusion of life and the blank staring, as well as the motif of the predator and the night killer of helpless prey. Norman's hobby is taxidermy: he likes to stuff birds, and the last bird to be stuffed (clearly a vulgarism for sex, for which Marion's murder is a demented substitute) is a (Marion) Crane from Phoenix—the mythic bird that rises from its own ashes, as does Mother Bates. Norman, birdlike, munches Kandy Korn and is photographed from a low angle, eating like a chicken. The knife-slashing of the two murders is done to the accompaniment of shrieking violins, imitating bird sounds. (Bernard Herrmann scored entirely for strings; his symphonic structure for the music is in the direct tradition of Sibelius's Fourth Symphony and much of Mahler.)

Psycho points forward to and in fact necessitates Hitchcock's next film (and a greater one still), *The Birds*. Here, the birds are at once unseeing, only *apparently* alive. Stuffed birds, they have no power to hurt—only Norman, their "creator," can do that. It's the ultimate gothic convention, exploited to its last dark implication.

The final horror of the film is that the dead one is the only victor, and Hitchcock leaves us in no doubt about the triumph of the kingdom of death. What Marion imagined during her nighttime drive (that the money would be replaced "with her fine soft flesh") has become horribly true. At the center of the film is the legendary shower murder, which focuses virtually everything discussed so far. In it, we receive the *impression* of violence, brutality and despair without being nauseated by color, blood and detail. The curtain of life and death is torn, marking a life's extinction, and Marion's eyes stare at the worst horror of all, which she knows but we do not yet: that the shy young man who just gave her supper has burst in upon her in a granny dress and a fright wig and slashed her to ribbons. Like the awful realization that Marion and Sam's last meeting was a casual farewell in the dingy hotel room, so here the tragedy catches like a thief in the night. Marion's staring eye becomes, then, an indictment of our watching; staring in exploitation, Hitchcock admits, is seeing nothing. The death of the person we identified with is at once punishment and derailment, and henceforth we have nowhere to "go" but with Norman.

The triumph of the kingdom of death: it's all there in the *Eroica* symphony in Norman's room, that work that mocks the funeral march and questions Napoleon's deadly exploits. Hitchcock, inspired, boldly adopted the satanic voice for *Psycho:* he affirms by indirection, negating all the negations, looking evil squarely in the face and calling it evil. And the psychiatrist's "explanation" of it all at the end—far from cleansing the wounds and making everything comprehensible—is in fact reversed and itself mocked by what follows. No academic analysis can explain away the final horror of what we see and hear: the complete annihilation of Norman's personality, forever swallowed up in his own death-in-life, with Mother the only victor. Once we hear all this business about matricide and schizophrenia and split personalities, we can't shake it off so easily. Nothing, in the final analysis, is analyzable at all. The madness is inscrutable, capricious, apparently unpreventable. "Things go crazy from time to time," as *Shadow of a Doubt* had it. And to avoid the cliché that would have perhaps been indulged by most other directors, Hitchcock refuses to show us Sam and Lila departing the courthouse together as dawn breaks. We're left staring into Norman's mad smile—no, *Mother's* mad smile, and the doctor's words are only jargon. We're left with the incomprehensible horror, all of it ignited by the most ordinary events: the need for cash, an intense love affair, the fate of poor Mrs. Bates, once widowed with a five-year-old child to support and victimized by a hotel man from the East "who could've tricked her into anything." And a lonely, overprotected child who felt an alienation of affection and, as a teenager, succumbed to some unimaginable moment of madness.

For most, a first viewing of *Psycho* is marked by suspense, even mounting terror, and by a sense of decay and death permeating the whole. Yet, for all its overt terror, repeated viewings leave one mostly with a profound sense of sadness. For *Psycho* describes, as perhaps no other American film before or since, the inordinate expense of wasted lives in a world so comfortably familiar as to appear initially unthreatening: the world of office girls and lunchtime liaisons, of half-eaten cheese sandwiches, of motels just off the main road, of shy young men and maternal devotion. But these become the flimsiest veils for moral and psychic disarray of horrifying proportions.

Psycho postulates that the American dream can easily become a nightmare, and that all its facile components can play us false. Hitchcock reveals the fraudulence of the fantasy that a woman can flee to her lover and begin an Edenic new life, forgetting the past: love stolen at midday, like cash stolen in late afternoon, amounts to nothing. He shatters the notion that intense filial devotion can conquer death and cancel the past, and he treats with satiric, Swiftian vengeance the two great American psychological obsessions: the role of Mother, and the embarrassed secretiveness that surrounds both lovemaking and the bathroom.

These concerns, these vulnerabilities, raise Marion Crane and Norman Bates almost to the level of prototypes—thus Hitchcock's insistence on audience manipulation and the resulting identification of viewer with character. It's this that accounts for the film's continuing power to touch us, its terror and its poignancy undiluted after three decades and multiple screenings. Broader in scope than the bizarre elements of its plot indicate, *Psycho* has the dimensions of great tragedy, very like the *Oresteia* and *Crime and Punishment*. In method and content, in the sheer economy of its style and its brave, uncompromising moralism, it's one of the great works of modern American art.

34

THE BIRDS

(PRODUCED 1962, RELEASED 1963)

Make a bloody attack; spread your wings,
Assail them, surround them all . . .
The birds are a prophetic divining Apollo.

ARISTOPHANES, *THE BIRDS*

Rod Taylor, Tippi Hedren, Jessica Tandy.

hree years elapsed between the release of *Psycho* and that of *The Birds*, the longest interval by far in Alfred Hitchcock's career to that time. The delay owed neither to lassitude nor indecision, but to the meticulous preparation of script and the careful study of the enormous technical challenges Hitchcock set for himself and his associates. There were, for example, many meetings with cinematographer Robert Burks, with special-effects expert Lawrence Hampton, with artist Albert Whitlock and photographic advisor Ub Iwerks, and with Ray Berwick, responsible for training over a thousand gulls and crows.

The result is perhaps Hitchcock's least accessible motion picture, for it reveals its richness like a demanding art novel or a complex symphony, only after considerable effort. Even ardent Hitchcockians are among those mystified and disappointed by this picture, although *The Birds* is certainly among his half-dozen masterpieces and one of the purest, most darkly lyrical films ever created. Part of the problem may be Hitchcock's refusal to compromise, for *The Birds* is nothing like a traditional narrative with a beginning, a middle and a firm conclusion. Working with writer Evan Hunter, the director took only the premise of Daphne du Maurier's short story for his basis; the screenplay became instead not a linear narrative (the typical structure of film) but rather a tragic poem whose episodes are like stanzas emotionally reinforcing a single theme. (Discussing *The Birds* with the author of this book, Federico Fellini called it an apocalyptic poem and affirmed it as his own favorite among Hitchcock's works and one of the cinema's greatest achievements.)

Hitchcock combined live action, animation, mechanical birds, live trained birds, and complex composite photography to produce an amazing series of shots—over fourteen hundred in this film, more than twice the usual number in a feature. But the deepest logic of *The Birds* is not exposed by elaborating its technical accomplishments, nor by detailing the harrowing experiences everyone sustained during production. More important and more enduring than any of this is the fact that the movie is a profound meditation on human relationships and on the myopic emotional vision that informs most of them. Precisely because the film operates *completely on the level of symbol,* it seems to masquerade as a bizarre, unclassifiable work. Some viewers still take it as a horror story, but in fact it has none of the characteristics of that genre. Others think it's a parable on the bomb, with all that destruction from the air. Still others see it as a weird tale of rebellious nature. But any interpretation along these lines is doomed to failure, for none takes into account the film's images, the rise and fall of the action and the crucial rotation of dialogues with eruptions of mysterious chaos. Hitchcock rigorously planned the structure, and to it he constantly referred. He had attached wide sheets of paper to his office walls, on which were graphs designating the rise and fall of each sequence, and the alternations of dialogue with action.

The film occurs over a five-day period, from Thursday to Monday, and except for the establishing sequence in San Francisco all the action is set in the coastal town of Bodega Bay, two hours north. Melanie Daniels (Tippi Hedren), a rich San Francisco socialite, meets the brash lawyer Mitch Brenner (Rod Taylor) in a city pet shop. Despite his flippant manner, she finds him attractive and drives to his weekend home in Bodega Bay (two hours north of San Francisco) to deliver a gift of lovebirds for his young sister Cathy (Veronica Cartwright)—and, it seems, to pursue him as well. On Melanie's arrival, she learns that Mitch shares the house with his mother Lydia (Jessica Tandy). She's injured when a sea gull swoops at her and scratches her forehead and, invited to dine with the Brenners, Melanie also attends Cathy's birthday party next afternoon. That night she stays with the local schoolteacher Annie Hayworth (Suzanne Pleshette), who was once in love with Mitch. Annie explains to Melanie the reason for Lydia's cool attitude toward any woman who comes into Mitch's life: she's a widow who endured a breakdown when her husband died five years earlier, and she's terrified of being abandoned.

As the delicate human relations of the story become more

The attack at the children's party.

complex, a series of bird attacks upsets life in Bodega Bay: a bird
smashes into Annie's front door, gulls terrorize the children at
Cathy's party, a flock of sparrows swoops down the chimney of
the Brenner living room, a neighboring farmer is pecked to death,
schoolchildren are besieged by attacking crows as they leave school
and Annie herself is killed while protecting youngsters. Eventually, Melanie and the Brenners become virtual prisoners, caged in
the house, and when Melanie is brutally attacked (in a sequence
that seems to repeat the shower murder of *Psycho*), her condition
makes it imperative that they attempt to leave the town. During
a lull in the attacks, the birds "allow" Mitch, Melanie, Lydia and
Cathy to depart, and the final frames show them driving slowly
away before (it is implied) the next savage onslaught. Hitchcock
refused to allow the words "The End" to appear, since indeed the
story does not have a conclusion. Like a poem, it simply stops.

Birds had long been agents and markers of chaos in Hitchcock's
films. The most important examples occurred in *Blackmail* (Alice

The attack on fleeing schoolchildren.

is awakened in the morning and feels the anguish of her plight as her pet bird chirps noisily away, filling her room with disorienting sound); *Sabotage* (the birds are the film's single most significant motif, linked to the terrorists, to the doomed Stevie and finally to the Disney cartoon that synthesizes the film's content); *Young and Innocent* (a flock of gulls indicates a corpse washed ashore, and young children refer to "rooks pecking at [the fugitive's] eyes"); *The Lady Vanishes* and *Jamaica Inn* (fluttering, crying birds attend the leading couple's fights for survival); *Saboteur* (stuffed birds and bird prints in the blind man's cabin presage danger for Barry Kane); *Vertigo* (the name "Elster" means mockingbird in German, and Judy Barton disguised as Madeleine Elster is just that—and wears a bird pin as talisman); and most of all *Psycho,* a film impossible to discuss without reference to its multiple, controlling bird imagery.

Bird-watching and the careful identification of species were of course national pastimes during Hitchcock's youth and were part of his school training as a country gentleman. One of the most famous late Victorian paintings synthesized the common artistic currency and identified the connection between birds and unpredictable eruptions of chaos. In Edward Burne-Jones's "Love and the Pilgrim" (painted 1896–97), Love is a garlanded angel—a giant "lovebird"—inviting a dark-robed pilgrim who emerges from a thicket to take the angel's hand and follow. The country journey ahead indicates thorns and brambles and there are numerous small birds in the thicket left behind and a large flock overhead—birds prevented from attacking only because of Love's protecting wings. But ever since early medieval times, birds had been representations of ill luck; in Victorian art and poetry, they became markers of discord.

The Birds seems to begin as an irrelevant romantic comedy that only shifts gears after about forty minutes. But these early sequences in fact are necessary for everything that follows. We're shown characters who treat relationships like brittle, amusing jokes, who tease and toy with one another, who refuse to take one another's feelings seriously. The decent and searching but still restless and shallow playgirl Melanie Daniels and the self-assured, emotionally withdrawn Mitch are prototypes of youthful brash-

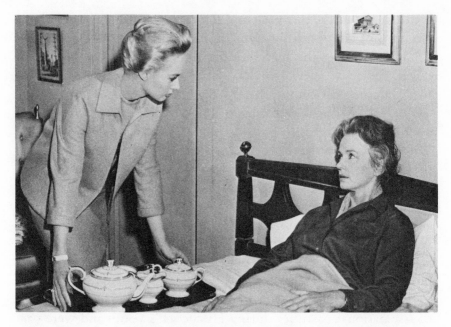

The fragility of the genteel life. (Tippi Hedren and Jessica Tandy.)

ness and almost neurotic independence. Their emotional lives and capacities for love are dangerously stifled, her charitable work is done from a comfortable distance (she helps to finance a foreign child's education), and her life as she describes it is an exercise in social and intellectual dilettantism (studies in linguistics one day of the week, "misdirecting travelers" at an airport another day, a charity lunch a third day). Neither wicked nor pathetic, she simply lacks depth and purpose, and on one level her ordeal in this story comprises her moral education. "Back in your gilded cage, Melanie Daniels," remarks Mitch at the pet shop; and the phrase "Poor thing!"—twice attached to birds by Annie Hayworth and Mrs. Bundy the ornithologist—is finally used by Lydia to describe Melanie after the great attic attack. On another level, of course, *The Birds* is the story of her search for her lost mother, a woman who abandoned her years ago and whom she "refinds" at the end in Lydia Brenner, the very woman who at first seems to reject her.

To appreciate just how the birds operate as markers of the chaos unleashed by shallow human relations, it's important to consider precisely when each attack occurs. This can be conveniently schematized (as Hitchcock himself did during preproduction): the attack of the gull on Melanie's head follows her coy teasing of Mitch; the gull crashes into Annie's door after Annie discusses her loneliness; the attack at Cathy's eleventh birthday party immediately follows Melanie's discussion of her own childhood abandonment at the age of eleven; the sparrows invade the Brenner living room as a frightened Lydia encourages Melanie (whose presence she fears) to leave Bodega Bay; the discovery of Dan Fawcett's dead body focuses Lydia's ordeal; the great attack on the schoolchildren follows Lydia's talk about her fear of abandonment and the loss of her children. And so on for the entire film, which may be most accurately described as a series of dialogues about loneliness and people's fear of and experience of abandonment—dialogues then localized and represented by the attacks of birds. The mysterious events, then, have nothing to do with capricious nature (much less a hostile or impassive deity); on the contrary, the bird attacks are poetic representations of everything shallow and undermining in human relationships. In this regard, it's important that we're not dealing with exotic birds—or bats or dark and stormy nights; there's nothing gothic about this picture, nothing removed. The birds are sparrows, sea gulls, crows, finches—all of them familiar.

Human relationships, the film postulates, are fragile and not ordinarily taken with the seriousness that prevents us from wounding one another—thus Hitchcock's insistence on three types of frailty that are multiplied elsewhere in the story: the teasing games Melanie and Mitch employ in the opening sequence (each playing dumb and trying to best the other); on Lydia's fear of abandonment ("I don't want to be left alone! I don't think I could bear to be left alone!" she sobs to Melanie) and Mitch's cross-questioning of Melanie at the bird shop, at the Tides Cafe and outside her car (where he wants to see her again because "I think it might be fun," to which she replies, "That's not enough for me!"). Accordingly, everyone is put through an ordeal because everyone suffers from that frailty, and the bird attacks are kinds of objective correlatives for the results of those weaknesses.

In this regard, it's also important to note that the major sufferers are children: they inherit the "sins of the fathers," as it were. From Melanie's tearful recollection of losing her mother (who, as a variant on Norman Bates's mother, "ditched us when I was eleven and ran off with a hotel man from the East") to the attack on children at the party and at the school, Hitchcock created episodes which contradict the frequently heard interpretation that the attacks are punishments for specific sins. It would be more accurate to say that the attacks are emblematic of *original sin,* the basic selfishness and weakness to which everyone is susceptible, to which every generation contributes and which causes even the innocent to suffer by virtue of their mere presence in the world. Our world is rightly represented, in *The Birds,* by the broken teacups which mark the film from the Brenner living room to the Fawcett kitchen. An avenging God may not be blamed for the chaos; it's the result of human sinfulness. Additionally, all possible explanations for the attacks are laughingly dismissed during the dialogues at the Tides Cafe: it's not the end of the world; Melanie's not a witch; the birds can't be dispatched by seizing guns and "blasting them off the face of the earth." The birds are, then, human forces of deception and abuse, representing all the unacknowledged frailties and imperceptions with which, however unwillingly, we hurt each other. The culprits of the story are not psychotics, nor people who murder or steal; they're folks just like us, people who hold one another with less honor than they deserve, who without commitments tease and play and act selfishly, refusing to go deeper than the shallows. It's a world typified by the children's game of blindman's bluff, an image carried forward from *Young and Innocent* ("which I added to that film as a deliberate symbol," Hitchcock told this author).

These imperceptions are localized and clarified in *The Birds* when we understand further just how deliberately it's a tract on the quality of our inner vision. Over two dozen times, characters say "I see," or "You see," the words like a refrain punctuating every stanza of this cinematic poem, just as every sequence concludes with a character staring out into space. Hitchcock chose to push to its limits the shocking image of Mother Bates's empty eye sockets in *Psycho,* an image logically extended here in a triple jump-cut to the pecked-out eyes of the dead farmer Dan Fawcett—and to Melanie's wide, unseeing stare after being attacked. Lashing out and beating at nothing while Mitch tries to calm her, she gazes

Rod Taylor, Jessica Tandy, Tippi Hedren, Veronica Cartwright—waiting.

straight out at the camera, at us, her eyes frantic with terror, thus making her the literal representation of Norman Bates's remark that we all "scratch and claw, but only at the air, only at each other."

Unseeing gazes and faulty vision needing correction—the point is impossible to ignore in *The Birds*. Attempting not to be seen by Mitch, Melanie is spied through his binoculars. Children play a game of blindman's bluff seconds before the birds attack. A schoolchild's shattered eyeglasses fill the frame during the great attack (a fulfillment of an historic image in Eisenstein's *Potemkin* and of Miriam's death in *Strangers on a Train*). A client of Mitch's shot his wife, who objected to his watching television. The episodes of *The Birds* move forward with a vengeance beyond the concerns of *Psycho,* and the only hope is with Cathy's lovebirds— "They haven't harmed anyone" is the film's bold, final line. But

whereas *Psycho*'s world was swallowed up in death, *The Birds* leaves open the possibility of salvation. A battered but surviving family makes its way through the thickening darkness, each member strengthened by its ordeal and their collective endurance, and the lonely Melanie embraced by Lydia, whose comfort and smile alone rouse her from shock. There's hope because they take with them the lovebirds, for these alone "haven't harmed anyone."

35

MARNIE

(PRODUCED 1963–64; RELEASED 1964)

Margaret, are you grieving
Over Goldengrove unleaving? . . .
It is the blight man was born for,
It is Margaret you mourn for.

GERARD MANLEY HOPKINS,
"SPRING AND FALL:
TO A YOUNG CHILD"

Tippi Hedren and Sean Connery.

The film opens with a close-up of a yellow purse, tightly clutched under a woman's arm. The film concludes with the word "purse," part of the old nursery song, "Mother, mother, I am ill—send for the doctor over the hill . . . Mumps! said the doctor. Measles! said the nurse. Nothing! said the lady with the alligator purse." And between these two moments we have one of Alfred Hitchcock's most underrated motion pictures, a tale that routs out a crippling fantasy life. When you stop to think about it, Alfred Hitchcock made his last emotional statement on film with *Marnie*. The somewhat forlorn *Torn Curtain* and *Topaz* followed in 1966 and 1969, then the icy anger of *Frenzy* in 1972 and the pleasant dessert *Family Plot* in 1976. But none of these has the wholeness of feeling, the

overt tenderness or the sheer poetry of *Marnie*. A complex, haunting parable about childish adulthood, it is not at all the lurid, facile
psychodrama as some have maintained. It was clearly a very personal work for the director, and it offers, in Tippi Hedren's astonishing second movie role, one of the finely honed, multileveled
displays of film acting of the 1960s.

The script (written with Jay Presson Allen and others who are
uncredited) was based on Winston Graham's novel of the same
name; as usual, however, Hitchcock altered it so that it might
conform to his own fervid sensibilities. *Psycho* told the fate of a
blond thief and *The Birds* of a monumentally cool blonde; *Marnie*
is pathologically frigid and a compulsive thief. Talk about "following a train of thought," as Barbara Bel Geddes said in *Vertigo*.

Among other values, *Marnie* is of course the midpoint of a
quartet on the sex-theft complex that began with *To Catch a Thief*,
continued through *Psycho,* and concludes with *Family Plot*. But to
place the film in context does not of itself justify my large claims
for it. The enduring value of *Marnie* lies rather in its exploration
of the relationship of past to present and the search for authentic
personality. A crippling fantasy life is finally confronted, no matter
how painful and demanding, and the film might quite accurately
be called a meditation on the healing of memories. Whereas *Psycho*
diagnosed a malignant psychological disease and *The Birds* applied
the surgeon's knife, *Marnie* begins the healing process. It is above
all a film about coming to terms with oneself—something of which
Norman Bates was incapable and the people of *The Birds* can only
begin to do at the finale. Thus the role of Mother is central to
these three films, for she is literally the bearer of oneself and the
repository of the past.

Margaret Edgar, who is called Marnie (Tippi Hedren), is a compulsive thief who moves from job to job, changing her name and
appearance. When she's hired by publisher Mark Rutland (Sean
Connery), who recognizes her from a previous brief business encounter, she ignores his amorous attentions and vanishes with a
large sum of cash from his company's safe. Mark discovers and
balances the loss and then finds Marnie. He blackmails her into
marriage, only to discover that she is also pathologically frigid.
When Mark forces himself on her, the poor woman attempts

suicide. Finally, in an attempt to solve the dual mystery of her compulsive thefts and her sexual confusion, Mark finds Marnie's mother Bernice Edgar (Louise Latham) and in a final confrontation between mother and daughter it emerges that Bernice was a prostitute who took the blame for Marnie's childhood killing of a sailor she thought was attacking her mother. The blocking of this memory has caused a psychoneurotic condition, and the story ends as Marnie leaves her mother's home, wishing to solve her emotional problems and to remain with Mark.

In adapting Winston Graham's novel, Hitchcock and Allen did more than change the setting from England to the American East Coast. Since the novel was a first-person narrative written by Marnie from prison, viewpoint was limited entirely to her. But in the film there is as much concern for Mark's curious psychology, for he's a man sexually obsessed with a woman who rejects him, and he continues to pursue her precisely because she's a thief (a theme introduced in Frances Stevens' attraction to John Robie in *To Catch a Thief*). Marnie's emotional states, her courage, her resourcefulness, her essentially sympathetic nature—all these are Hitchcock's invention. And we are never permitted to so identify with her that we cannot observe the ambiguities of her relationship to Mark with his exploitive comment, "I've trapped you and caught you and by God I'm going to keep you. I've really caught a wild thing this time!"

In this regard, Mark is as much the cause of Marnie's pain as he is her hope for the future, whereas in the novel a psychiatrist (boringly) fulfills the healing function. Even if we grant that Mark is the strongest hero of Hitchcock's later films, we must also admit that his methods can hardly be endorsed. He's manipulative, exploitive and, as Hitchcock always insisted, as psychologically sick in his way as Marnie in hers.

Another major change from the novel is the survival of Bernice Edgar, who conveniently dies in the original tale while Marnie is en route to visit her. Their final confrontation and the mutual confession of love at the end introduces the tenderest note of hope and fulfills Marnie's question at the film's beginning: "Why don't you love me, Momma? I've always wondered why you don't. You don't give me one part of the love you give Jessie [a neighborhood child Bernice cares for]." The answer comes at the end, after Marnie whispers, "You *must* have loved me, Momma—you *must* have loved me!" Bernice, also tearfully, replies, "Why sugar-pop, you're the only thing I ever did love!" Seldom is such emotion nakedly presented in Hitchcock's films, and it's hard not to suggest that this, too—a tone so uncharacteristic of him—is one of the reasons *Marnie* is flatly rejected by many critics. Like Marnie's relationship with Mark, the mother-daughter relationship will have to be worked out in time—after the healing of memories—and it is time that Marnie has hitherto both denied and abused.

Little has been solved at the conclusion, and the dimensions of the problem have been only exposed, but the finale is open-ended and suffused with the glow of hope. That is why *Marnie* is fundamentally not a psychological case history at all; it rather illumines the therapeutic ground plan and the wholeness of feeling that precedes arrival at a healthier emotional state.

Hitchcock also changed the novel's Terry Holbrook, a man who turns Marnie over to the police because of his jealousy of her relationship with Mark; because there's enough sexual specialism in the story already, the gay Terry has become the film's Lil Mainwaring (Diane Baker), the tart brunette who's Mark's sister-in-law and equally jealous. Likewise Lucy Nye, the mother's elderly companion in the novel, has become the film's young Jessie (Kimberly Beck). This change establishes an understated but significant reference to Marnie's childhood, for both have long blond hair the camera examines in close-up several times. In the book it's Lucy Nye who tells Marnie the truth about her mother, whereas in the film Marnie herself must *reenter and reexperience the past in memory*. Thus she (not others, as in the book) must kill the wounded horse Forio, an action directly linked to the traumatic incident of her childhood by Marnie's repetition of "There—there now" when she mercifully shoots the horse and when she allows the memory of her killing of the sailor to reemerge from repressed memory. Additionally, Graham presented Marnie's mother as murdering an illegitimately conceived child. Hitchcock wisely omitted this unnecessary detail and has focused attention on Mother as a far more sympathetic figure. Finally, the book's Mrs. Rutland has become the film's Mr. Rutland (Alan Napier), so that

Mark may have the parent Marnie lacks—just as was the case with Mitch and Melanie in *The Birds*. A readable little book, therefore, was immeasurably deepened in its transference to the screen and the conclusion is infinitely more compassionate, humane and hopeful.

At the center of the film is the troubled relationship between Marnie and Mark, who is able to help her because he is relatively free of the past—"relatively" because he still wears the wedding band from his first marriage. During the storm which frightens Marnie, his late wife's art is broken when a tree crashes through a window into the room. "Well, we all have to go sometime," he says calmly. Later, Marnie refers to those items as "all you had left of your wife," but he corrects her: "I said it was all I had left that had *belonged* to my wife." The distinction is important, and the ability to distinguish enables him to help her.

The first word heard in the film—"Robbed!"—is uttered directly out at us by Rutland's accountant, Strutt (Martin Gabel). But he's not the only one so exploited. Marnie was, too, and her mother before her, as Bernice makes clear in a painful monologue after

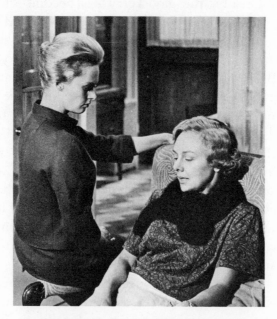

"A decent girl don't have need for no man."
(Tippi Hedren and Louise Latham.)

The theft of Rutland money and (below) the fear of discovery.

"Oh, Forio, if you want   The shooting of Forio.
to bite someone, bite me!"

the dream-remembrance. "You know how I got you, Marnie?
There was this boy—Billy—and I wanted Billy's basketball
sweater. And he said if I let him, I could have his sweater. So I
let him. And then when you got started he run away. But I still
got that old basketball sweater—and I got you, Marnie—and I
wouldn't let them take you away from me! I promised God that
if He'd let me keep you, I'd raise you different from myself—
decent." From the beginning, others had tried to *buy* affection
from her mother, and she bartered with them; and in a way it's
the same now with little Jessie, whose love Bernice buys with a
pecan pie. Theft is a chain reaction, a family trait which seeps
beyond the confines of one household.

Larceny is often related to sexual pathology, and so the film
uses three classically Freudian images to make the connection: the
purse (familiar from significant shots in *Suspicion*), the horse and
the tree crashing through the window, which is linked to the
porthole on the honeymoon cruise. "Oh, Forio!" Marnie says
affectionately to her beloved horse, "If you want to bite someone,

bite me!" (Again, one recalls Lina in *Suspicion,* happy only when she's on horseback.)

The connection between water, sex and death is a venerable complex of ideas, and Hitchcock makes rich use of it in *Marnie.* She and Mark endure a destructive rainstorm through which they then drive. Mark is associated with sailing and cruises—and thus with the paying clients of Bernice, who are sailors; in each case, the men are both lustful and protective, and the dream-remembrance shows the sailor (Bruce Dern) comforting the frightened young Marnie (Melody Thomas) with the identical gesture of Mark in the present. Like the sailor, too, Mark is beaten by Bernice. The final confrontation occurs in another rainstorm that drenches Marnie and Mark and is associated with the specifically Baptist training Marnie received: "And His tears will wash thy

At the stable—reminiscent of *Vertigo.*
(Tippi Hedren and Sean Connery.)

The final dream-remembrance.
(Louise Latham, Sean Connery,
Tippi Hedren.)

sins away and make thee over again," Marnie remembers of her
Sunday school education.

Marnie and Mark are both fascinated by animals, each of them
more or less in touch with their own physicality. While Mark
reads *Animals of the Seashore,* Marnie paces in her stateroom, rather
like the jaguarundi Mark proudly trained. She also identifies with
the hunted fox—and all of it is linked to her pathetic desire for
death ("Me!" is her word-association with Mark's cry "Death!"
during their psychological game-playing). And in this regard, the
red suffusions that fill the screen when Marnie is traumatized refer
not only to the deeply repressed memory of the sailor's bloodstained T-shirt; they also imply feminine maturity and loss of
virginity—precisely the realities of which Marnie is terrified and
which she tries to avoid.

The hope for a resolution of her trauma lies, then, not in simple
textbook counseling, nor in a facile application of what Mark has
read about behavioral psychology—but rather in reentering the
experience and confronting its meaning. The ending of *Marnie,*
far more hopeful than that of *Psycho* and more directly affirmative
even than *The Birds,* shows us an emotional landscape once burnt,
now resown. Marnie will come to terms with her mother, we feel
sure, and while the final chant of the children outside the Edgar
house does not augur an easy outcome, it's a kind of expression

With Mariette Hartley, Tippi Hedren and S. John Launer, Hitchcock lightens the tone for a moment. Then (below, with cinematographer Robert Burks) it's back to business.

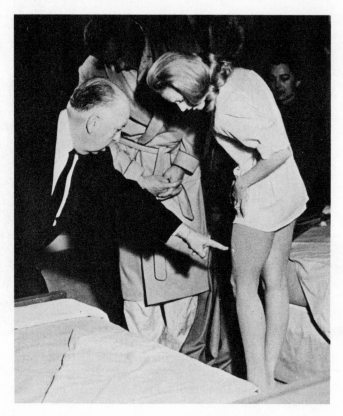

Hitchcock points to chalk mark on Miss Hedren's legs;
the camera will shoot below that for illusion of nudity.

of Marnie's own fear, and of her now expressed desire to be saved.

The richness of this film derives very greatly from Tippi Hedren, who gave a remarkably nuanced performance (under particularly trying circumstances that are detailed in *The Dark Side of Genius*). Miscalculated by most American critics at the time (but not by British or French writers), she brought an unruffled calm and understatement to an hysterical dramatic situation. Hedren conveyed considerable emotional range, and one remembers with perhaps especial appreciation the robbery scenes, the scene aboard ship and the final confrontation with actress Louise Latham. One has only to listen to her little-girl falsetto (complete with Southern accent), as she recalls the childhood trauma, her pain over Forio's death, and the complex of emotions offered in the bedroom dialogue with Mark after her nightmare. Here was a young actress with quickly polished skills, developing a credible character (one of the

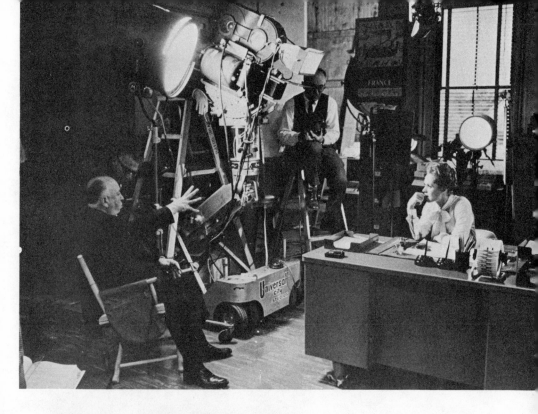

A rehearsal for the shot
in which Marnie spills red ink
on her blouse.

Hitchcock sketches a
rectangle in the air,
indicating what will
fill the screen.

Shooting the conclusion of the hunt sequence.

most demanding in all Hitchcock's films), memorably rendered by a woman in only her second picture.

And so *Marnie* remains, always controversial, ever (at least to this writer) almost unbearably moving in its final scenes. By illuminating the corners of one woman's fears, it comes close to a description of the delicate balance between sickness and health in everyone. Never descending to the bathetic, it has that stance toward life that also characterized the injunction to acceptance addressed to another Margaret, in Hopkins's extraordinary lyric:

> Now no matter, child, the name:
> Sorrow's springs are the same.
> Nor mouth had, no nor mind, expressed
> What heart heard of, ghost guessed:
> It is the blight man was born for,
> It is Margaret you mourn for.

36

TORN CURTAIN

(PRODUCED 1965–66; RELEASED 1966)

Some say the world will end in fire,
Some say in ice.

ROBERT FROST,

''FIRE AND ICE''

Julie Andrews as Sarah.

After a decade of successes, the release of *Torn Curtain* was a disappointment for just about everyone, and none more than Hitchcock himself, who agreed that it lacks the interest, wit and style of his recent works. It's a good example of a picture with some intellectual substance and a great deal of polish and dignity but little emotional power apart from one touching sequence. And since emotional power is invariably the mark of Hitchcock's creative genius, *Torn Curtain* has to be judged a minor achievement.

Working with the director, Brian Moore fashioned an original screenplay which hinges on an aspect of the cold war that has dated hopelessly since 1990: the separation of the two Germanys. Michael Armstrong (Paul Newman), an American nuclear physicist, pretends to be a defector to East Germany in order to learn a secret formula (the MacGuffin, of course) from a certain Dr. Lindt (Ludwig Donath). His assistant and fiancée Sarah Sherman (Julie Andrews) follows him behind the Iron Curtain, and at last he confides the truth in her. A series of adventures follow: Michael must murder Gromek (Wolfgang Kieling), a man who discovers his true purpose; the couple are briefly aided by an eccentric Polish countess (Lila Kedrova); and they finally elude pursuers at a ballet performance of *Francesca da Rimini,* reaching safety at last on a Scandinavian ship and returning to the free West.

The title of the film refers ostensibly to the "tearing" of the Iron Curtain which Michael effects by infiltrating East Germany under false pretenses. But it refers equally well to his dramatic interruption of the ballet performance and to Lindt's blackboard containing the secret formula, which he unsuccessfully tries to hide beneath another board, slammed down like a concealing curtain. What really engage our interest in this picture, however, are the admirable structure, the themes of journey and displacement, the centrality of the fire imagery and the mythological parallel which

Mort Mills and Paul Newman.

momentarily illuminates the meaning of the story and its characters.

Like *Foreign Correspondent* and Hitchcock's other "travel/espionage" films, this has a logically cyclical structure, opening in Scandinavia, moving to East Berlin, to Leipzig, then back to East Berlin and finally back to Scandinavia. This is more than a neat framework: it defines the meaning and the meaninglessness of Michael's espionage mission. What he really learns has to do with his need of other people—Sarah particularly, for at the end he is at last able to respond to her earlier question, "Aren't I of use to you anymore?" It is, after all, she who matters, not the secret formula. The message was the same regarding the specifications for a line of fighter planes in *The 39 Steps;* the tune containing the secret clause in *The Lady Vanishes;* the clause of the treaty in *Foreign Correspondent;* the espionage activities in *Notorious;* the politics of

After the swim to safety.

The Man Who Knew Too Much; and the microfilm in *North by Northwest*. Relationships matter, not political secrets.

The cyclic journey is also a kind of treadmill of displacements, for Michael and Sarah arrive as strangers in hostile territory and must be continually on the move—from luxury liner to airplane to private car to taxi (which brings Michael to the farm, the murder of Gromek and the structural and thematic midpoint of the film), then to bicycle, to bus and to boat. The modes of transportation, one notes, become progressively uncomfortable and dangerous after Gromek's death, until the final escape is made in theatrical costume baskets, from which the couple must jump into chilly waters and swim to a nearby ship.

The voyage behind the Iron Curtain becomes a trip to a hellish underworld where the predominant color, aptly, is red, suggesting the "Red" world of cold war Communism and the infernal (or perhaps, more accurately, the purgatorial) fires through which Michael and Sarah must pass. Red objects always crowd the frame: kiosks, lampposts, clothes, posters, books, pens, signs, flowers in parks and on dining tables, carpets, costumes, even wigs (on Madame Luchinska and on the stagehand). This constant use of red must have been both a problem and a minimal satisfaction to Hitchcock, for whom *Torn Curtain* was rewarding only insofar as it was an experiment in lighting and color. "I tried for the first time to change the style of color lighting," he said. "We shot the whole film through a gray gauze. We almost attained the ideal, shooting with natural lights."

Red also has the hellish connotation because of its association with fire, the controlling image and motif throughout the film. The credits appear against a flame, and the faces of the principals emerge from gray smoke. Throughout, Gromek's cigarette lighter functions badly for him (although it works just fine for Michael after Gromek's murder). Lindt lights several cigars with a large flame, and Mr. Jakobi (David Opatoshu), the leader of the freedom bus, lights a cigarette for a passenger to distract the police from recognizing Michael and Sarah. The final fire imagery appears in the ballet sequence. As Michael watches the infernal fires round Paolo and Francesca (from the fifth canto of Dante's "Inferno," where the poet meets the pathetic lovers in hell), the flames suggest

As usual with his actors, Hitchcock draws a screen,
then "sketches in" what will fill it.

to him an avenue of escape. He shouts "Fire!" and creates sufficient
panic to enable him and Sarah to flee.

If their journey is infernal, it's also a kind of Orphic descent
and return. In the classical myth, Orpheus claimed he didn't seek
out the secrets of the underworld; his only purpose, he explained
to the guardian spirits of the dead, was to rescue his Eurydice.
The situation of *Torn Curtain* is an ironic inversion of that. Sarah's
loyalty, her refusal to believe in Michael's defection, redeems them
both and enables them to benefit from those they meet. And
Michael indeed seeks out the secrets of this "red world." He's a
kind of Orpheus manqué, and his new Eurydice is the redeeming
figure of Sarah. Their trial by fire, furthermore, links them to the
ballet's Paolo and Francesca. And again like Orpheus and Eurydice, Michael and Sarah are forced out of their former isolation and
must endure crowds. Initially, we see them huddling under blankets and rejecting dinner invitations but later, just as Orpheus had
to encounter the infernal crowds, Michael must battle crowds at
the university, on the bus, at the post office and at the theater.
But alas, this intriguing mythic subtext simply cannot save *Torn*

Curtain from its own lethargy, and the film is so firmly rooted in an ad hoc political situation (now no longer compelling) that the characters tend to be ciphers.

At the opening—aboard, significantly, the *M/S Meteor,* reinforcing the fire imagery—a breakdown in the ship's heating system causes everyone to bundle up against the cold (it's literally a cold war, if you please). The thermostat reads zero centigrade, and Michael and Sarah shiver in bed under gray blankets while other passengers break the solid ice in their water glasses. Emerging later from his cabin, Michael is addressed: "The heat's on again," to which he replies, "I'll say." This neatly introduces the theme of heat against cold, for he has just received a cable which will plunge him into a fiery mission of espionage in a "red-hot" country. Then, in the cold countryside, Michael kills Gromek, with the help of the farmer's wife (Carolyn Conwell).

The progress of the story, then, takes Michael and Sarah from

Hitchcock with his co-star for the
cameo appearance in *Torn Curtain.*

cold to warmth, and the final frames show them warming themselves near a stove aboard ship. They've endured the cold war, a trial by fire in miniature. The fire imagery, in other words, points on the positive side to what lies at journey's end—warmth and Michael's passage from cool, mathematical, academic speculation to the heart of action. He enacts the Orphic drama.

The last sequence focuses all this quite clearly, as the couple must plunge into the water for escape, crossing back over the Stygian waters to the "upper world" of light and warmth. In the last shot, the lovers seem to be in the identical situation as at the opening, but Sarah's laughter suggests a closeness that was tentative when she nervously wondered about their future at the beginning.

But for all its color and its interesting subtexts (and the magnificent wordless pursuit through the Leipzig museum), *Torn Curtain* finally fails to move. Even the poignant scenes with Countess Luchinska seem gratuitous, salvaged only by Lila Kedrova's funny-touching characterization as she yearns for her "sponsors to the United States of America."

37

TOPAZ

(PRODUCED 1968–69, RELEASED 1969)

*Where yellow is emphasized and compensatory,
there is likely to be superficiality.*

THE *LÜSCHER COLOR TEST*

Karin Dor and John Vernon.

W̲hereas *Torn Curtain* was received lukewarmly, *Topaz* was not: audiences and critics were hot with resentment and disappointment, rating it as a disaster, and the general consensus since 1969 has been that here Hitchcock strayed beyond his form. *Topaz* simply lacked the suspense and shocks to which audiences had become addicted. Additionally, it had a narrative line of uncommon complexity, and there were few climactic moments to break up the interminable talk. It has, however, more than a few redeeming qualities.

Based on Leon Uris's sprawling novel (film rights to which were owned by Universal Pictures, whose executives virtually forced the project on Hitchcock after two years of indolence) and on the allegedly factual account of Thyraud de Vosjoli, *Topaz* was produced under what Samuel Taylor, the author of the final screenplay, called

> dreadful circumstances . . . While he was in production, Hitchcock threw out Mr. Uris's original screenplay—it was literally unusable. He called me and I flew to London on twenty-four hours' notice and started writing a whole new screenplay for him while he was beginning to shoot. It was all written—although Hitchcock knew the story line—a few days ahead of every shot. Scenes were written, then photographed. That was quite stimulating, but quite difficult.

This was also, of course, quite contrary to Hitchcock's traditional methods, since he ordinarily worked out every element of a picture well in advance of shooting, secluding himself with the writer until the script was completed and perfected. Only then did he emerge for conferences with designers, wardrobe artists and the rest of his crew—and after all this preproduction, filming began. The forfeiture of this preparation time was one of the reasons for the failure of *Topaz*. "If we'd had more time," Taylor concluded, "obviously it would have been much better. When we got back to California, we were still casting. The Cuban lady wasn't cast until the very last minute."

The story is set in 1962, amid the complexities of the Cuban missile crisis. Michael Nordstrom (John Forsythe), an American intelligence agent in Copenhagen, helps Boris Kusenov (Per-Axel Arosenius), a noted Russian security officer on holiday with his family, to defect from Russia to the West. On their arrival in Washington, American agents then learn from Kusenov that the Russians are involved in Cuban military strategy, and that there is a Communist spy group—code-named "Topaz"—within the highest levels of French (and therefore NATO) security. Details of the Russian-Cuban pact are available, since Rico Parra (John Vernon), one of Castro's senior assistants, is in America and Uribe (Don Randolph), Parra's secretary, can be blackmailed for this information. Parra, however, will not talk to an American, and so Nordstrom seeks aid from André Dévereaux (Frederick Stafford), a friend attached to the French embassy; Dévereaux in turn is helped by a West Indian florist, Philippe Dubois (Roscoe Lee Browne), who photographs the secret treaty.

Against the wishes of his wife Nicole (Dany Robin), Dévereaux goes to Cuba to uncover more information about Russian plans. He is there reunited with his sometime mistress, Juanita de Cordoba (Karin Dor). The widow of a national hero and also Parra's mistress, she is the leader of a resistance network, glad to assist Dévereaux in his pro-American, anti-Communist efforts. But her servants are arrested and tortured when their surveillance cameras are found, and Parra himself murders Juanita. Dévereaux escapes with vital pictures and returns to Washington, where he learns that his family has gone back to France. Shortly thereafter he is summoned by his government, which is suspicious of his involvements.

In Paris, Dévereaux tries to learn the identity of the Frenchman who heads Topaz ("Columbine" by code name). The man turns out to be Nicole's lover, Jacques Granville (Michel Piccoli), who has already implicated NATO economist Henri Jarre (Philippe Noiret) and has killed him so as to suggest suicide. At the end, Granville, discovered, returns home and kills himself, and the final frames show a newspaper headline announcing the resolution of the Cuban crisis.

Topaz begins in a typical Hitchcock manner: place and date appear on-screen, and the camera moves from a vast overview of Copenhagen to a private residence. Thenceforward, the film's structure is elliptical: to Washington, to New York, to Cuba to Washington to Paris. The title is important and suggests how the film is in fact a kind of series of color correlatives. The topaz is a yellow quartz, and the spy group with that name is located in France: hence yellow is constantly associated in the film with French people. The lamp shades, chairs and flowers in the Dévereaux residence in Georgetown are yellow; Nordstrom brings a large bouquet of yellow chrysanthemums to their suite in New York; the Harlem florist who helps the Frenchman wears a yellow smock; when Juanita agrees to help André she changes to a yellow skirt; yellow roses decorate Granville's room. All this would be mere coincidence were there not production files indicating Hitch-

In the florist's refrigerator.
(Roscoe Lee Browne and Frederick Stafford.)

cock's specific directions and his meticulous work with production designer Henry Bumstead.

But the French-based Topaz is at the same time part of a Communist plot, and so Hitchcock has brilliantly combined red with the vivid yellows: Parra's bright red beard; a red attaché case contains the Russian–Cuban treaty; Granville wears a red dressing gown; André's son sketches Jarre with a red pencil; red and yellow Picasso Harlequins are framed nearby, and a red and yellow Tif-

The spies' camera hidden in the sandwich.
(John Roper, Karin Dor, Lewis Charles, Anna Navarro.)

fany lamp shade stands in the foreground. Thus Hitchcock darkens
the apparently optimistic yellows with the color then linked to
Communism, bloodshed and death.

Equally important is the use of lavender, a color with poignant
emotional overtones. Dubois pins a lavender requiem motto across
a funeral bouquet, and in the next sequence Nicole wears a floor-
length lavender dressing gown as her husband leaves for his mistress. When we first see Juanita she wears red (she is, after all,
ostensibly pro-Castro), but when her lover arrives she changes to
yellow, thus identifying herself with the French, and for the scene
of her murder she wears lavender.

There are other typically Hitchcockian grace notes in *Topaz:* the contrast between the St. Regis and the Theresa Hotels in Manhattan; the bathroom as the place where twice secrets are revealed (at the Theresa and on the airplane), just as in *Torn Curtain* and *Psycho,* among others; a gull flies off with the sandwich bread that conceals the Mendozas' camera, leading Parra's men to the fleeing couple; a chicken which concealed another camera is blithely eaten for dinner and boldly offered to Parra when he interrupts the lovers at table.

The political bias of *Topaz* is not as simplistic as it seems on first viewing. Hitchcock has never been quite comfortable with overtly political, one-sided statements, and the politics of his films are always merely a cyclorama against which he probes issues of human moral concern at once more specific and more universal than international politics. (This is obviously so in *Secret Agent, Foreign Correspondent, Saboteur, Lifeboat* and *Notorious.*) In *Sabotage* and *North by Northwest* we are not even told the details of the political issue at stake; in *The 39 Steps* we are told only that the secret involves a line of fighter planes. But the MacGuffin continues to operate amid political issues, and there are several indications that in *Topaz* he had in mind, at least as a subtheme, the shared responsibility of the United States for the suffering and deaths in the story.

The motif of flowers is also worth noting. In the opening sequence, the tour guide at a Copenhagen studio comments on the details of floral sculptures on statuettes. The image is carried forward at the Harlem florist; Nordstrom brings flowers to the Frenchman's suite; the rooms in Cuba are banked with flowers, as are those in Paris. Every set is ablaze with floral arrangements, and the unifying sequence for their significance is the florist scene: each episode, in other words, has the faint redolence of death. The florist was also Samuel Taylor's invention, and there is no parallel for it in the Uris novel.

The intimate relationships in the film have a sad intensity, too. Juanita's kisses are passionate—almost desperate—and the scene in which her lover departs for the last time is especially poignant in light of her subsequent death. Afterwards, when her servants are caught taking photos of the Russian ships and missile installations, they are hideously tortured in a pose deliberately resembling the Michelangelo *Pietà*. Then, when Parra learns his mistress is a traitor, he returns to her home in one of the most carefully designed sequences in Hitchcock's films. Juanita descends the staircase slowly, he embraces her, clasps her hands and kisses them, then quietly insists that he will have to turn her over for punishment. The camera, all the while, travels round them 180 degrees, and slowly begins an upward climb until we see them as if from God's viewpoint, directly overhead. A revolver shot rings out and Juanita, head thrown back and eyes open wide, sinks slowly to the white marble floor, her lavender robe splaying round her like a dark, fatal lily pad. (The effect was achieved by inserting wire spokes in the gown.) By involving and exploiting her, Dévereaux has indirectly caused Juanita's death; he has also alienated his wife, who has ironically taken as *her* lover the head of Topaz! Dévereaux's face registers grief, loss and confusion when on the airplane he opens the book Juanita gave him (signed "With all my love, Juanita—October 1962") and, moments later, discovers the microfilm pasted beneath the endpapers. Her parting gift is the secrets he wanted, but they are passed on at the cost of her life.

The bitterest irony of *Topaz* is the moral dilemma expressed by Kusenov toward the end. Initially diffident and scornful of American capitalism, he is now master of his castle, smoking expensive cigars, pouring tea from an elegant service, walking in the lovely gardens before dinner and suggesting to Dévereaux, "If your problem is whether to obey your conscience or your government—don't go. These people—the Americans—will give you a new life." The irony of this cynicism is that we soon learn Kusenov is in fact a double agent.

Hitchcock filmed two endings besides the one we have: in one, Granville is killed by a sniper during a duel with Dévereaux; in the second, Granville escapes to the East and to safety with his Communist colleagues. But the ending as we have it is the best. The newspaper announcement of the resolution to the Cuban missile crisis is hardly a triumph, for it is followed in the final montage with the tortured and murdered people who were involved, all those caught in the cogs of the mad machines of the superpowers—

the Mendozas, savagely tortured in jail; Jarre, shot through the head and tossed out his window atop a yellow car; Juanita, sacrificed more because of jealousy than politics. Hitchcock's moral cynicism, his deep distrust of politics and his contempt for international big business have perhaps never been so uncompromisingly revealed.

"The problem with *Topaz,* which I don't like," Hitchcock told this writer, "is that you have all those foreigners speaking English. It's a big letdown." But it has a strange and tenebrous beauty, and in the last analysis the picture may be one of the finest flawed films of a decade that gave us so many "relevant" but superficial and simplistic movies. Amid such wasted celluloid, Hitchcock's *Topaz* gleams brightly.

38

FRENZY

(PRODUCED 1971, RELEASED 1972)

O, who can . . . cloy the hungry edge of appetite
By bare imagination of a feast?

RICHARD II

Jon Finch and Barry Foster.

After the disappointments expressed by critics over *Torn Curtain* and *Topaz,* the huge success of *Frenzy* placed Alfred Hitchcock back at the top of his popularity with this first-rate thriller, as notable for its juicily macabre humor as for the horror of its major theme. He and screenwriter Anthony Shaffer took Arthur La Bern's novel *Goodbye Piccadilly, Farewell Leicester Square* for their basis and turned it into something quite different.

Frenzy may, first of all, be profitably considered as the fourth in a tetralogy that began with *Shadow of a Doubt* and developed in *Strangers on a Train* and *Psycho.* In all four, Hitchcock examined a pair of complementary personalities—only apparently opposites, actually matched aspects of a single character. Once again, inno-

cence and guilt are interrelated, and there are several levels of
disturbing moral ambiguity. But perhaps the film's most remarkable achievement is its brilliantly sustained metaphor of food—
the act of eating and its antithesis, hunger.

The plot is straightforward. Hot-tempered Richard Blaney
(Jon Finch), down on his luck, is suspected of being London's
notorious rapist-murderer who has been eluding police, and an
indictment seems near when his estranged wife Brenda (Barbara
Leigh-Hunt) is added to the list of victims. The incriminating
evidence is a necktie identical to his, which has been used for the
stranglings. When Blaney's girlfriend Babs Milligan (Anna Massey) also falls victim, he's arrested.

The case is under the direction of Inspector Oxford (Alec
McCowen) who, in the course of his investigation, must contend
with the no less criminal gourmet cooking of his eccentric wife
(Vivien Merchant). The murderer, as the audience has known since
early on, is Blaney's friend, Covent Garden wholesale grocer Bob
Rusk (Barry Foster).

Jon Finch and Anna Massey.

"You're my kind of girl."

. . .

Scenes set at dinners have been central to the Hitchcock filmography. One thinks of the three meals of *Sabotage,* the formal dinners of *Notorious, The Paradine Case* and *Marnie,* the dinners in *Shadow of a Doubt,* the supper in *Psycho* and so forth. For Hitchcock there was always an ambivalence, a conflict about food and eating, and in *Frenzy* food becomes at last the main character. It constantly interrupts our view, carried back and forth in great sacks of produce by workmen until, at the end, a human body is stuffed into a sack of potatoes. This visual association lifts the picture to the level of metaphor, for it's really about the kind of exploitation that becomes the devouring of people.

The idea is ruthlessly elaborated in the film. Blaney crushes grapes underfoot; inedible "gourmet food" is prepared by Mrs. Oxford; her husband is forced to eat heartily away from home; and Brenda Blaney—one of the film's two positive figures (both are women)—buys dinner for her ex-husband and then becomes the lunch of her victim. People become food for their victims. "Don't squeeze the goods until they're yours," the grocer Rusk says to Brenda—and at once he fulfills the market motto, raping her (making her his) and then strangling her, squeezing her to death. She becomes his goods, his lunch, his food, and once she's dead he picks his teeth after taking one last bite from her apple. All this was prepared when Rusk and his buddy spoke at the Globe pub of a lot of rotten potatoes, concluding: "And they say there's people starving in this world." This is why Inspector Oxford, of course, speaks of catching the killer "before his appetite is whetted again"—and this he says as he tries to cut into the tiny quail his wife serves him as a substitute for a real dinner. The opening words of the film begin the motif, when the politician Sir George says, "Ladies and gentlemen, I'm pleased to tell you that these ravishing sights will soon be restored to you"—and so they will momentarily, when we witness a ravishing—and that the Thames River above County Hall "will be clear of industrial effluents, free of the waste products with which we have for so long polluted our rivers and canals." And then at once we see a woman's body, naked and floating to shore, and the link between dross and human life is made at precisely the moment of Sir George's ironic promise.

Blaney is Hitchcock's least attractive innocent, a man capable of Rusk's crime even more than Guy Haines (in *Strangers on a Train*) was capable of Bruno's. Angry, hard-drinking, violent when married to Brenda, he finally plans a worse crime—a premeditated revenge murder worse even than anything the demented Rusk could have hatched. Blaney has himself admitted to a hospital in order to escape more easily and murder the man responsible for his predicament. But Rusk, as we clearly understand, simply actualized Blaney's potential for violence and abuse: whereas Blaney exploited Brenda and let her pay for his dinner, Rusk literally makes Brenda his free meal. Thus the "R" of Rusk's tiepin is neatly ambiguous, marking Richard as well as Rusk. A further link is supplied by potatoes. Because Blaney's clothes have the smell of potatoes (he slept with a potato sack over him at the Salvation Army), he must have them cleaned at the Coburg Hotel, and at once he jumps into bed (in the sack) with Babs. Later, Rusk packs Babs's body in a sack of potatoes, and the smell of potatoes on his clothes and on his brush gives him away to Inspector Oxford.

This complex of ideas—food-sex-death—is further highlighted by the grotesque scenes in which Rusk tries to pry the pin loose from Babs's dead fingers, a moment balanced by Oxford's attempt to slice into the tiny quail with his knife. Describing Rusk's breaking of Babs's dead fingers to remove the incriminating tiepin, Mrs. Oxford breaks a breadstick as her husband says "broke the fingers." Pretty it isn't; morally savage, certainly.

Everyone in the modern, bustling world of *Frenzy* is hungry indeed, despite the glut of food in this fallen "garden," Covent Garden. As Rusk says, he's from Kent, "the garden of England"; and Felix Forsythe (Bernard Cribbins) says at the Globe pub, "This is Covent Garden, not the Garden of Love." But now the paradise has gone to rot; it's the place where sour fruit is sold and people become food for each other.

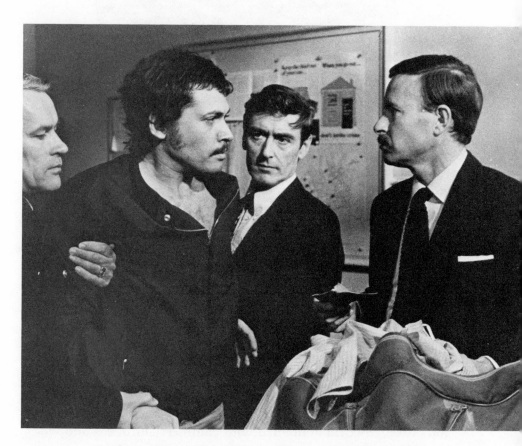

Alec McCowen (right) as Inspector Oxford.

Rehearsing the potato truck sequence.

Frenzy describes, in its brilliantly icy, angry moral outrage, a world in which Hitchcock apparently lost hope, and it's important to see the failure of love and friendship in every single relationship in the story—even the couple just matched at the Blaney Bureau, who share only the dangerous hobby of beekeeping. People exist, in this picture, only as food for one another's maniacal appetites. "Oh, get stuffed!" mutters Babs to the unkind Felix in a line Hitchcock added latterly to the screenplay; the line takes us back to *Psycho* and its stuffing of birds and women—and forward to the last sequences of poor Babs herself, stuffed in a potato sack. Brenda buys Blaney a meal, Oxford longs for one, Babs becomes one. The "getting stuffed" is, then, no mere vulgar metaphor: it suggests directly the link between eating and exploitation, and the perversity of each one out of control. *Frenzy* speaks, then, in the demonic voice: deceitful, devouring relationships are all too typical of a fallen world of fruits and vegetables and Covent Garden hustle and bustle, a world gone mad with commercialism, sex and violence. It's a place where people are very hungry indeed.

39

FAMILY PLOT

(PRODUCED 1975, RELEASED 1976)

The world, dear Agnes,
is a strange affair.

MOLIÈRE,
L'ÉCOLE DES FEMMES

William Devane, Karen Black, Alfred Hitchcock,
Barbara Harris, Bruce Dern.

Critics and the public were astonished, in the spring of 1976, when Alfred Hitchcock's fifty-third feature film was released, for it demonstrated a control, a sure-handed wit and a tight sense of structure. After all, he was seventy-six, he had had a pacemaker inserted during preproduction, and he suffered a variety of painful ailments, including arthritis. If his movie had turned out to be a little tired, well, that would have been excused. But he offered a great surprise, for the film has an extraordinary youth and zest and, thanks to Ernest Lehman's polished screenplay (wisely departing from its basis, Victor Canning's novel *The Rainbird Pattern*), Hitchcock's final film was a small but significant gem.

Rich, elderly Julia Rainbird (Cathleen Nesbitt) enlists the aid

Barbara Harris as Madame Blanche. Cathleen Nesbitt as Julia Rainbird.

Fran (Karen Black) examines the Constantine diamond.

of spiritualist Blanche Tyler (Barbara Harris) in an effort to locate her sole surviving heir, a lost nephew. Attracted by the promise of a ten-thousand-dollar reward, Blanche and her boyfriend—taxi-driver and aspiring actor George Lumley (Bruce Dern)—set out to find the missing man. At the same time, jewelry merchant Arthur Adamson (William Devane) and his mate Fran (Karen Black) are profitably engaged in a series of kidnappings and fantastic diamond thefts. The paths of the couples accidentally intertwine, and it turns out that Adamson, though unaware of it, is really the Rainbird heir. After a series of bizarre incidents, including the attempted murders of Blanche and Lumley, Adamson and Fran are captured, and Blanche and Lumley happily survive.

The title of the film, as always with Hitchcock, deserves some scrutiny. (Until the last week of shooting, in July 1975, it was known as *Deceit*. But Hitchcock thought that was a weak title, and, perhaps aware of an earlier movie called *Deception*, accepted the change.) It's an amusing title, and the ambiguity covers multiple possibilities.

First, Julia Rainbird instigated a family plot forty years earlier

Lumley (Bruce Dern) suspects that Edward Shoebridge may not be dead.

Maloney and his wife (Ed Lauter
and Katherine Helmond).

when she persuaded her sister Harriet to give up her illegitimate
son to spare the family public disgrace. Second, there is the family
plot hatched by the Rainbird heir as a child, when he was known
as Edward Shoebridge and plotted the murder of his adoptive
parents. Third, there is the family plot in which Harry and Sadie
Shoebridge are buried. Young Eddie and his crony Joe Maloney
had set fire to the Shoebridge home, and the murder was designed
to look as if the boy had died in the blaze, too. As we learn,
however, Eddie Shoebridge—with his name changed to Arthur
Adamson—is not in the family burial plot at all.

Although the film exploits several modern concerns and in-
terests (psychism, kidnapping, electronic gadgetry in Adamson's
secret room), it's thematically very much mainstream Hitchcock—
as perhaps only Ernest Lehman, who had crafted *North by Northwest* almost two decades earlier—would have known. Four themes
are especially prominent.

First, the link between theft and sex, comically described in
To Catch a Thief and more tragically in *Psycho* and *Marnie*. Kid-

At Abe and Mabel's Cafe.

napping and diamond-stealing make Fran in *Family Plot* feel strange and "tingly," and then sexually aroused. *Marnie* forged the same link dramatically in the association of compulsive theft with derailed sexuality and acquisitiveness as a substitute for mature love. "When a child—a child of any age—can't get love, it takes what it can get, any way it can get it." Thus Mark Rutland (Sean Connery) in *Marnie*.

Second, there is the Hitchcock tradition of the search for a missing person. The pursuit, or the disclosure of a hidden personality, was an important element in *The 39 Steps, The Lady Vanishes, Spellbound, Vertigo, North by Northwest* and *Psycho*. Here, it's the search for the Rainbird heir, now known as Arthur Adamson—a kidnapper who "steals" prominent people (a shipping magnate, a bishop) who are worth great ransoms. But the irony is neat, for Adamson doesn't know that he's worth much more than those he kidnaps. He resorts to an attempt on the lives of Blanche and Lumley (and then of Blanche alone) to cover up the *false* identity—Eddie Shoebridge—he thinks is his real identity, and under which he had plotted the death of his adoptive parents. All these resonances add special poignancy to the moment in the cemetery when Mrs. Maloney, who has given Lumley a crucial clue, kicks the Eddie Shoebridge tombstone, crying, "Fake! Fake!"

It's easy to see how the irony is carried further. Adamson hides in his basement the people he has kidnapped. Like the basement of *Psycho,* it's a kind of hiding place for acquired identities (the Freudian id couldn't be more literal). Adamson, then, deals not ultimately in jewelry but in the glitter of famous people whom he kidnaps and then returns in exchange for diamonds. As we've seen in earlier films, jewelry is invariably a symbol of spurious value, of the apparent versus the real—consider, in this regard, *The Ring, Shadow of a Doubt, Lifeboat, Under Capricorn, Stage Fright, To Catch a Thief* and *Vertigo.*

Third, Hitchcock gives free rein to his obsession with the motif of the influence of the dead on the living. The whole adventure is precipitated by Miss Rainbird's guilt ("I am seventy-eight years old and I want to go to my grave with a quiet conscience") and by her troublesome nightmares, for her dead sister Harriet disturbs her sleep, "always whining and complaining" about the lost child

Julia forced her to give up. The dead often come back to haunt the living in Hitchcock's films—*Notorious, The Trouble with Harry, Vertigo* and especially *Psycho*—and one of the structural niceties of *Family Plot* is that Blanche, a fake medium, abets the adventure by her "profession" of linking the dead with the living.

Detailed even more finely is the fourth theme, that of role-playing. As in *The 39 Steps, Stage Fright, North by Northwest* and elsewhere, everyone is playing a part. In a story about the disclosure of a missing person's real identity, we follow here the activities of people who constantly assume false identities: Blanche is a fake medium; Lumley is an aspiring actor who role-plays ("McBride, a lawyer") but who's called a "real amateur" by Joe Maloney (Ed Lauter); Adamson forces Fran to wear disguises and to assume the name "The Trader" in her role as her aide; Adamson plays the role of a respectable jeweler.

Structurally, this is the purest film Hitchcock made since *The Birds*. It begins and concludes at night and with a tight close-up of Blanche—eyes closed in the first scene, winking in the last. The comparisons between the two sets of couples (delineated fully below) are unfolded similarly: first we are shown the female doing

Adamson (William Devane) is told the good and the bad news by Fran.

The cemetery sequence.

her part as a fake (Blanche as a medium, Fran as a blonde). Then
their respective men are introduced, each in a lengthy dialogue in
their automobiles (Lumley's taxi, Adamson's black sedan). Then
we move from the opening dialogue between Blanche and Lumley
to the Fran/Adamson story as Fran crosses a street and is nearly
hit by Lumley's taxi. The runaway car sequence which nearly kills
Blanche and Lumley is perfectly balanced by another daylight
sequence, the quick getaway Adamson and Fran make after kidnapping the bishop. The film's structure is also neat in the introduction of Julia's sleeping problems: she tried to get sleeping pills
without prescription at a pharmacy, while Adamson drugs his
victims into coma for their abduction and release.

But perhaps the most interesting aspect of the film is the contrast of couples. The fundamental identification is that of Blanche
with Adamson, for both are motivated by greed. They're also
linked by her use of a crystal ball as a "cover," and by his use of
the crystal chandelier as "cover"—as the hiding place for dia-

monds. Furthermore, each is linked to an unseen and unreal personality—Eddie Shoebridge and Henry, Blanche's "control" in her seances. Finally, it's interesting to note that the only homes we enter are those of Blanche and Adamson (except for Miss Rainbird's parlor): Lumley and Fran, whose identities derive from and are very much dependent on their lovers, are never seen in their own homes. (Fran is even deprived of a surname.) And in the final scene, Blanche fools Lumley into believing that she is really psychic—just as Fran was fooled about Adamson's "Eddie Shoebridge" identity, which he kept from her. The basis of the whole adventure, as so often in Hitchcock's films, began with a childhood incident (as in *Downhill, Spellbound* and *Marnie*) and involved a breach of trust (as in *Strangers on a Train* and *Frenzy*). "Isn't it touching," Adamson remarks to Maloney, "how a perfect murder has kept our friendship alive all these years."

The guilty persons in the story receive proper retributions. As punishment for setting the fire that killed the Shoebridges and for buying the fake tombstone, Maloney dies in the flames of his auto wreck—after warning Lumley to "be careful with those matches" at the filling station. And he's buried in the same cemetery as the Shoebridges, close by the family plot. Similarly, Adamson and

Bruce Dern: he's "the most entertaining man, the best actor."

Barbara Harris, about Hitchcock: he's "serene."

Fran are locked in the basement room, apt retribution for locking up their kidnap victims.

The structural midpoint of *Family Plot* links the complex of ideas—sleep/danger/death/loss of identity—in the haunting cemetery pursuit of Mrs. Maloney (Katherine Helmond). The shot suggests a human chess game, the paths evoking a painting by Mondrian sprung to life. (The sequence was shot in two days of drizzle, without artificial light, at the Pioneer Cemetery in Sierra Madre, California.) *Family Plot* is, in fact, a series of chases within the framework of the pursuit of a missing man.

How was it to work with Hitchcock on his final film? During the last week of shooting on *Family Plot,* the author of this book put that question to several members of the company.

Bruce Dern: I've made thirty films, and he's the best director I've ever worked for. He's also the most entertaining man, the best actor. He's got style and personality, and he's full of stories.

William Devane: he "knows what he wants."
Karen Black: he's "always thinking of his audience."

Of course, people say he allows no freedom to actors. But there's all the freedom in the world once you understand the ground rules. He explains what the shot is supposed to say and what you're supposed to do. Then you give it! If you couldn't do it, you wouldn't be working for him in the first place. Nothing is left to chance except the actor's improvisation. He's concerned that the actor keep it fresh, alive, new. He wants each shot to entertain him—then he knows the audience will be entertained.

Barbara Harris: Hitchcock makes radical remarks about actors, but he is actually very serene and thoughtful with them.

William Devane: He knows what he wants. For this role, he gave me an image of William Powell and told me to keep it as light as possible. So what I do is to play the clothes. I put the clothes on and let them do the work.

Karen Black: Hitchcock has an inner placidity. Everything has been figured out before he does it on the set, and he's always thinking of his audience, of how they will respond to each detail. That's why audiences love Hitchcock. He's a great man. He has ebullience of spirit, lightness of heart, charm. People feel different around him. I wanted to play Blanche, but especially I wanted the chance to work with Hitchcock.

Leonard South, director of cinematography: He's a master technician. He knows the photographer's problems because he knows exactly how it's done. To get a director with as much art and technical talent is very rare. Hitchcock makes it easy for a cameraman. Most directors, if artistic, have no technical knowledge. I've worked with him since *The Paradine Case,* and he's uncanny.

Edith Head: he's a "super-perfectionist."

Leonard South: he "makes it easy for a cameraman."

He asks what lens you have on the camera, then he looks at the scene and he knows what will appear on the screen. He's rarely wrong. And he never moves the camera without a reason. When it moves, it's because the audience should be looking around with the actors. He's very specific about that.

Edith Head, costumes: He's a super-perfectionist. When I go to him to have a discussion on clothes, he looks at me with that inscrutable smile and says, "There it is, my dear Edith—in the script." In Hitchcock's films, our concern is to change actors into characters, not to do fashion shows. Working with him has been the most important part of my career. Each of his pictures has its own nuance and chemistry. He always gets what he wants. He demands respect, and everything is so calm around him. You can't categorize Hitchcock. He's—Hitchcock!

STORYBOARD

Throughout his career Hitchcock has plotted the action of his films by the use of a storyboard, a series of sketches developed from the final shooting script depicting each bit of action. The storyboard is a constant guide for the director and his cinematographer as filming takes place, but Hitchcock often makes modifications—which accounts for the absence, in the film, of some of the elements in the two sequences from the *Family Plot* storyboard shown on the following pages.

Of all the episodes in *Family Plot,* the runaway-car sequence and the cemetery pursuit provided the greatest technical challenges and have already been called classic Hitchcock moments. I am grateful to Mr. Hitchcock for his permission to publish this valuable material, which provides a rare glimpse into the specifics of his technique. The illustrator of the storyboard for *Family Plot* was Thomas J. Wright.

To assist the reader in understanding the shorthand of film language, the major abbreviations used are here explained:

L.S.—long shot, full figures of the subjects and more

L.&B.—Lumley and Blanche (characters in the film)

P.O.V.—a point of view shot, i.e., what a character sees

Int/Ext—interior or exterior

Process—a process shot is one in which actors play in front of a screen onto which a background (usually exterior) is projected

Obj.—an objective shot, i.e., not a point of view shot

O.S.—off-screen; a voice is heard, the speaker is not seen

C.U.—a close-up shot

Insert—a shot photographed separately, inserted later

THE RUNAWAY-CAR SEQUENCE

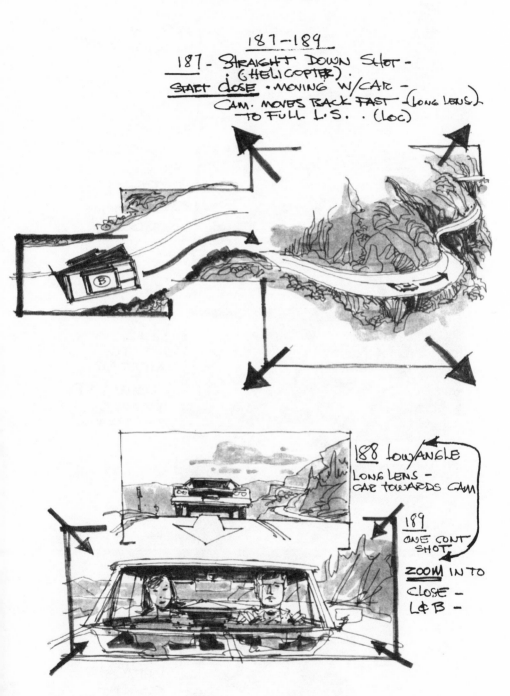

187-189
187 - STRAIGHT DOWN SHOT -
      (HELICOPTER).
START CLOSE - MOVING W/CAR -
CAM. MOVES BACK FAST (LONG LENS).
    TO FULL L·S· · (LOC)

188 LOW/ANGLE
LONG LENS -
CAR TOWARDS CAM

189
ONE CONT
SHOT
ZOOM INTO
CLOSE -
L & B -

190 — 193

190
P.O.V.
MOVING SHOT

190.
CONT SHOT
CAR AROUND
BEND —

191
CUT TO
INT/CAR.
CLOSE L & B
PROCESS.

192
P.O.V.. ?
BOULDER.
—

193
INT/CAR
2 SHOT
PROCESS.

194—197

194
OBJ. SHOT
LOW ANGLE —
CAR OUT OF FRAME →

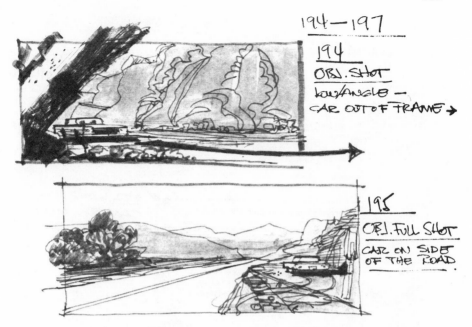

195
OBJ. FULL SHOT
CAR ON SIDE
OF THE ROAD.

196 REVERSE ANGLE

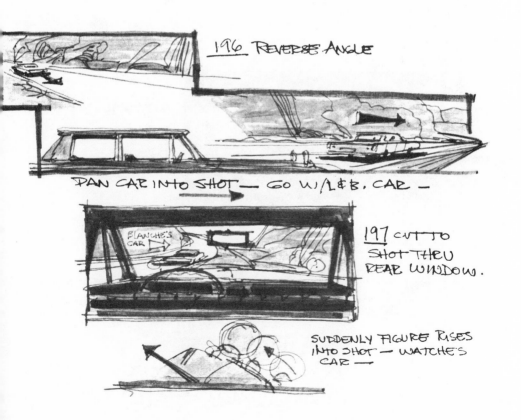

PAN CAR INTO SHOT — GO W/ L & B. CAR —

BLANCHE'S CAR →

197 CUT TO
SHOT THRU
REAR WINDOW.

SUDDENLY FIGURE RISES
INTO SHOT — WATCHES
CAR —

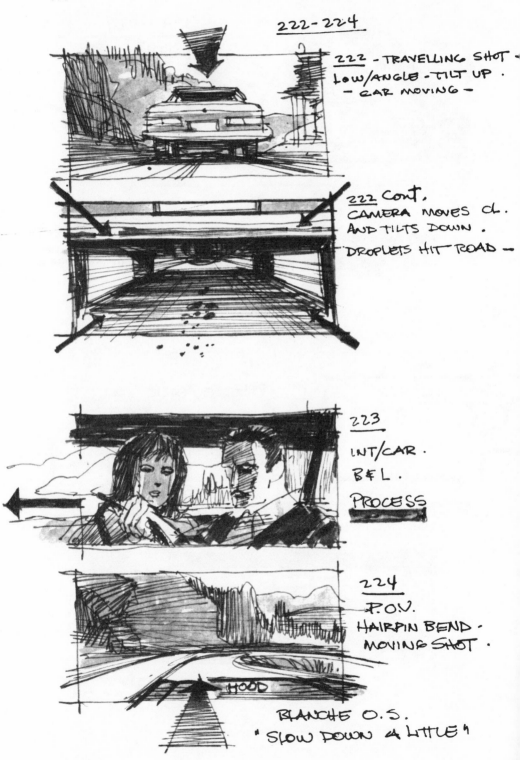

222-224

222 - TRAVELLING SHOT -
LOW/ANGLE - TILT UP.
- CAR MOVING -

222 CONT.
CAMERA MOVES CL.
AND TILTS DOWN.
DROPLETS HIT ROAD -

223
INT/CAR.
B&L.
PROCESS

224
P.O.V.
HAIRPIN BEND.
MOVING SHOT.

HOOD

BLANCHE O.S.
"SLOW DOWN A LITTLE"

225 — 228

225
MOVING
P.O.V.

HAIRPIN CORVE —

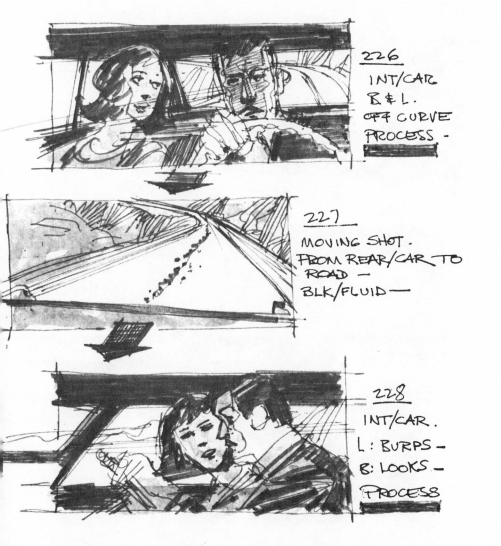

226
INT/CAR
B & L.
OFF CURVE
PROCESS —

227
MOVING SHOT.
FROM REAR/CAR TO
ROAD —
BLK/FLUID —

228
INT/CAR.
L: BURPS —
B: LOOKS —
PROCESS

229 — 231

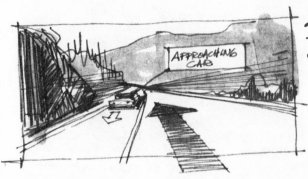

229 P.O.V.
CAR APPROACHES —

229. cont
INTER/CUT.
CLOSE 2 SHOT.
B & L.
PROCESS

230
QUICK C.U.
LUMLEY.
LOOKS DOWN
TOWARDS FOOT
PROCESS.

231. INSERT
BIG C.U.
LUMLEYS FOOT.

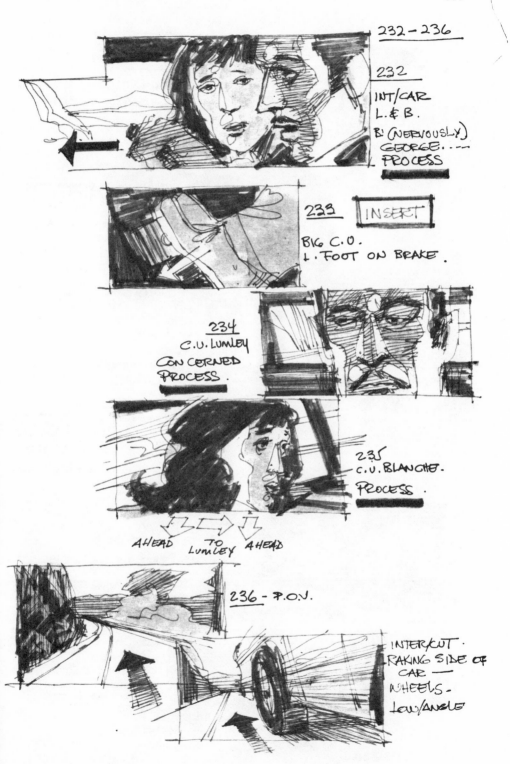

232 - 236

232
INT/CAR
L. & B.
B: (NERVOUSLY)
GEORGE....
PROCESS

233   INSERT
BIG C.U.
L. FOOT ON BRAKE.

234
C.U. LUMLEY
CONCERNED
PROCESS.

235
C.U. BLANCHE.
PROCESS.

AHEAD   TO   AHEAD
      LUMLEY

236 - P.O.V.

INTERCUT.
RAKING SIDE OF
CAR —
WHEELS.
LOW/ANGLE

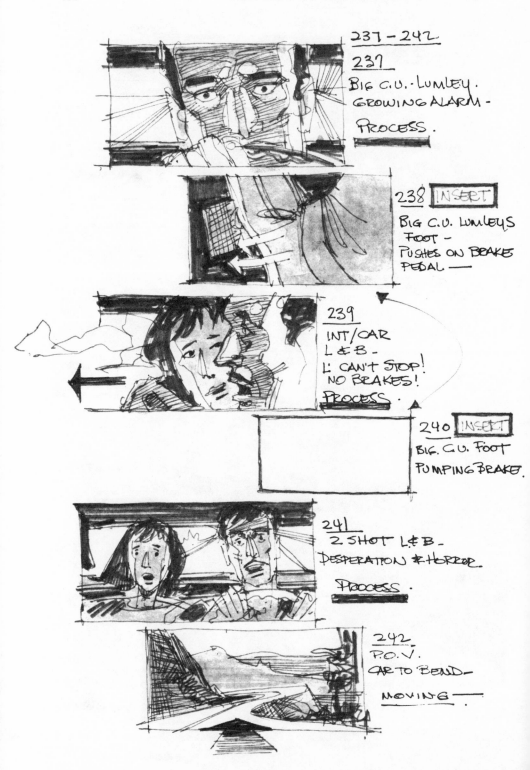

237-242

237
BIG C.U. LUMLEY.
GROWING ALARM -
PROCESS.

238 INSERT
BIG C.U. LUMLEYS
FOOT -
PUSHES ON BRAKE
PEDAL —

239
INT/CAR
L & B -
L: CAN'T STOP!
NO BRAKES!
PROCESS.

240 INSERT
BIG. C.U. FOOT
PUMPING BRAKE.

241
2 SHOT L & B -
DESPERATION & HORROR.
PROCESS.

242
P.O.V.
CAR TO BEND -
MOVING —

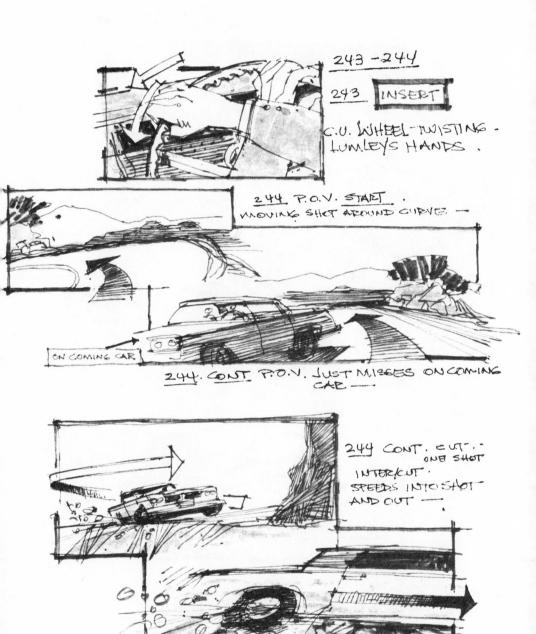

243 -244

243 INSERT

C.U. WHEEL TWISTING -
LUMLEY'S HANDS .

244 P.O.V. START .
MOVING SHOT AROUND CURVE. —

ON COMING CAR

244. CONT P.O.V. JUST MISSES ON COMING
CAR —

244 CONT. CUT -
ONE SHOT
INTERCUT .
SPEEDS INTO SHOT
AND OUT —

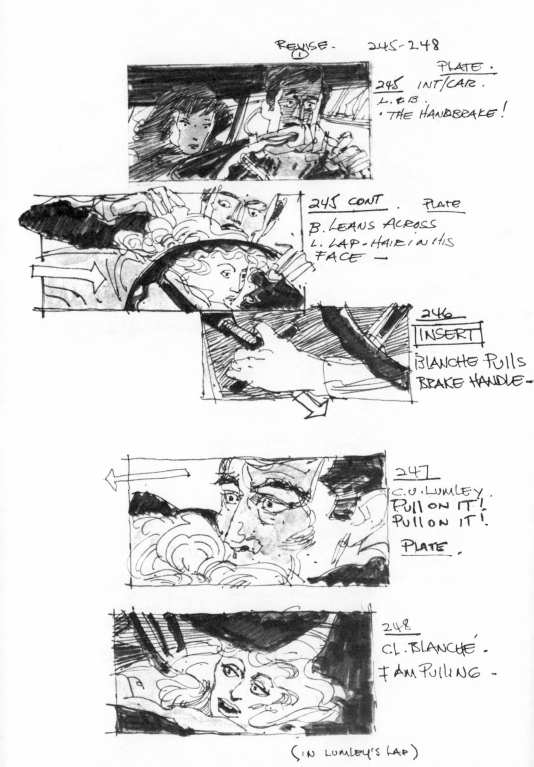

REVISE.   245-248
①

PLATE.
245 INT/CAR.
L. & B.
· THE HANDBRAKE!

245 CONT.   PLATE
B. LEANS ACROSS
L. LAP - HAIR IN HIS
FACE —

246
INSERT
BLANCHE PULLS
BRAKE HANDLE —

247
C.U. LUMLEY.
PULL ON IT!.
PULL ON IT!.
PLATE.

248
C.U. BLANCHE.
I AM PULLING —

(IN LUMLEY'S LAP)

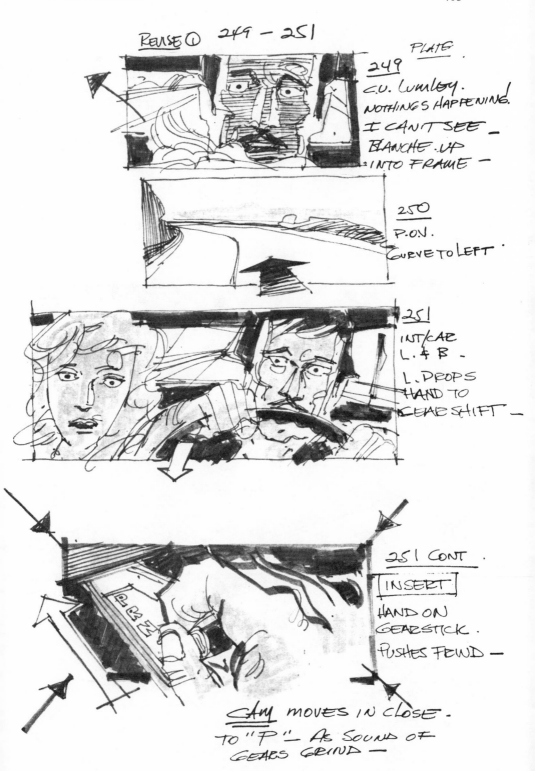

REUSE ① 249 — 251

PLATE.

249
C.U. LUMLEY.
NOTHINGS HAPPENING.
I CAN'T SEE
BLANCHE. UP
INTO FRAME —

250
P.O.V.
CURVE TO LEFT.

251
INT/CAR
L. & B.
L. DROPS
HAND TO
GEAR SHIFT —

251 CONT.
[INSERT]
HAND ON
GEARSTICK.
PUSHES FEWD —

CAM MOVES IN CLOSE.
TO "P". AS SOUND OF
GEARS GRIND —

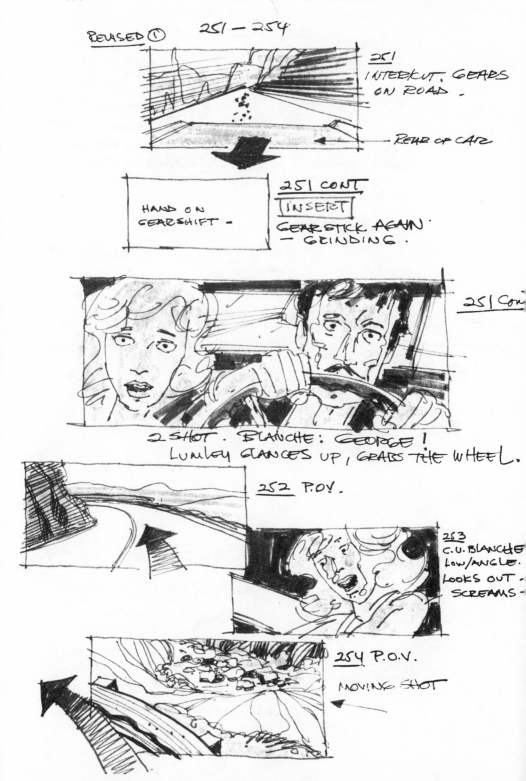

REVISED ① 251 — 254

251
INTERCUT. GEARS
ON ROAD.

← REAR OF CAR

HAND ON
GEARSHIFT —

251 CONT
INSERT
GEAR STICK AGAIN.
— GRINDING.

251 Cont

2 SHOT. BLANCHE: GEORGE!
LUMLEY GLANCES UP, GRABS THE WHEEL.

252 P.O.V.

253
C.U. BLANCHE
LOW/ANGLE.
LOOKS OUT.
— SCREAMS —

254 P.O.V.

MOVING SHOT

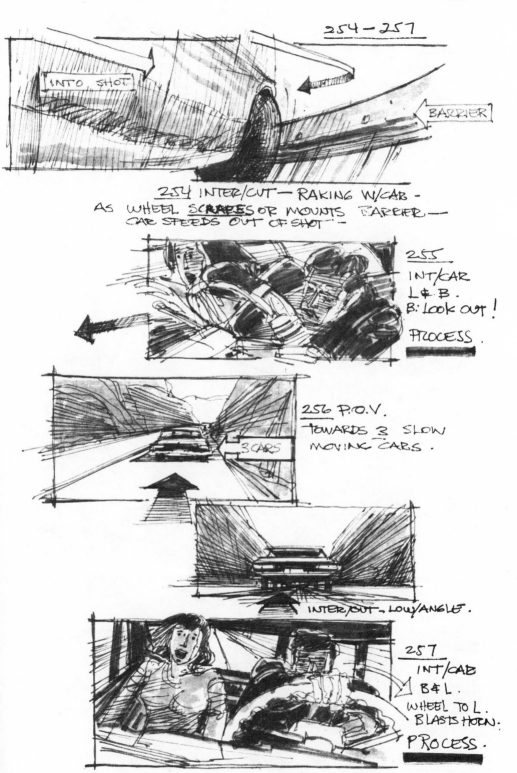

254 — 257

254 INTER/CUT — RAKING W/CAB —
AS WHEEL SCRAPES OR MOUNTS BARRIER —
CAR SPEEDS OUT OF SHOT —

INTO SHOT

BARRIER

255
INT/CAR
L & B.
B: Look out!

PROCESS.

256 P.O.V.
TOWARDS 3 SLOW
MOVING CARS.

3 CARS

INTER/OUT - LOW/ANGLE.

257
INT/CAB
B & L.
WHEEL TO L.
BLASTS HORN.
PROCESS.

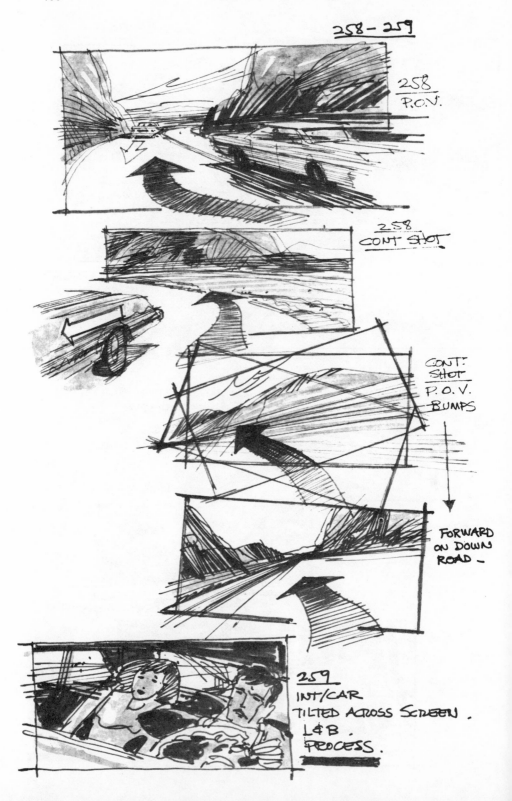

258 - 259

258
P.O.V.

258
CONT SHOT

CONT:
SHOT
P. O. V.
BUMPS

FORWARD
ON DOWN
ROAD —

259
INT/CAR
TILTED ACROSS SCREEN.
L & B.
PROCESS.

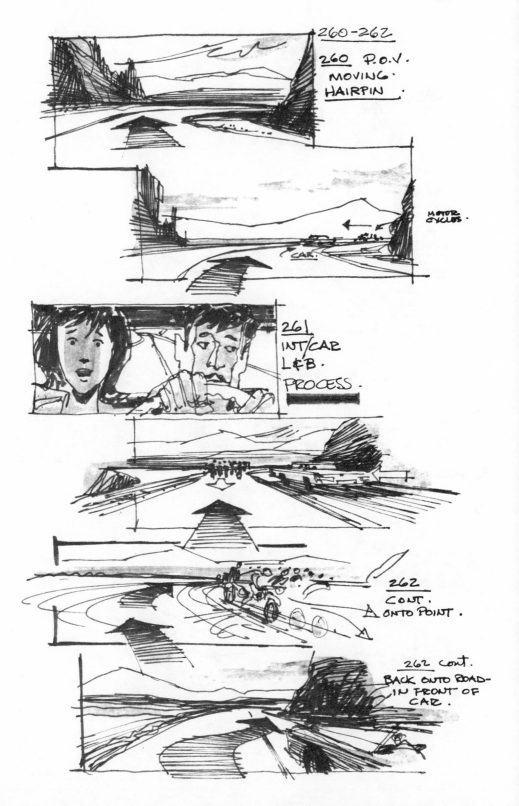

260-262

260 P.O.V.
MOVING.
HAIRPIN.

MOTOR
CYCLES.

CAR.

261
INT/CAR
L&B.
PROCESS.

262
CONT.
Δ ONTO POINT.

262 CONT.
BACK ONTO ROAD-
IN FRONT OF
CAR.

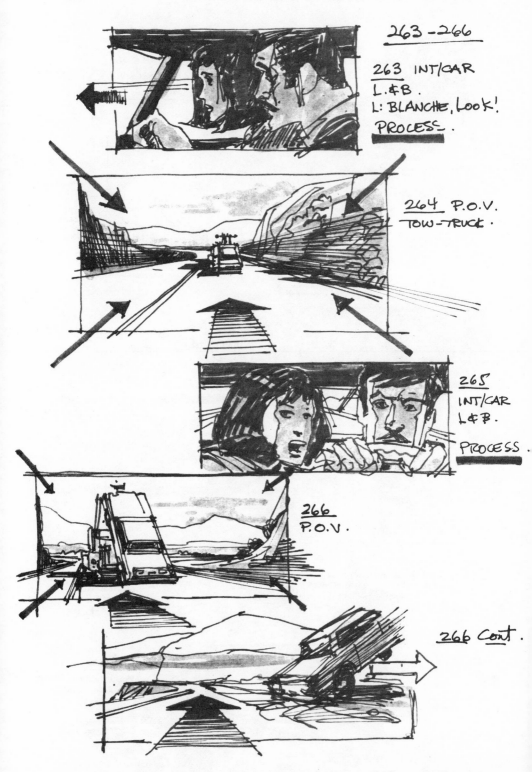

263-266

263 INT/CAR
L.&B.
L: BLANCHE, LOOK!
PROCESS.

264 P.O.V.
TOW-TRUCK.

265
INT/CAR
L&B.

PROCESS.

266
P.O.V.

266 Cont.

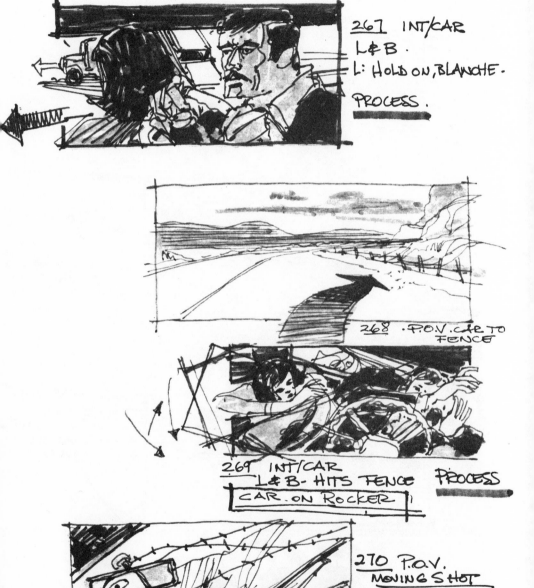

267 INT/CAR
L & B.
L: HOLD ON, BLANCHE.

PROCESS.

268 · P.O.V. CAR TO
FENCE

269 INT/CAR
L & B. HITS FENCE   PROCESS
CAR · ON ROCKER

270 P.O.V.
MOVING SHOT
THROUGH WINDSHIELD ·

PROCESS.

· OR ·
· REAL ·

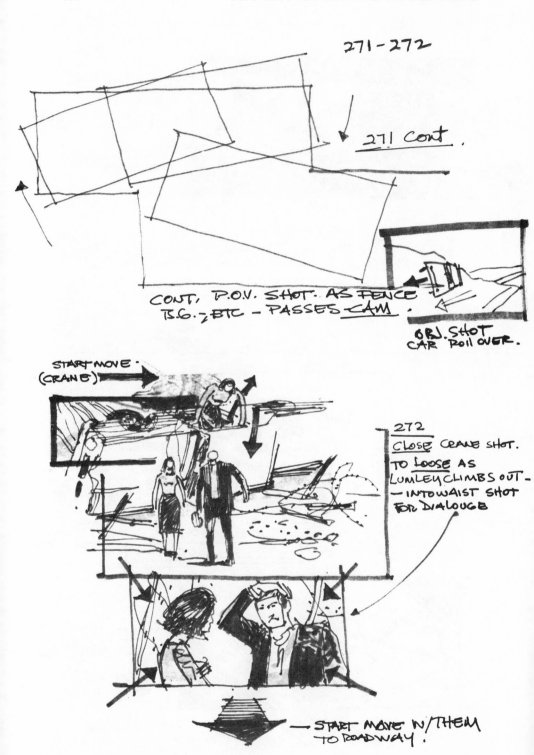

271-272

271 Cont.

CONT, P.O.V. SHOT. AS FENCE
B.G. & ETC - PASSES CAM.

OBJ. SHOT
CAR ROLL OVER.

START MOVE·
(CRANE)

272
CLOSE CRANE SHOT.
TO LOOSE AS
LUMLEY CLIMBS OUT·
— INTO WAIST SHOT
FOR DIALOUGE

— START MOVE W/THEM
TO ROADWAY.

272A - 272B . ADDED.

272A

START

START CLOSE - PAN CAR ⟶
NO SIGN OF ACTIVITY -

272B

CUT TO INSIDE
CLOSE - HEEL OF
BLANCHES SHOE IN
LUMLEY'S CHEEK —

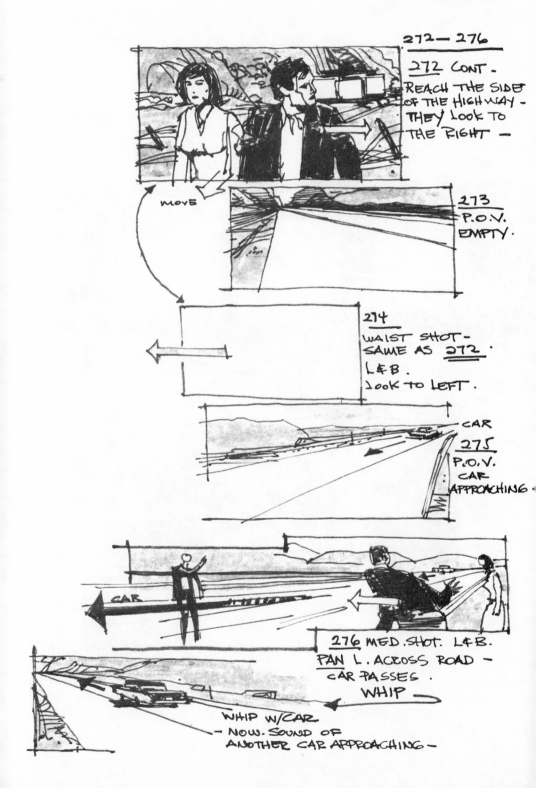

272—276

272 CONT.
REACH THE SIDE
OF THE HIGHWAY.
THEY LOOK TO
THE RIGHT —

MOVE

273
P.O.V.
EMPTY.

274
WAIST SHOT.
SAME AS 272.
L&B.
LOOK TO LEFT.

CAR
275
P.O.V.
CAR
APPROACHING.

CAR

276 MED. SHOT. L&B.
PAN L. ACROSS ROAD —
CAR PASSES.
WHIP

WHIP W/CAR
— NOW. SOUND OF
ANOTHER CAR APPROACHING —

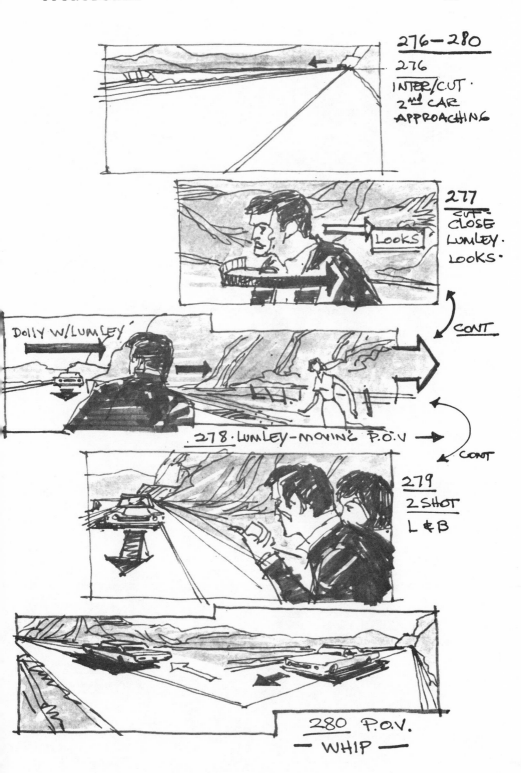

276—280

276
INTER/CUT.
2ⁿᵈ CAR
APPROACHING

277
CUT.
CLOSE
LUMLEY.
LOOKS.

LOOKS

CONT

Dolly W/LUMLEY

278 · LUMLEY — MOVING P.O.V

CONT

279
2 SHOT
L & B

280 P.O.V.
— WHIP —

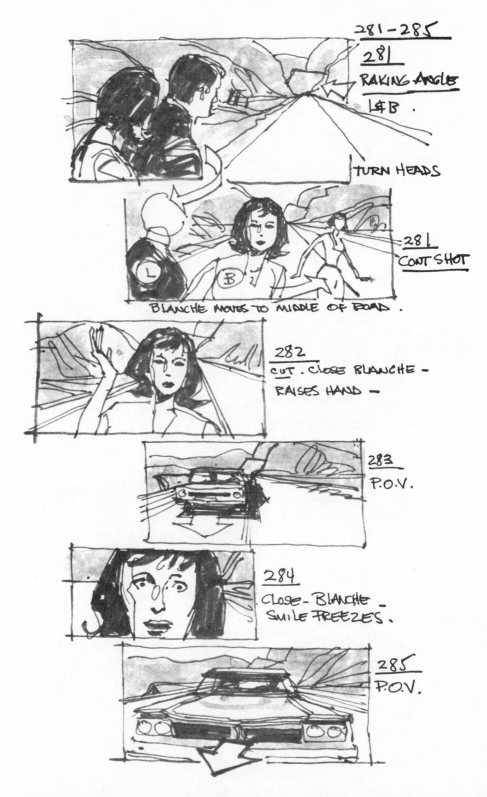

281-285

281
RAKING ANGLE
L&B.

TURN HEADS

281
CONT SHOT

BLANCHE MOVES TO MIDDLE OF ROAD.

282
CUT. CLOSE BLANCHE -
RAISES HAND -

283
P.O.V.

284
CLOSE - BLANCHE -
SMILE FREEZES.

285
P.O.V.

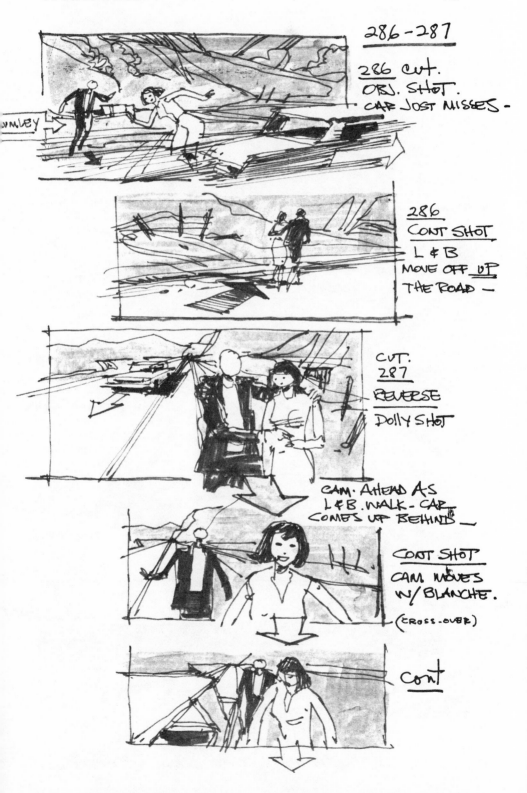

286-287

286 CUT.
OBJ. SHOT.
CAR JUST MISSES -

UMLEY →

286
CONT SHOT.
L & B
MOVE OFF UP
THE ROAD -

CUT.
287
REVERSE
DOLLY SHOT

CAM. AHEAD AS
L & B. WALK - CAR
COMES UP BEHIND -

CONT SHOT
CAM. MOVES
W/ BLANCHE.
(CROSS-OVER)

CONT

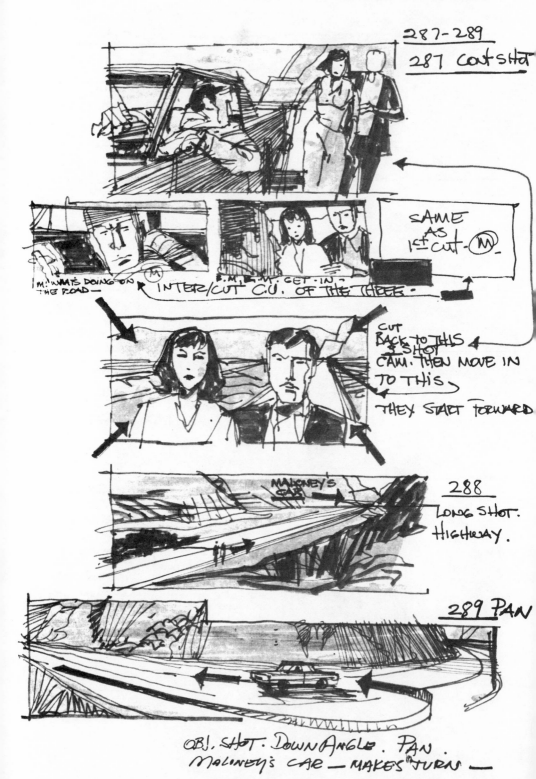

287-289
287 Cont Shot

SAME
AS
1st CUT - Ⓜ

M: WHAT'S DOING ON
THE ROAD —
INTER/CUT C.U. OF THE THREE
B.M.B.M. GET IN

CUT
BACK TO THIS
¾ SHOT
CAM. THEN MOVE IN
TO THIS
THEY START FORWARD

MALONEY'S
CAR
288
LONG SHOT.
HIGHWAY.

289 PAN

OBJ. SHOT. DOWN ANGLE. PAN.
MALONEY'S CAR — MAKES TURN —

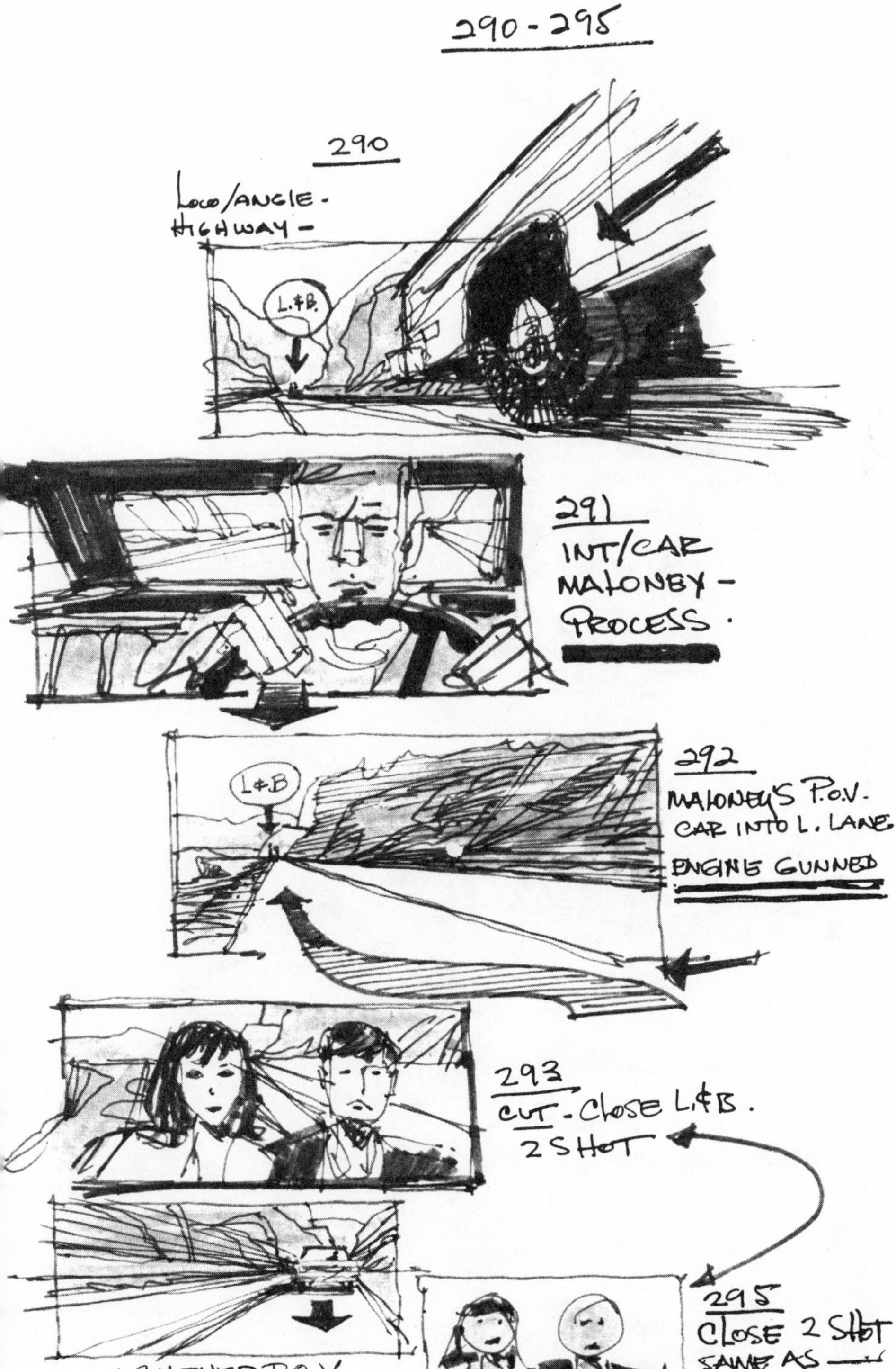

290-295

290

Loco/ANGLE.
HIGHWAY —

L.&B.

291
INT/CAR
MALONEY —
PROCESS.

292
MALONEY'S P.O.V.
CAR INTO L. LANE
ENGINE GUNNED

L&B

293
CUT-CLOSE L&B.
2 SHOT

294 THEIR P.O.V.

295
CLOSE 2 SHOT
SAME AS —

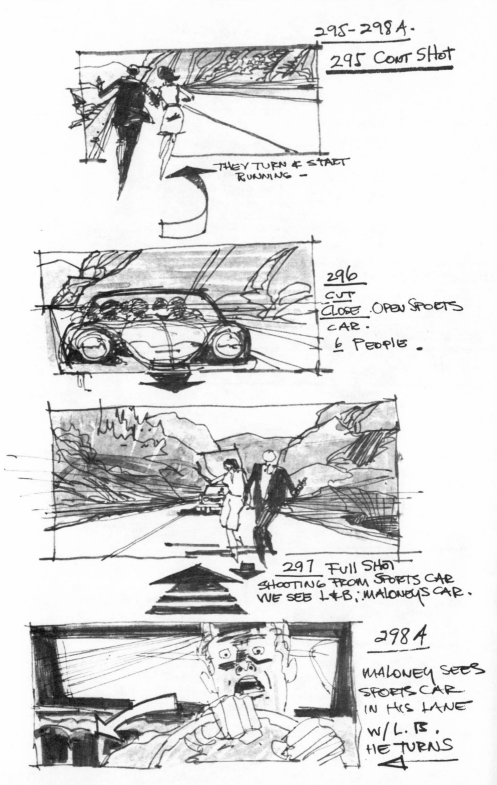

295-298A.

295 CONT SHOT

THEY TURN & START
RUNNING —

296
CUT
CLOSE . OPEN SPORTS
CAR.
6 PEOPLE.

297 FULL SHOT
SHOOTING FROM SPORTS CAR
WE SEE L & B; MALONEYS CAR.

298A

MALONEY SEES
SPORTS CAR
IN HIS LANE
W/ L. B.
HE TURNS

298 - 299B

<u>298</u> OBJ. SHOT
<u>low/ANGLE</u>
SPORTS CAR
TURNS

<u>299</u>
FLASH. BIG C.U.
MALONEY.
HORRIFIED
SPORTS CAR
IN HIS LANE
AGAIN

<u>299A</u>
ADDED CUT - P.O.V.
SPORTS CAR.

<u>299B</u> ADDED.
MALONEY TURNS
BACK.

300 - 302 . REVISED

300
FLASH CUT
MALONEYS CAR
SWERVES TO
L.

301
FLASH CUT
MALONEY.

302
OBJ. SHOT
MALONEY'S
CAR OVER THE
EDGE.

303 — 306

303

Quick cut.
OPEN SPORTS
CAR.
— STOPS —
ZOOMS OFF.

304

Quick cut
Low/angle

L & B. to EDGE — LOOK DOWN

305

P.O.V.
MALONEY'S CAR
IN FLAMES —

306

2 SHOT
L & B.
SLIGHT HIGH
ANGLE.

MOVE TO CAM —

THE CEMETERY PURSUIT SEQUENCE

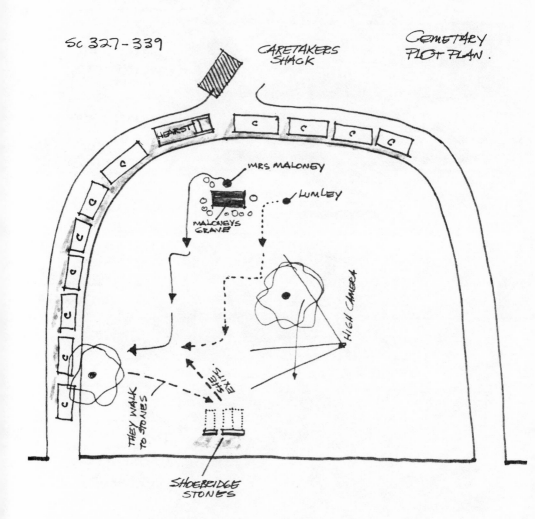

Sc 327-339

CARETAKERS SHACK

CEMETARY PLOT PLAN.

HEARST

c   c   c   c

c

c

c

c

c

c

c

MRS MALONEY

LUMLEY

MALONEYS GRAVE

HIGH CAMERA

THEY EXIT

THEY WALK TO STONES

SHOEBRIDGE STONES

327-330

PAN ➝

EXT: BARLOW CREEK CEMETERY   (D)   327.

SADIE
SHOEBRIDGE
etc.

EDWARD
SHOEBRIDGE

➝

OPEN CLOSE
2 ■ HEAD STONES —
PAN ➝ SEE CARS, HEARSE, MOURNERS,
         TO HEAD, SHOULDERS OF LUMLEY

328
CONT.

➝

➝

WAIST SHOT — GROUP AROUND GRAVE [PARSONS VOICE]

CAM MOVES THRU MOURNERS TO MRS. MALONEY —
— STARING OFF INTO DISTANCE —

➝

329.

L

[PARSON]

HER P.O.V. — SEES THE WATCHING
          LUMLEY —

330
CLOSE-UP
— MRS. MALONEY.

331-333

<u>331</u>

P.O.V.
LUMLEY

HER P.O.V. TO LUMLEY · STEPS FORWARD.

<u>332</u>
WAIST SHOT
MRS. MALONEY
GLANCES AROUND
STARTS TO EASE
AWAY FROM
GROUP ⎯

MRS. MALONEY

MRS MALONEY

<u>333</u>

⎯ VERY HIGH SHOT - THRU TREE ⎯
<u>MRS. MALONEY</u> MOVING AWAY FROM GROUP ⬅
THEN <u>LUMLEY</u> STARTS ⬅
<u>MOURNERS</u> MOVE OFF TO <u>CARS</u> ON ROAD
<u>CAM</u> STARTS TO <u>PAN</u> ⬅⎯ w/ MALONEY & LUMLEY

333-335

333. CONT. PAN ◄ HIGH SHOT.

MRS MALONEY

MRS. MALONEY, LUMLEY · WALKING ◄

:BRIDGE
:ONES.

334

CUT TO FULL FIG. MRS. MALONEY
SHOOTING ON HER BACK. SHE STOPS
SOUND OF LUMLEY'S FOOTSTEPS ─

335

REVERSE/ANGLE -
LUMLEY LOOKS
OFF ─

PAN   CAM STARTS PAN

335-336

335 CONT. PAN◀

— LUMLEY WALKS TO MRS MALONEY —
MRS. M: CAN'T YOU LEAVE ME ALONE ?......
    L: THATS NOT SO MRS M. YOU'VE GOT IT ALL WR⟨
✳ <u>SHE TURNS TO FACE HIM</u> —

336.

—Ⓛ

WAIST SHOT .
<u>MRS. MALONEY , LUMLEY .</u>
<u>SHE STARTS TO</u> <u>CAM</u> WHICH STARTS
TO DOLLY BACK WITH THEM ————

336 CONT

SHE STEPS ABRUPTLY, CAM STOPPING
W/HER, AND SHE TURNS TO LUMLEY.
THEY ARE NOW 2 BIG HEADS, IN PROFILE —
L: BUT WAIT A MINUTE......
SHE HURRIES AWAY FROM HIM —
336 CONT
PULL BACK

STONE TOPPLES
SLIGHTLY

CAM PULLS BACK
HOLDING 2 STONES (SHOEBRIDGE).
ON THE LEFT — MRS. MALONEY TO
HEADSTONES, KICKS EDDIES STONE
SOBBING: FAKE! FAKE!

(THE STONE TOPPLES SLIGHTLY TO)
(ONE SIDE BUT DOESN'T FALL)
OVER

337-339.

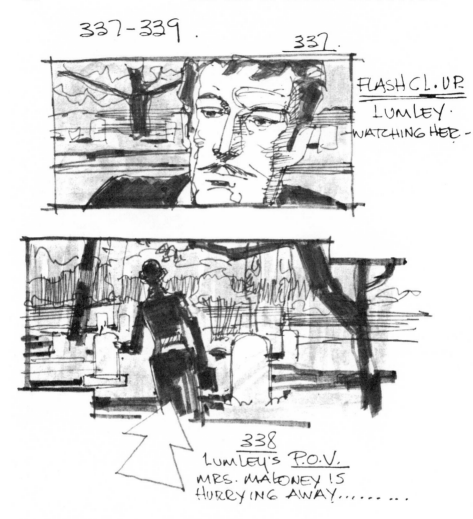

337.

FLASH CL. UP.
LUMLEY.
WATCHING HER -

338
LUMLEY'S P.O.V.
MRS. MALONEY IS
HURRYING AWAY........

339
WAIST SHOT
LUMLEY.

A HITCHCOCK ALBUM

Dates refer to the time of the photo, not the release year of the relevant film.

Alfred Hitchcock as a studio apprentice, about 1923.

Hitchcock's first cameo appearance (with his back to camera) in the newspaper office at the beginning of *The Lodger* (1926).

On the set of *Secret Agent* (1935) with John Gielgud and Peter Lorre.

With Sylvia Sidney and John Loder, during filming of *Sabotage* (1936).

Reading script revisions for *The Lady Vanishes* (1937) with Margaret Lockwood.

Publicity photo released by the Selznick studio for Hitchcock's arrival in America, 1939.

At home in Bel-Air with Alma and Pat, 1940.

With Cary Grant and Ingrid Bergman during production of *Notorious* (1945).

Lining up the first interior shot of *The Paradine Case* (1947).

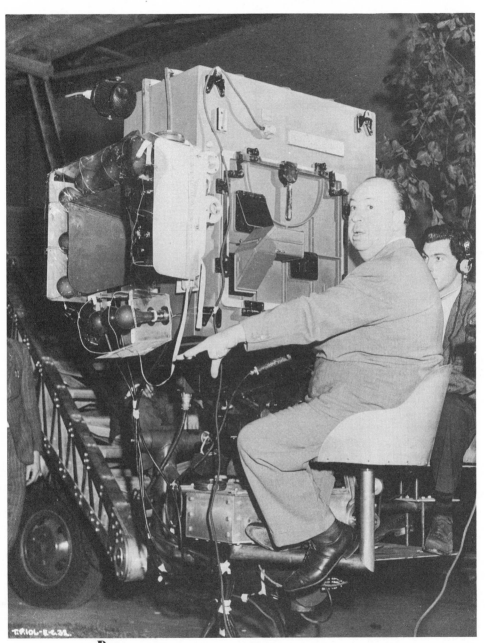

Directing a crane shot for *Under Capricorn* (1948).

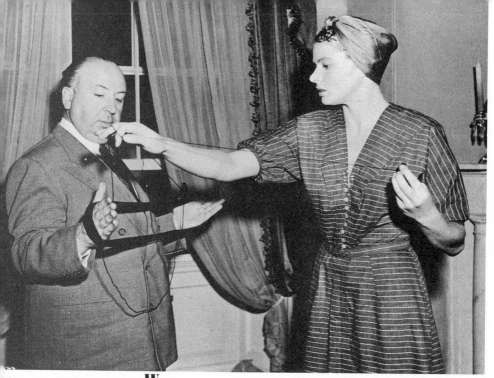

With Ingrid Bergman during a break in *Under Capricorn*.

Setting up the intricate below-carousel shot in the climactic scene of *Strangers on a Train* (1950).

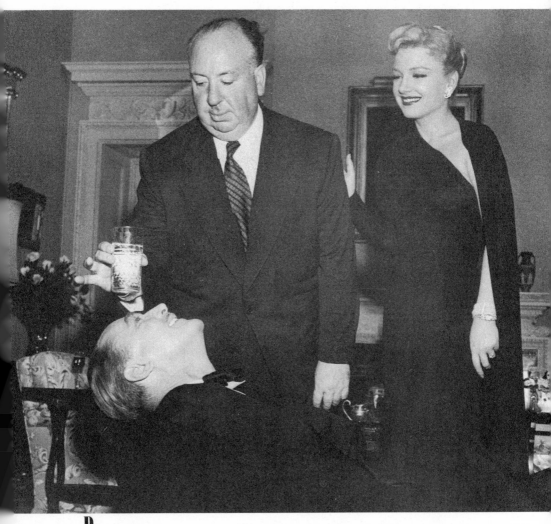

Preparing Brian Aherne and Anne Baxter for the party scene
of *I Confess* (1952).

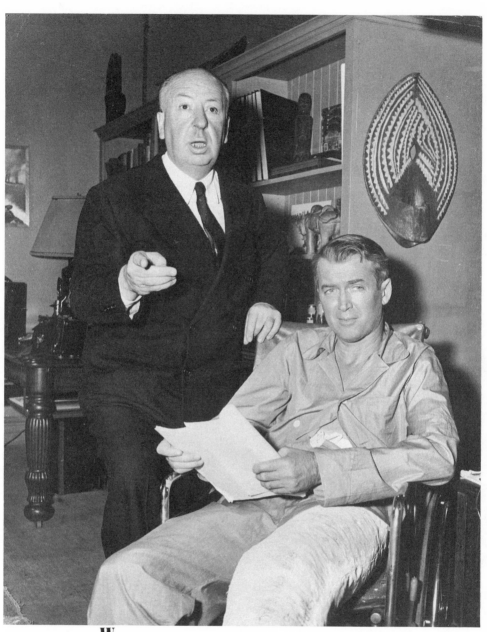

With James Stewart, filming *Rear Window* (1953).

10336-2/76

With Grace Kelly, on the set of *To Catch a Thief* (1954).

Directing Grace Kelly and Cary Grant for the first kissing scene (at threshold of the hotel room) in *To Catch a Thief* (1954).

With Daniel Gélin and Doris Day during production of *The Man Who Knew Too Much* (1955).

As Henry Fonda and Anthony Quayle wait, Hitchcock directs a close-up of Vera Miles in *The Wrong Man* (1956).

On the set of *North by Northwest* at MGM (1958).

A light moment on the set of *Psycho*, with Janet Leigh (1959).

Cast and crew of *The Birds* at a surprise birthday party for thirteen-year-old Veronica Cartwright (1962).

With Peggy Robertson, directing the opening shots of *Frenzy* on the Thames embankment (1971).

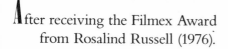

After receiving the Filmex Award from Rosalind Russell (1976).

Sarah, Hitchcock's West Highland terrier, was perhaps the only creature in Hollywood that refused to take direction from the master.

FILMOGRAPHY

The abbreviations that follow are used in designating those associated in the production of each film.

> *P:* Producer(s)
> *AP:* Associate producer(s)
> *Sc:* Screenplay by
> *b/o:* based on
> *DP:* Director(s) of photography
> *Ed:* Editor(s)
> *AD:* Art director(s)/production designer(s)
> *S:* Set designer(s)
> *W:* Wardrobe and costumes by
> *M:* Musical score composed by
> *SE:* Special effects supervisor(s)
> *ad:* Assistant director(s)
> *C:* Continuity supervisor(s)
> *Int:* Interior studio sets
> *B/W:* Filmed in black and white
> *Col:* Filmed in color

There are two dates given after each feature-film title: *prod.* indicates the year in which the film was made; *rel.* specifies the year of the first release for public screening.

SILENT FEATURES

The Pleasure Garden (A Gainsborough-Emelka Picture; *prod.* 1925/*rel.* 1927) *P:* Michael Balcon. *Sc:* Eliot Stannard, b/o the novel by Oliver Sandys. *DP:* Baron [Giovanni] Ventimiglia. *Int:* Emelka. *B/W.*

Cast:

Patsy Brand	Virginia Valli
Jill Cheyne	Carmelita Geraghty
Levett	Miles Mander
Hugh Fielding	John Stuart
Native girl	Nita Naldi

and with Frederick Martini and Florence Helminger.

The Mountain Eagle (A Gainsborough-Emelka Picture; *prod.* 1925/*rel.* 1927)
P: Michael Balcon. *Sc:* Eliot Stannard. *DP:* Baron [Giovanni] Ventimiglia. *Int:*
Emelka. *B/W*

Cast:	Pettigrew	Bernard Goetzke
	Beatrice	Nita Naldi
	Fear o' God	Malcolm Keen
	Edward	John Hamilton

(Released in the U.S.A. as *Fear o' God*.)

The Lodger: A Story of the London Fog (A Gainsborough Picture; *prod.*
1926/*rel.* 1927)
P: Michael Balcon. *Sc:* Eliot Stannard, b/o the novel *The Lodger* by Marie Belloc
Lowndes. *DP:* Baron [Giovanni] Ventimiglia. *ad:* Alma Reville. *AD:* C. Wilfrid
Arnold, Bertram Evans. *Ed/titling:* Ivor Montagu. *Title designs:* E. McKnight
Kauffer. *Int:* Islington. *B/W*.

Cast:	The landlady	Marie Ault
	Her husband	Arthur Chesney
	Daisy Bunting, a mannequin	June
	Joe, a police detective	Malcolm Keen
	The lodger	Ivor Novello

Downhill (A Gainsborough Picture; *prod./rel.* 1927)
P: Michael Balcon. *Sc:* Eliot Stannard, b/o the play by David LeStrange (pseud.
of Ivor Novello and Constance Collier). *DP:* Claude McDonnell. *Ed:* Ivor Montagu. *Int:* Islington. *B/W/*

Cast:	Roddy Berwick	Ivor Novello
	Tim Wakely	Robin Irvine
	Lady Berwick	Lillian Braithwaite
	Julia	Isabel Jeans
	Archie	Ian Hunter

(Released in the U.S.A. as *When Boys Leave Home*.)

Easy Virtue (A Gainsborough Picture: *prod./rel.* 1927)
P; Michael Balcon. *Sc:* Eliot Stannard, b/o the play by Noël Coward. *DP:* Claude
McDonnell. *Ed:* Ivor Montagu. *Int:* Islington. *B/W*.

Cast:	Larita Filton	Isabel Jeans
	Her husband	Franklyn Dyall
	The artist	Eric Bransby Williams
	Counsel for the plaintiff	Ian Hunter
	John Whittaker	Robin Irvine
	His mother	Violet Farebrother
	and with Benita Hume.	

The Ring (A British International Picture; *prod./rel.* 1927)
P: John Maxwell. *Sc:* Alfred Hitchcock. *C:* Alma Reville. *DP:* John J. Cox. *Int:*
Elstree. *B/W*.

Cast:	Jack Sanders	Carl Brisson
	Nellie	Lillian Hall Davis
	The champion	Ian Hunter

and with Harry Terry, Gordon Harker, Forrester Harvey and Tom Helmore.

The Farmer's Wife (A British International Picture; *prod.* 1927/*rel.* 1928)
P: John Maxwell. *Sc:* Alfred Hitchcock, b/o the play by Eden Phillpotts. *DP:*
John J. Cox. *Ed:* Alfred Booth. *Int:* Elstree. *B/W*.

Cast: Farmer Sweetland   Jameson Thomas
Araminta Dench   Lillian Hall Davis
Churdles Ash   Gordon Harker
Thirza Tapper   Maud Gill
Widow Windeat   Louise Pounds
and with Olga Slade and Antonia Brough.

Champagne (A British International Picture: *prod/rel.* 1928)
P: John Maxwell. *Sc:* Eliot Stannard. Adaptation: Alfred Hitchcock, b/o an original story by Walter C. Mycroft. *DP:* John J. Cox. *AD:* C. W. Arnold. *ad:* Frank Mills. *Int:* Elstree. *B/W.*
Cast: The girl   Betty Balfour
The boy   Jean Bradin
The man   Theo von Alten
The father   Gordon Harker

The Manxman (A British International Picture: *prod.* 1928/*rel.* 1929)
P: John Maxwell. *Sc:* Eliot Stannard, b/o the novel by Hall Caine. *DP:* John J. Cox. *ad:* Frank Mills. *Int:* Elstree. *B/W.*
Cast: Pete   Carl Brisson
Philip   Malcolm Keen
Kate   Anny Ondra
Her father   Randle Ayrton

SOUND FEATURES

Blackmail (A British International Picture; *prod./rel.* 1929)
P: John Maxwell. *Sc:* Alfred Hitchcock, b/o the play by Charles Bennett. *Dialogue:* Benn W. Levy. *DP:* John J. Cox. *AD:* C. W. Arnold. *Ed:* Emile de Ruelle. *ad:* Frank Mills. *M:* Campbell and Connelly. *Int:* Elstree. *B/W.*
Cast: Alice White   Anny Ondra (voice: Joan Barry)
Mrs. White   Sara Allgood
Mr. White   Charles Paton
Detective Frank Webber   John Longden
Tracy, the blackmailer   Donald Calthrop
The artist   Cyril Ritchard
The landlady   Hannah Jones
The neighbor   Phyllis Monkman
Chief inspector   Harvey Braban

Juno and the Paycock (A British International Picture; *prod./rel.* 1930)
P: John Maxwell. *Adaptation:* Alfred Hitchcock and Alma Reville, b/o the play by Sean O'Casey. *DP:* John J. Cox. *AD:* Norman Arnold. *Int:* Elstree. *B/W.*
Cast: Juno   Sara Allgood
Captain Boyle   Edward Chapman
Mrs. Madigan   Marie O'Neill
Joxer   Sidney Morgan

Murder! (A British International Picture; *prod./rel.* 1930)
P: John Maxwell. *Adaptation:* Alfred Hitchcock and Walter Mycroft, b/o the novel and play *Enter Sir John* by Clemence Dane and Helen Simpson. *DP:* John J. Cox. *AD:* J. F. Mead. *ad:* Frank Mills. *Sc:* Alma Reville. *M:* John Reynders. *Ed:* René Harrison, Emile de Ruelle. *Int:* Elstree. *B/W.*
Cast: Diana Baring   Norah Baring
Sir John Menier   Herbert Marshall

Gordon Druce   Miles Mander
Handel Fane   Esmé Percy
and with Edward Chapman, Phyllis Konstam, Hannah Jones and Una
O'Connor.
(Hitchcock also directed a German version, *Mary,* starring Walter Abel.)

The Skin Game (A British International Picture; *prod.* 1930–1931/*rel.* 1931)
P: John Maxwell. *Adaptation:* Alfred Hitchcock. *Sc:* Alma Reville, b/o the play
by John Galsworthy. *DP:* John J. Cox. *AD:* J. B. Maxwell. *ad:* Frank Mills. *Int:*
Elstree. *B/W.*
Cast: Mr. Hillcrest   C. V. France
Mrs. Hillcrest   Helen Haye
Mr. Hornblower   Edmund Gwenn
Jill   Jill Esmond
and with John Longden and Phyllis Konstam.

Number Seventeen (A British International Picture; *prod.* 1931/*rel.* 1932)
P: John Maxwell. *Sc:* Alma Reville, Alfred Hitchcock, and Rodney Ackland,
b/o the play by J. Jefferson Farjeon. *DP:* John J. Cox, Bryan Langley. *AD:* C.
W. Arnold. *ad:* Frank Mills. *Ed:* A. C. Hammond. *M:* A. Hallis. *Int:* Elstree.
B/W.
Cast: Ben   Leon M. Lion
The girl   Anne Grey
The detective   John Stuart
and with Donald Calthrop, Barry Jones, Ann Casson, Henry Caine and
Garry Marsh.

Rich and Strange (A British International Picture; *prod./rel.* 1932)
P: John Maxwell. *Adaptation:* Alfred Hitchcock. *Sc:* Alma Reville. *DP:* John J.
Cox, Charles Martin. *Additional dialogue:* Val Valentine. *AD:* C. W. Arnold. *Ed:*
René Harrison, Winifred Cooper. *ad:* Frank Mills. *M:* Hal Dolphe. *Int:* Elstree.
B/W.
Cast: Fred Hill   Henry Kendall
Emily Hill   Joan Barry
Commander Gordon   Percy Marmont
The "princess"   Betty Amann
The old maid   Elsie Randolph
(Released in the U.S.A. as *East of Shanghai.*)

Waltzes from Vienna (A Tom Arnold Production; *prod./rel.* 1933)
P: Tom Arnold. *Sc:* Alma Reville and Guy Bolton, b/o the play by Bolton. *M:*
Johann Strauss. *AD:* Alfred Junge. *S:* Peter Proud. *Int:* Lime Grove. *B/W.*
Cast: Rasi   Jessie Matthews
Strauss the younger   Esmond Knight
Strauss the elder   Edmund Gwenn
The prince   Frank Vosper
The countess   Fay Compton
(Released in the U.S.A. as *Strauss's Great Waltz.*)

The Man Who Knew Too Much (A Gaumont-British Picture; *prod./rel.* 1934)
P: Michael Balcon. *AP:* Ivor Montagu. *Sc:* Edwin Greenwood and A. R. Raw-
linson, b/o a story by Charles Bennett and D. B. Wyndham Lewis. *Additional
dialogue:* Emlyn Williams. *DP:* Curt Courant. *AD:* Alfred Junge. *Ed:* H. St.C.
Stewart. *M:* Arthur Benjamin. *Int:* Lime Grove. *B/W.*
Cast: Bob Lawrence   Leslie Banks

Jill Lawrence	Edna Best
Betty Lawrence	Nova Pilbeam
Abbott	Peter Lorre
Ramon	Frank Vosper
Clive	Hugh Wakefield
Louis Bernard	Pierre Fresnay
Nurse Agnes	Cicely Oates

and with D. A. Clarke Smith and George Curzon.

The 39 Steps (A Gaumont-British Picture; *prod./rel.* 1935)

P: Michael Balcon. *AP:* Ivor Montagu. *Adaptation:* Charles Bennett, b/o the novel *The Thirty-Nine Steps* by John Buchan. *C:* Alma Reville. *Dialogue:* Ian Hay. *DP:* Bernard Knowles. *AD:* O. Werndorff. *Ed:* D. N. Twist. *M:* Louis Levy. *Int:* Lime Grove. B/W.

Cast:	Richard Hannay	Robert Donat
	Pamela	Madeleine Carroll
	Annabella Smith	Lucie Mannheim
	Prof. Jordan	Godfrey Tearle
	The crofter	John Laurie
	His wife	Peggy Ashcroft
	Mrs. Jordan	Helen Haye
	The sheriff	Frank Cellier
	Mr. Memory	Wylie Watson

and with Gus MacNaughton, Jerry Verno and Peggy Simpson

Secret Agent (A Gaumont-British Picture; *prod.* 1935/*rel.* 1935)

P: Michael Balcon. *AP:* Ivor Montagu. *Sc:* Charles Bennett, from the play by Campbell Dixon b/o stories by W. Somerset Maugham. *Dialogue:* Ian Hay, Jesse Lasky, Jr. *C:* Alma Reville. *DP:* Bernard Knowles. *AD:* O. Werndorff. *Ed:* Charles Frend. *M:* Louis Levy. *Int:* Lime Grove. B/W.

Cast:	Edgar Brodie/Richard Ashenden	John Gielgud
	Elsa	Madeleine Carroll
	The General	Peter Lorre
	Marvin	Robert Young
	Caypor	Percy Marmont
	Mrs. Caypor	Florence Kahn

and with Charles Carson, Lilli Palmer and Michel Saint-Denis.

Sabotage (A Gaumont-British Picture; *prod./rel.* 1936)

P: Michael Balcon. *AP:* Ivor Montagu. *Sc:* Charles Bennett, b/o the novel *The Secret Agent* by Joseph Conrad. *Dialogue:* Ian Hay, Helen Simpson. *C:* Alma Reville. *DP:* Bernard Knowles. *Ed:* Charles Frend. *AD:* O. Werndorff. *M:* Louis Levy. Cartoon sequence from Walt Disney's *Who Killed Cock Robin? Int:* Lime Grove. B/W.

Cast:	Mrs. Verloc	Sylvia Sidney
	Mr. Verloc	Oscar Homolka
	Stevie	Desmond Tester
	Ted Spenser	John Loder
	Renee	Joyce Barbour

and with William Dewhurst, Martita Hunt and Peter Bull. (Released in the U.S.A. as *The Woman Alone*.)

Young and Innocent (A Gaumont-British Picture; *prod.* 1937/*rel.* 1938)

P: Edward Black. *Sc:* Charles Bennett, Edwin Greenwood, and Anthony Armstrong, b/o the novel *A Shilling for Candles* by Josephine Tey. *Dialogue:* Gerald

Savory. *C:* Alma Reville. *DP:* Bernard Knowles. *Ed:* Charles Frend. *AD:* Alfred
Junge. *M:* Louis Levy. *Int:* Limegrove and Pinewood. *B/W.*

Cast:	Erica Burgoyne	Nova Pilbeam
	Robert Tisdall	Derrick de Marney
	Col. Burgoyne	Percy Marmont
	Old Will	Edward Rigby
	Erica's aunt	Mary Clare
	Det. Insp. Kent	John Longden
	Guy	George Curzon
	Erica's uncle	Basil Radford
	Christine	Pamela Carme

(Released in the U.S.A. as *The Girl Was Young.*)

The Lady Vanishes (A Gaumont-British Picture; *prod.* 1937/*rel.* 1938)
P: Edward Black. *Sc:* Sidney Gilliat and Frank Launder, b/o the novel *The Wheel
Spins* by Ethel Lina White. *C:* Alma Reville. *DP:* John J. Cox. *Ed:* R. E. Dearing.
S: Vetchinsky. *M:* Louis Levy. *Int:* Islington. *B/W.*

Cast:	Iris Henderson	Margaret Lockwood
	Gilbert	Michael Redgrave
	Miss Froy	Dame May Whitty
	Dr. Hartz	Paul Lukas
	Mr. Todhunter	Cecil Parker
	His mistress	Linden Travers
	Caldicott	Naunton Wayne
	Charters	Basil Radford
	Baroness	Mary Clare
	The "nun"	Catherine Lacey

and with Josephine Wilson, Kathleen Tremaine, Emile Boreo and Googie
Withers.

Jamaica Inn (An Erich Pommer Production; *prod.* 1938/*rel.* 1939)
P: Erich Pommer. *Sc:* Sidney Gilliat and Joan Harrison, b/o the novel by Daphne
du Maurier. *C:* Alma Reville. *Additional dialogue:* J. B. Priestley. *DP:* Harry
Stradling, Bernard Knowles. *S:* Tom Morahan. *W:* Molly McArthur. *M:* Eric
Fenby. *Int:* Elstree. *B/W.*

Cast:	Sir Humphrey Pengallan	Charles Laughton
	Joss Merlyn	Leslie Banks
	Patience, his wife	Marie Ney
	Mary, his niece	Maureen O'Hara
	Harry	Emlyn Williams
	Salvation	Wylie Watson
	Thomas	Mervyn Johns

and with Edwin Greenwood and Stephen Haggard.

Rebecca (A Production of the Selznick Studio; *prod.* 1939/*rel.* 1940)
P: David O. Selznick. *Sc:* Robert E. Sherwood and Joan Harrison, b/o the novel
by Daphne du Maurier. *Adaptation:* Philip MacDonald, Michael Hogan. *DP:*
George Barnes. *M:* Franz Waxman. *AD:* Lyle Wheeler. *S:* Joseph B. Platt. *SE:*
Jack Cosgrove. *Ed:* James Newcom, Hal Kern. *ad:* Edmond Bernoudy. *Int:*
Selznick Studios. *B/W.*

Cast:	Maxim de Winter	Laurence Olivier
	His wife	Joan Fontaine
	Mrs. Danvers	Judith Anderson
	Jack Favell	George Sanders
	Mrs. Van Hopper	Florence Bates

Giles Lacey   Nigel Bruce
Beatrice Lacey   Gladys Cooper
and with C. Aubrey Smith, Melville Cooper, Leo G. Carroll, Forrester
Harvey, Reginald Denny, Lumsden Hare, Philip Winter and Edward
Fielding.

Foreign Correspondent (A Wanger Production; *prod./rel.* 1940)
P: Walter Wanger. *Sc:* Charles Bennett, Joan Harrison. *Dialogue:* James Hilton,
Robert Benchley. *M:* Alfred Newman. *AD:* Alexander Golitzen. *DP:* Rudolph
Maté. *SE:* Paul Eagler. *Ed:* Otho Lovering, Dorothy Spencer. *Special production
effects:* William Cameron Menzies. *S:* Julia Heron. *W:* I. Magnin. *ad:* Edmond
Bernoudy. *Int:* Goldwyn Studios.*B/W.*
Cast: Johnny Jones/Huntley Haverstock   Joel McCrea
        Carol Fisher   Laraine Day
        Stephen Fisher   Herbert Marshall
        ffolliott   George Sanders
        Van Meer   Albert Basserman
        Stebbins   Robert Benchley
        Rowley   Edmund Gwenn
        Mr. Powers   Harry Davenport
        Krug   Eduardo Ciannelli
        and with Eddie Conrad, Frances Carson, Martin Kosleck, Gertrude W.
Hoffman, Emory Parnell, Ian Wolfe, Eily Malyon and E. E. Clive.

Mr. and Mrs. Smith (An RKO Radio Picture; *prod.* 1940/*rel.* 1941)
P: Harry E. Edington. *Story and sc:* Norman Krasna. *M:* Edward Wand. *DP:*
Harry Stradling. *AD:* Van Nest Polglase. *SE:* Vernon L. Walker. *W:* Irene. *S:*
Darrell Silvera. *Ed:* William Hamilton. *ad:* Dewey Starkey. *Int:* RKO Studios.
B/W.
Cast: Ann Krausheimer Smith   Carole Lombard
        David Smith   Robert Montgomery
        Jeff Custer   Gene Raymond
        His parents   Philip Merivale, Lucile Watson
        Chuck Benson   Jack Carson

Suspicion (An RKO Radio Picture; *prod./rel.* 1941)
P: Harry E. Edington. *Sc:* Samson Raphaelson, Joan Harrison, and Alma Reville,
b/o the novel *Before the Fact* by Francis Iles. *DP:* Harry Stradling. *M:* Franz
Waxman, *SE:* Vernon L. Walker. *AD:* Van Nest Polglase. *S:* Darrell Silvera.
Ed: William Hamilton. *ad:* Dewey Starkey. *Int:* RKO Studios. *B/W.*
Cast: Lina McLaidlaw   Joan Fontaine
        Johnny Aysgarth   Cary Grant
        General McLaidlaw   Sir Cedric Hardwicke
        Mrs. McLaidlaw   Dame May Whitty
        Beaky Thwaite   Nigel Bruce
        Mrs. Newsham   Isabel Jeans
        and with Heather Angel, Auriol Lee and Leo G. Carroll.

Saboteur (A Frank Lloyd Production for Universal; *prod./rel.* 1942)
P: Frank Lloyd. *AP:* Jack H. Skirball. *Sc:* Peter Viertel, Joan Harrison, Dorothy
Parker. *DP:* Joseph Valentine. *AD:* Jack Otterson, Robert Boyle. *Ed:* Otto Lud-
wig. *M:* Frank Skinner. *ad:* Fred Rank. *Int:* Universeal. *B/W.*
Cast: Barry Kane   Robert Cummings
        Pat Martin   Priscilla Lane
        Charles Tobin   Otto Kruger

Mrs. Van Sutton   Alma Kruger
Fry   Norman Lloyd

Shadow of a Doubt (A Jack H. Skirball Production for Universal; *prod.* 1942/
rel. 1943)
P: Jack H. Skirball. *Sc:* Thornton Wilder, Sally Benson, and Alma Reville, b/o
an original story by Gordon McDonell. *DP:* Joseph Valentine. *M:* Dimitri Tiomkin. *AD:* John B. Goodman, Robert Boyle. *S:* R. A. Gausman, E. R. Rob-
inson. *Ed:* Milton Carruth. *W:* Adrian / Vera West. *ad:* William Tummell. *Int:*
Universal. *B/W.*
Cast: Uncle Charlie Oakley   Joseph Cotten
          Charlie Newton   Teresa Wright
          Jack Graham   MacDonald Carey
          Emma Newton   Patricia Collinge
          Joe Newton   Henry Travers
          Herb Hawkins   Hume Cronyn
          Ann Newton   Edna May Wonacott
          Roger Newton   Charles Bates
          Fred Saunders   Wallace Ford
          and with Eily Malyon and Estelle Jewell.

Lifeboat (A 20th Century-Fox Picture; *prod.* 1943/*rel.* 1944)
P: Kenneth MacGowan. *Sc:* Jo Swerling, c/o a story by John Steinbeck. *DP:*
Glen MacWilliams. *AD:* James Basevi, Maurice Ransford. *S:* Thomas Little,
Frank E. Hughes. *Ed:* Dorothy Spencer. *SE:* Fred Sersen. *Technical adviser:*
Thomas Fitzsimmons (National Maritime Union). *M:* Hugo W. Friedhofer. *W:*
René Hubert. *Int:* 20th Century-Fox. *B/W.*
Cast: Constance Porter   Tallulah Bankhead
          Kovac   John Hodiak
          Gus   William Bendix
          Willi   Walter Slezak
          Alice MacKenzie   Mary Anderson
          Stanley Garrett   Hume Cronyn
          Charles J. Rittenhouse   Henry Hull
          Mrs. Higgins   Heather Angel
          Joe Spencer   Canada Lee

Spellbound (A Selznick International Picture; *prod.* 1944/*rel.* 1945)
P: David O. Selznick. *Sc:* Ben Hecht, b/o the novel *The House of Dr. Edwardes*
by Francis Beeding. *Adaptation:* Angus MacPhail. *DP:* George Barnes. *M:* Miklos
Rozsa. *AD:* James Basevi. *Ed:* Hal Kern. *SE:* Jack Cosgrove. *S:* Emile Kuri.
Dream sequence based on designs by Salvador Dalí. *ad:* Lowell J. Farrell. *Psychiatric
adviser:* May E. Romm, M.D. *Int:* Selznick Studios. *B/W.*
Cast: Dr. Constance Petersen   Ingrid Bergman
          John Ballantine   Gregory Peck
          Dr. Murchison   Leo G. Carroll
          Garmes   Norman Lloyd
          Mary Carmichael   Rhonda Fleming
          Dr. Alex Brulov   Michael Chekhov
          Dr. Fleurot   John Emery
          and with Bill Goodwin, Art Baker, and Wallace Ford.

Notorious (An RKO Radio Picture; *prod.* 1945–1946/*rel.* 1946)
P: Alfred Hitchcock. *Sc:* Ben Hecht. *DP:* Ted Tetzlaff. *SE:* Vernon L. Walker,
Paul Eagler. *AD:* Albert S. D'Agostino, Carroll Clark. *S:* Darrell Silvera, Claude

Carpenter. *M:* Roy Webb. *Ed:* Theron Warth. *W:* Edith Head. *ad:* William Dorfman. *Int:* RKO. *B/W.*

Cast:	
Alicia Huberman	Ingrid Bergman
T. R. Devlin	Cary Grant
Alexander Sebastian	Claude Rains
Madame Sebastian	Leopoldine Konstantin
Paul Prescott	Louis Calhern
Dr. Anderson	Reinhold Schunzel
Eric Mathis	Ivan Triesault
Joseph	Alex Minotis
Hupka	Eberhard Krumschmidt
Commodore	Sir Charles Mendl
Walter Beardsley	Moroni Olsen
Dr. Barbosa	Ricardo Costa

The Paradine Case (A David O. Selznick/Vanguard Film; *prod.* 1946/*rel.* 1947)
P: David O. Selznick. *Sc:* David O. Selznick, b/o the novel by Robert Hichens. *Adaptation:* Alma Reville. *DP:* Lee Garmes. *Production designer:* J. MacMillan Johnson. *AD:* Tom Morahan. *S:* Joseph B. Platt, Emile Kuri. *SE:* Clarence Slifer. *ad:* Lowell J. Farrell. *W:* Travis Banton. *M:* Franz Waxman. *Ed:* Hal Kern, John Faure. *Int:* RKO. *B/W.*

Cast:	
Mrs. Paradine	Valli
Anthony Keane	Gregory Peck
Gay, his wife	Ann Todd
Lord Horfield	Charles Laughton
Lady Horfield	Ethel Barrymore
Sir Simon Flaquer	Charles Coburn
Judy Flaquer, his daughter	Joan Tetzel
André Latour	Louis Jourdan

and with Leo G. Carroll, John Williams and Isobel Elsom.

Rope (A Transatlantic Picture; *prod./rel.* 1948)
P: Alfred Hitchcock, Sidney Bernstein. *Adaptation:* Hume Cronyn, b/o the play by Patrick Hamilton. *Sc:* Arthur Laurents. *DP:* Joseph Valentine, William V. Skall. *AD:* Perry Ferguson. *S:* Emile Kuri, Howard Bristol. *Ed:* William H. Ziegler. *ad:* Lowell J. Farrell. *M:* Francis Poulenc, Leo F. Forbstein. *Int:* Warner Brothers. *Col.*

Cast:	
Rupert Cadell	James Stewart
Brandon	John Dall
Philip	Farley Granger
Mr. Kentley	Sir Cedric Hardwicke
Mrs. Atwater	Constance Collier
Kenneth	Douglas Dick
Mrs. Wilson	Edith Evanson
Janet	Joan Chandler
David Kentley	Dick Hogan

Under Capricorn (A Transatlantic Picture; *prod.* 1948/*rel.* 1949)
P: Alfred Hitchcock, Sidney Bernstein. *Adaptation:* Hume Cronyn. *Sc:* James Bridie, from the play by John Colton and Margaret Linden b/o the novel by Helen Simpson. *DP:* Jack Cardiff. *AD:* Tom Morahan. *W:* Roger Furse. *Ed:* A. S. Bates. *ad:* C. Foster Kemp. *C:* Peggy Singer. *M:* Richard Addinsell. *Int:* Elstree. *Col.*

Cast:	
Sam Flusky	Joseph Cotten
Lady Henrietta Flusky	Ingrid Bergman

Charles Adare   Michael Wilding
Milly   Margaret Leighton
Governor   Cecil Parker
Corrigan   Denis O'Dea

Stage Fright (A Warner Brothers–First National Picture; *prod.* 1949/*rel.* 1950)
P: Alfred Hitchcock. *Adaptation:* Alma Reville. *Sc:* Whitfield Cook, b/o the novel
Man Running by Selwyn Jepson. *DP:* Wilkie Cooper. *AD:* Terence Verity. *Ed:*
E. B. Jarvis. *M:* Leighton Lucas. *C:* Peggy Singer. *Int:* Elstree. *B/W.*
Cast: Charlotte Inwood   Marlene Dietrich
          Eve Gill   Jane Wyman
          Wilfrid Smith   Michael Wilding
          Jonathan Cooper   Richard Todd
          Commodore Gill   Alastair Sim
          Mrs. Gill   Sybil Thorndike
          Nellie Good   Kay Walsh
          Chubby Bannister   Patricia Hitchcock
          and with Joyce Grenfell, Miles Malleson, Hector MacGregor, Ballard
          Berkeley and André Morell.

Strangers on a Train (A Warner Brothers–First National Picture, *prod.* 1950/
rel. 1951)
P: Alfred Hitchcock. *Adaptation:* Whitfield Cook. *Sc:* Raymond Chandler and
Czenzi Ormonde, b/o the novel by Patricia Highsmith. *DP:* Robert Burks. *AD:*
Edward S. Haworth. *Ed:* William Ziegler. *S:* George James Hopkins. *SE:* H.
F. Koenekamp. *M:* Dimitri Tiomkin. *Int:* Warner Brothers. *B/W.*
Cast: Bruno Anthony   Robert Walker
          Guy Haines   Farley Granger
          Miriam Haines   Laura Elliott
          Ann Morton   Ruth Roman
          Barbara Morton   Patricia Hitchcock
          Senator Morton   Leo G. Carroll
          Mrs. Anthony   Marion Lorne
          and with Jonathan Hale and Norma Varden.

I Confess (A Warner Brothers–First National Picture; *prod.* 1952/*rel.* 1953)
P: Alfred Hitchcock. *Sc:* George Tabori and William Archibald, b/o the play
Nos Deux Consciences by Paul Anthelme. *DP:* Robert Burks. *AD:* Edward S.
Haworth. *Ed:* Rudi Fehr. *S:* George James Hopkins. *ad:* Don Page. *M:* Dimitri
Tiomkin. *Int:* Warner Brothers. *B/W.*
Cast: Father Michael Logan   Montgomery Clift
          Ruth Grandfort   Anne Baxter
          Inspector Larrue   Karl Malden
          Pierre Grandfort   Roger Dann
          Otto Keller   O. E. Hasse
          Alma Keller   Dolly Haas
          Willy Robertson   Brian Aherne

Dial M for Murder (A Warner Brother–First National Picture; *prod. 1953/rel.*
1954)
P: Alfred Hitchcock. *Sc:* Frederick Knott, b/o his play. *DP:* Robert Burks. *AD:*
Edward Carrera. *Ed:* Rudi Fehr. *S:* George James Hopkins. *ad:* Mel Dellar. *M:*
Dimitri Tiomkin. *Int:* Warner Brothers. *Col.* and 3-D.
Cast: Tony Wendice   Ray Milland
          Margot Wendice   Grace Kelly

Mark Halliday	Robert Cummings
Lesgate (Swann)	Anthony Dawson
Inspector Hubbard	John Williams

and with Leo Britt, Patrick Allen, George Leigh, George Alderson and Robin Hughes.

Rear Window (A Paramount Release; *prod.* 1953/*rel.* 1954)
P: Alfred Hitchcock. *Sc:* John Michael Hayes, b/o the short story by Cornell Woolrich. *DP:* Robert Burks. *AD:* Hal Pereira, Joseph MacMillan Johnson. *SE:* John P. Fulton. *S:* Sam Comer, Ray Moyer. *ad:* Herbert Coleman. *Ed:* George Tomasini. *W:* Edith Head. *M:* Franz Waxman. *Int:* Paramount. *Col.*

Cast:		
	L. B. Jeffries	James Stewart
	Lisa Carol Fremont	Grace Kelly
	Stella	Thelma Ritter
	Tom Doyle	Wendell Corey
	Lars Thorwald	Raymond Burr
	Mrs. Thorwald	Irene Winston
	Miss Lonelyhearts	Judith Evelyn
	The composer	Ross Bagdasarian
	Miss Torso	Georgine Darcy
	Miss Sculptress	Jesslyn Fax

and with Sara Berner, Frank Cady, Rand Harper, Havis Davenport and Anthony Ward.

To Catch a Thief (A Paramount Picture; *prod.* 1954/*rel.* 1955)
P: Alfred Hitchcock. *Sc:* John Michael Hayes, b/o the novel by David Dodge. *DP:* Robert Burks. *Second-unit director:* Herbert Coleman. *AD:* Hal Pereira, Joseph MacMillan Johnson. *SE:* John P. Fulton. *Second-unit DP:* Wallace Kelley. *Process photography:* Farciot Edouart. *S:* Sam Comer, Arthur Krams. *Ed:* George Tomasini. *ad:* Daniel McCauley. *M:* Lyn Murray. *W:* Edith Head. *Int:* Paramount. *Col.*

Cast:		
	John Robie	Cary Grant
	Frances Stevens	Grace Kelly
	Jessie Stevens	Jessie Royce Landis
	H. H. Hughson	John Williams
	Danielle Foussard	Brigitte Auber
	Bertani	Charles Vanel

and with René Blancard.

The Trouble with Harry (A Paramount Release; *prod.* 1954/*rel.* 1955)
P: Alfred Hitchcock. *Sc:* John Michael Hayes, b/o the novel by J. Trevor Story. *DP:* Robert Burks. *ad:* Howard Joslin. *Ed:* Alma Macrorie. *M:* Bernard Herrmann. *W:* Edith Head. *AP:* Herbert Coleman. *Int:* Paramount. *Col.*

Cast:		
	Capt. Albert Wiles	Edmund Gwenn
	Sam Marlowe	John Forsythe
	Jennifer Rogers	Shirley MacLaine
	Miss Graveley	Mildred Natwick
	Mrs. Wiggs	Mildred Dunnock
	Arnie Rogers	Jerry Mathers
	Calvin Wiggs	Royal Dano
	Millionaire	Parker Fennelly
	Harry	Philip Truex

The Man Who Knew Too Much (A Paramount Release; *prod.* 1955/*rel.* 1956)
P: Alfred Hitchcock. *AP:* Herbert Coleman. *Sc:* John Michael Hayes, b/o a story by Charles Bennett and D. B. Wyndham Lewis. *DP:* Robert Burks. *Ed:* George

Tomasini. *AD:* Hal Pereira, Henry Bumstead. *SE:* John P. Fulton. *S:* Sam Comer, Arthur Krams. *W:* Edith Head. *ad:* Howard Joslin. *M:* Bernard Herrmann; "Storm Cloud Cantata" by Arthur Benjamin and D. B. Wyndham Lewis. *Songs:* "Whatever Will Be" and "We'll Love Again" by Jay Livingston and Ray Evans. *Int:* Paramount. *Col.*

Cast:		
	Dr. Ben McKenna	James Stewart
	Jo McKenna	Doris Day
	Hank McKenna	Christopher Olsen
	Mr. Drayton	Bernard Miles
	Mrs. Drayton	Brenda de Banzie
	Rien, the assassin	Reggie Nalder
	Louis Bernard	Daniel Gélin

and with Ralph Truman, Mogens Wieth, Hilary Brooke, Carolyn Jones, Alan Mowbray, Richard Wattis and Alix Talton.

The Wrong Man (A Warner Brothers-First National Picture; *prod./rel.* 1956)
P: Alfred Hitchcock. *AP:* Herbert Coleman. *Sc:* Maxwell Anderson and Angus MacPhail, b/o story by Anderson. *DP:* Robert Burks. *Ed:* George Tomasini. *AD:* Paul Sylbert. *ad:* Daniel J. McCauley. *S:* William L. Kuehl. *M:* Bernard Herrmann. *Int:* Warner Brother. *B/W.*

Cast:		
	Christopher Emmanuel Balestrero	Henry Fonda
	Rose Balestrero	Vera Miles
	Frank O'Connor	Anthony Quayle
	Mrs. Balestrero	Esther Minciotti
	Lt. Bowers	Harold J. Stone
	Tomasini	John Heldabrand
	Mrs. James	Doreen Lang
	Constance Willis	Laurinda Barrett
	Betty Todd	Norma Connolly
	Olga Conforti	Lola D'Annunzio
	Gene Conforti	Nehemiah Persoff
	Gregory Balestrero	Robert Essen
	Robert Balestrero	Kippy Campbell
	Judge	Dayton Lummis
	Det. Matthews	Charles Cooper
	Miss Dennerly	Peggy Webber
	Daniell	Richard Robbins

Vertigo (A Paramount Release; *prod.* 1957/*rel.* 1958)
P: Alfred Hitchcock. *AP:* Herbert Coleman. *Sc:* Alec Coppel and Samuel Taylor, b/o the novel *D'entre les morts* by Pierre Boileau and Thomas Narcejac. *DP:* Robert Burks. *Ed:* George Tomasini. *AD:* Hal Pereira, Henry Bumstead. *S:* Sam Comer, Frank McKelvey. *M:* Bernard Herrmann. *Titles:* Saul Bass. *SE:* John P. Fulton. *ad:* Daniel McCauley. *W:* Edith Head. *Special sequence:* John Ferren. *Int:* Paramount. *Col.*

Cast:		
	John "Scottie" Ferguson	James Stewart
	"Madeleine Elster" (Judy Barton)	Kim Novak
	Midge Wood	Barbara Bel Geddes
	Gavin Elster	Tom Helmore
	Pop Liebl	Konstantin Shayne

and with Henry Jones, Raymond Bailey, Ellen Corby and Lee Patrick.

North by Northwest (An MGM Picture; *prod.* 1958/*rel.* 1959)
P: Alfred Hitchcock. *AP:* Herbert Coleman. Written by Ernest Lehman. *DP:* Robert Burks. *Ed:* George Tomasini. *AD:* Robert Boyle, William A. Horning,

Merrill Pye. *S:* Henry Grace, Frank McKelvey. *SE:* A. Arnold Gillespie, Lee LeBlanc. *Titles:* Saul Bass. *M:* Bernard Herrmann. *Int:* MGM. *Col.*

Cast:	Roger O. Thornhill	Cary Grant
	Eve Kendall	Eva Marie Saint
	Philip Vandamm	James Mason
	Clara Thornhill	Jessie Royce Landis
	The Professor	Leo G. Carroll
	Lester Townsend	Philip Ober
	Leonard	Martin Landau
	Valerian	Adam Williams
	Licht	Robert Ellenstein

and with Josephine Hutchinson, Doreen Lang, Les Tremayne, Philip Coolidge, Edward Binns, Pat McVey, Nora Marlowe, Ned Glass and Malcolm Atterbury.

Psycho (A Paramount Release; *prod.* 1959-1960/*rel.* 1960)
P: Alfred Hitchcock. *Sc:* Joseph Stefano, b/o the novel by Robert Bloch. *DP:* John L. Russell. *Ed:* George Tomasini. *AD:* Joseph Hurley, Robert Clatworthy. *S:* George Milo. *Titles:* Saul Bass. *M:* Bernard Herrmann. *W:* Helen Colvig. *SE:* Clarence Champagne. *ad:* Hilton A. Green. *Int:* Revue Studios. *B/W.*

Cast:	Norman Bates	Anthony Perkins
	Marion Crane	Janet Leigh
	Lila Crane	Vera Miles
	Sam Loomis	John Gavin
	Arbogast	Martin Balsam
	Al Chambers	John McIntire
	Mrs. Chambers	Lurene Tuttle
	Psychiatrist	Simon Oakland
	Cassidy	Frank Albertson
	Caroline	Pat Hitchcock
	Mr. Lowery	Vaughn Taylor
	Highway patrolman	Mort Mills
	"California Charlie"	John Anderson

The Birds (A Universal Release; *prod.* 1962/*rel.* 1963)
P: Alfred Hitchcock. *Sc:* Evan Hunter, b/o the short story by Daphne du Maurier. *DP:* Robert Burks. *Ed:* George Tomasini. *AD:* Robert Boyle *ad:* James H. Brown. *W:* Edith Head. *SE:* Lawrence A. Hampton. *Special photographic adviser:* Ub Iwerks. *Pictorial designs:* Albert Whitlock. *S:* George Milo. *Bird trainer:* Ray Berwick. *Titles:* James S. Pollak. *Asst. to AH:* Peggy Robertson. *Electronic sound production and composition:* Remi Gassmann, Oskar Sala; *consultant,* Bernard Herrmann. *Int:* Universal. *Col.*

Cast:	Melanie Daniels	Tippi Hedren
	Mitch Brenner	Rod Taylor
	Lydia Brenner	Jessica Tandy
	Annie Hayworth	Suzanne Pleshette
	Cathy Brenner	Veronica Cartwright
	Mrs. Bundy	Ethel Griffies
	Sebastian Sholes	Charles McGraw
	Mrs. MacGruder	Ruth McDevitt
	Al Malone	Malcolm Atterbury
	Deke Carter	Lonny Chapman
	Helen Carter	Elizabeth Wilson
	Traveling salesman	Joe Mantell
	Fisherman	Doodles Weaver

Postal clerk	John McGovern
Drunk	Karl Swenson
Man in elevator	Richard Deacon
Mother in Tides Cafe	Doreen Lang

Marnie (A Universal Release; *prod.* 1963–1964/*rel.* 1964)
P: Alfred Hitchcock. *Sc:* Jay Presson Allen, b/o the novel by Winston Graham.
DP: Robert Burks. *AD:* Robert Boyle. *ad:* James H. Brown. *W:* Edith Head.
Ed: George Tomasini. *Pictorial design:* Albert Whitlock. *S:* George Milo. *M:*
Bernard Herrmann. *Asst. to AH:* Peggy Robertson. *Int:* Universal. *Col.*

Cast:	Margaret (Marnie) Edgar	Tippi Hedren
	Mark Rutland	Sean Connery
	Lil Mainwaring	Diane Baker
	Bernice Edgar	Louise Latham
	Sidney Strutt	Martin Gabel
	Cousin Bob	Bob Sweeney
	Mr. Rutland	Alan Napier
	Susan Clabon	Mariette Hartley
	Rita	Edith Evanson
	Sam Ward	S. John Launer
	Mrs. Turpin	Meg Wyllie
	Sailor	Bruce Dern

Torn Curtain (A Universal Release; *prod.* 1965–1966/*rel.* 1966)
P: Alfred Hitchcock. Written by Brian Moore. *DP:* John F. Warren. *AD:* Hein
Heckroth, Frank Arrigo. *Pictorial design:* Albert Whitlock. *Ed:* Bud Hoffman. *ad:*
Donald Baer. *S:* George Milo. *W:* Edith Head, Grady Hunt. *M:* John Addison.
Asst. to AH: Peggy Robertson. *Int:* Universal. *Col.*

Cast:	Michael Armstrong	Paul Newman
	Sarah Sherman	Julie Andrews
	Countess Luchinska	Lila Kedrova
	Gromek	Wolfgang Kieling
	Ballerina	Tamara Toumanova
	Professor Lindt	Ludwig Donath
	Jakobi	David Opatoshu

and with Mort Mills, Carolyn Conwell, Arthur Gould-Porter and Gloria
Gorvin.

Topaz (A Universal Release; *prod.* 1968–1969/*rel.* 1969)
P: Alfred Hitchcock. *AP:* Herbert Coleman. *Sc:* Samuel Taylor, b/o the novel
by Leon Uris. *DP:* Jack Hildyard. *AD:* Henry Bumstead. *S:* John Austin. *W:*
Edith Head. *Ed:* William Ziegler. *M:* Maurice Jarre. *Asst. to AH:* Peggy Robertson. *Int:* Universal. *Col.*

Cast:	André Dévereaux	Frederick Stafford
	Michael Nordstrom	John Forsythe
	Nicole Dévereaux	Dany Robin
	Rico Parra	John Vernon
	Juanita de Cordoba	Karin Dor
	Jacques Granville	Michel Piccoli
	Henri Jarre	Philippe Noiret
	Michele Picard	Claude Jade
	Philippe Dubois	Roscoe Lee Browne

| Boris Kusenov | Per-Axel Arosenius |
| François Picard | Michel Subor |

Frenzy (A Universal Release; *prod.* 1971/*rel.* 1972)
P: Alfred Hitchcock. *Sc:* Anthony Shaffer, b/o the novel *Goodbye Piccadilly, Farewell Leicester Square* by Arthur La Bern. *DP:* Gil Taylor. *AP:* William Hill. *AD:* Syd Cain, Bob Laing. *ad:* Colin M. Brewer. *Ed:* John Jympson. *S:* Simon Wakefield. *M:* Ron Goodwin. *Asst. to AH:* Peggy Robertson. *Int:* Pinewood. *Col.*

Cast:	Richard Blaney	Jon Finch
	Bob Rusk	Barry Foster
	Brenda Blaney	Barbara Leigh-Hunt
	Babs Milligan	Anna Massey
	Inspector Oxford	Alec McCowen
	Mrs. Oxford	Vivien Merchant
	Hetty Porter	Billie Whitelaw
	Johnny Porter	Clive Swift
	Felix Forsythe	Bernard Cribbins
	Gladys	Elsie Randolph
	Sergeant Spearman	Michael Bates
	Monica Barling	Jean Marsh

Family Plot (A Universal Release; *prod.* 1975/*rel.* 1976)
P: Alfred Hitchcock. *Sc:* Ernest Lehman, b/o the novel *The Rainbird Pattern* by Victor Canning. *DP:* Leonard South. *AD:* Henry Bumstead. *S:* James W. Payne. *Ed:* J Terry Williams. *W:* Edith Head. *M:* John Williams. *SE:* Albert Whitlock *ad:* Howard G. Kazanjian, Wayne A. Farlow. *Asst. to AH:* Peggy Robertson. *Int:* Universal. *Col.*

Cast:	Fran	Karen Black
	Lumley	Bruce Dern
	Blanche	Barbara Harris
	Adamson	William Devane
	Maloney	Ed Lauter
	Julia Rainbird	Cathleen Nesbitt
	Mrs. Maloney	Katherine Helmond
	Grandison	Warren J. Kemmerling
	Mrs. Clay	Edith Atwater
	Bishop	William Prince
	Constantine	Nicolas Colasanto
	Vera Hannagan	Marge Redmond

BIBLIOGRAPHICAL NOTE

The following were the books most frequently consulted:

Durgnat, Raymond. *The Strange Case of Alfred Hitchcock*. Cambridge, Mass.: The M.I.T. Press, 1974.

Estève, Michel (ed.). *Alfred Hitchcock*. Etudes Cinématographiques 84/87. Paris: Minard-Lettres Modernes, 1971.

LaValley, Albert J. *Focus on Hitchcock*. Englewood Cliffs: Prentice-Hall, 1972.

Truffaut, François. *Hitchcock*. New York: Simon and Schuster, 1967.

Wood, Robin. *Hitchcock's Films*. London: A. S. Barnes, 1969.

The texts by Durgnat and LaValley contain more extensive bibliographies; the latter also includes popular newspaper and magazine listings.

INDEX

Italicized page numbers refer to illustrations.

ABOUT THE AUTHOR

DONALD SPOTO, who earned his Ph.D. degree from Fordham
University, is the author of (among other books) the internation-
ally bestselling biography *The Dark Side of Genius: The Life of
Alfred Hitchcock* (which won the Edgar Award as Best Nonfiction
Book of the Year, 1983); *The Kindness of Strangers: The Life of
Tennessee Williams;* and lives of Lotte Lenya and Preston Sturges.
His most recent book is *Laurence Olivier: A Biography,* and his
next will be *Blue Angel: The Life of Marlene Dietrich*. He has taught
at major universities in America and continues to lecture worldwide.